GAMER NATION

ALSO BY ERIC GEISSINGER

Virtual Billions: The Genius, the Drug Lord,
and the Ivy League Twins behind the Rise of Bitcoin

GAMER NATION

The Rise of MODERN GAMING
and the COMPULSION to PLAY AGAIN

Eric Geissinger

Prometheus Books

59 John Glenn Drive
Amherst, New York 14228

Published 2018 by Prometheus Books

Cover design by Jacqueline Nasso Cooke
Cover design © Prometheus Books

Inquiries should be addressed to
Prometheus Books
59 John Glenn Drive
Amherst, New York 14228
VOICE: 716–691–0133 • FAX: 716–691–0137
WWW.PROMETHEUSBOOKS.COM

22 21 20 19 18   5 4 3 2 1

Library of Congress Cataloging-in-Publication Data

Names: Geissinger, Eric, 1968- author.
Title: Gamer nation : the rise of modern gaming and the compulsion to play again / Eric
    Geissinger.
Description: Amherst, New York : Prometheus Books, 2018. | Includes index.
Identifiers: LCCN 2018003771 (print) | LCCN 2018018604 (ebook) |
    ISBN 9781633883802 (ebook) | ISBN 9781633883796 (hardback)
Subjects: LCSH: Video games—Social aspects—United States. | Video games—Psychological
    aspects. | Video game addiction—United States. | BISAC: GAMES / Video & Electronic.
    | PSYCHOLOGY / Psychopathology / Compulsive Behavior.
Classification: LCC GV1469.34.S52 (ebook) | LCC GV1469.34.S52 G45 2018 (print) |
    DDC 794.8—dc23
LC record available at https://lccn.loc.gov/2018003771

Printed in the United States of America

"You can deny, if you like, nearly all abstractions: justice, beauty, truth, goodness, mind, God. You can deny seriousness, but not play."

—Johan Huizinga, *Homo Ludens: A Study of the Play-Element in Culture*

CONTENTS

Introduction   11

What's "Play" and What's a "Game"?   12
Childish Play and Mature Games   18
The Unexpected Power of Games   20

**Chapter One: Birds Do It, Bees Don't Do It,
         but Some Pig-Faced Turtles
         Do It**   23

Birds at Play, or at Least Playing a Game   30
The Sad Tale of Pigface, and Happier Turtles   33
The Irresistible Appeal of Space [to] Geckos   36
More, More, and More   37
Giggling and Wrestling Rats   39

**Chapter Two: All Work and No Unstructured
         Play Makes Jane Whiny**   41

The Helicopter Parent Hypothesis   45
The Results of Unstructured Play, and the
         Inevitable Expansion of Perceived Harm   52
Something Is Up   57
Play Is Fundamental   66

Chapter Three: Massive Size Is Massive   67

YouTube Incentivizing Blandness   73
"Minecraft Is Love. Minecraft Is Life."   80

CONTENTS

Chapter Four: Anatomy of a Bestseller   87

How (Some) Things Are Done   91
Nothing's Good and (Pretty Much) Everything's Bad
     with Steven Johnson's *Everything Bad Is Good for You*   93
What Does the Book Actually Claim?   95
A Bestseller at Any Cost   99

**Chapter Five: *Candy Crush*(ing)
               the Competition, and
               Harpooning Whales**   103

Hate-Playing *Candy Crush*   103
Candy Crush Origins   106
The Good Old Days   108
How Las Vegas Sees the World   109
Learning from the Casinos   112
Slot Machines and *Tetris*   117
The (De)Evolution of Games   124
Old School Capitalism   125
Extracting Profit: When a Game Plays You   127
The Mechanics of Video-Game Manipulation   132
Others Jump on the Manipulation Bandwagon   136

**Chapter Six: Professional Leagues and the
              Rise of Esports—
              Are They Still Games?**   143

The Rise of EnVyUs   150
What to Make of *Overwatch* as a Spectator Sport?   161

CONTENTS

Chapter Seven: The Dangers of the Virtual   167

More and More Games   167
Nabokov's *The Luzhin Defense*   170
Taking Games Far Too Seriously   174
What's "Real Life" and What's "Virtual"?   179
Let's "Gamify" the World! Everyone Wins!   186
Games to Improve the World   195

Chapter Eight: Keep Us Safe by Giving Them Games   203

The Comic-Book Code Comes to Video Games   203
Games Inspiring the Good Life   208
The Benefits of Sports   210
The Town That Killed Football   218

Chapter Nine: Flooding the Colosseum   225

Having Too Much Fun to Work   226
Games Are Different   229
A Warning   231
Addiction and Distraction: It's Not Just Games   234
What Can Be Done? We Know but Don't Want to Know   237
What's to Come?   239

Acknowledgments   241

Notes   243

Index   269

INTRODUCTION

I can't remember the first game I ever played; it was probably something created on the spur of the moment with my two sisters near the small creek flowing through the forest behind our home. Water had to be diverted, blocked, and dammed using smooth brown sand, eroded from Triassic sediments, which clumped together in a satisfying way when dampened. You could grab a handful, mound it up, push it into position, and block for a moment the clear trickle of water that was all that generally flowed during the hottest months of a North Carolina summer. How high could the water be made to rise before it ate through the barrier? If we used rocks, was it possible to obstruct the creek for ten minutes or half an hour? The rules were defined: block the water. The opponent was clear: the water itself. The goal of the game: an unusually water-tight and long-lasting dam. When the water eventually broke through we moved on, still playing, still making up games.

Our specific game rules were as fluid as the water, changing as we roamed up and down the creek, exploring a deeper pool or a narrower and faster-flowing bottleneck. The game radically shifted when we discovered a huge crawdad slipping beneath a rock. This was a true challenge: this was a combat sport clearly defined, with a darting opponent, a vague possibility of danger (claws magnified out of proportion by the passage of time), and a definite goal—we were going to track down the darting crawdad, block its escape with sticks, and capture it. My older sister told me to run home and get a bucket, and I turned to my younger sister and told her to run home and get a bucket or we would let it escape, and she resisted, stubborn, and almost cried in frustration before whirling away. We ended up capturing it. We had plenty of experience with crawdads. Collectively, we all won. (Except the crawdad.)

There's nothing unusual about this or any of the other games we played. We were, at no point, spurred on or directed by adults. Spontaneously creating a game during play, and playing the created game, was as natural as breathing.

It's easy to overlook how deeply play permeates our lives. Play is in a unique category in its cross-cultural and cross-species universality. You can't talk to your cat, and you certainly can't tell your cat what to do, but you can enter into a game with your cat that is understood by both of you as a game, complete with special rules and a distinct start and end. You bat at its paw, and it bats at your hand with claws retracted, and it's fun for a while until the claws come out, which conclusively ends things. Game over.

WHAT'S "PLAY" AND WHAT'S A "GAME"?

What is play? And how does *play* relate to *games*? Scholars have made distinguished careers out of teasing apart the categories of "play" and "not play." University departments have been endowed and populated with academics looking into theories of "games" and "gaming." The literature is vast and has been a subject of serious investigation since the early 1800s, but for the purpose of this book I am using a broad definition of these two terms. Restrictive definitions omit common experiences that most people would readily define as *play* or a *game*, yet the definitions need to be narrow enough to be useful.

Play, n. (pleɪ) [OE. pleÆa (plæÆa, plaÆa), wk. n. from root of pleÆ(e)an, -ian, plæÆian, plaÆian to play]

Play requires freedom of motion and expression; it is a pleasurable open-ended activity often involving make-believe and worldbuilding; the player performs actions in a separate reality without material consequences.

Game, n. (geɪm) [Com. Teut.: OE. gamen, gǫmen str. ncut. = OFris. game, gome, OS., OHG. gaman (MHG. gamen) joy, glee, ON. gaman (Sw. gamman, Da. gammen)]

A game is an activity that must be: 1) circumscribed in time and space, 2) governed by rules, 3) uncertain in result, 4) nonproductive, and 5) occurring in a separate reality.

These definitions catch most, if not all, of our everyday expectations for what qualifies as *play* and what constitutes a *game*. Unfortunately, the limitations of the English language make it difficult to disentangle the two words: we have a paucity of ways to describe an activity involving humans participating in a game. That highly mangled sentence was required to avoid writing the words "playing a game." *Play* involves freedom, pleasure, creativity, and liberty from material concerns. *Games* do not necessarily incorporate these features of play, but there isn't another way to say it: can you "operate" a game? You can "participate" in a game, but is that active enough? I suppose you might "engage with a game"—but this discussion is hopeless, awkward, pedantic.

I'll keep saying "playing a game," but for clarity's sake I'll clearly distinguish between what it means to *play* and what it means to *play a game*. Just because you are playing a game does *not* mean you are experiencing play, as illustrated by the following absurd examples in three categories.

INTRODUCTION

Freedom and Coercion

After being kidnapped by an insane chess grandmaster you can still, albeit unhappily, play a game a chess at gunpoint. But you cannot *play* at gunpoint on pain of death. You might pretend to play without actually playing; you might convince your tormentor he is witnessing true play, but this merely depends upon mechanical acting skills. True play involves freedom, in particular freedom from coercion, because a critical element of play is choice. You choose when to play and you choose when play ends: when play ceases to be voluntary it abruptly reverts into something else.

Immaterial and Material

You can play a game of Russian roulette for money or fame, and stakes couldn't be higher: you either win and survive or you lose your life. The material consequences are extreme. True *play*, however, has no material consequences. You can't earn or lose money when playing (except by accident). You don't create bridges or paint somebody's fence (except inadvertently). Play generates a reality distinct from our everyday reality: this stick is actually a sword, and that tree is the tower of the castle, and it's incredibly important to hit every falling leaf at least once before it strikes the ground. Anything occurring in the play world is bounded by the fictional sphere of the play area, and if the "real world" impinges it's either incorporated into the fun, transformed into another aspect of the alternative reality, or it ends the play. Somebody's mother pokes her head into the treehouse and that's it. *She* can't be worked into the fiction, particularly after your friend's hand is securely gripped and he's led away.

Games also generate their own special realities, and some are seductive enough to swallow people's lives entirely, but there is no expectation that this separate reality will be free from material concerns or that the game won't impact the real world. You might love playing poker and wish to spend your life playing it, but after losing your loan shark's stake during a highly improbable river card suckout, "reality" might assert itself rather strongly the following morning in the form of a visitor carrying an assortment of brass knuckles and butterfly knives.

Pleasure and Mechanics

Play cannot be mandated. The onset of play is always spontaneous. You can put the ingredients together—fill a room with toys and children and cake and multicolored oversized beanbag chairs—but you can't arbitrarily blow a whistle and shout: *This is the party room, start to play—NOW!* The kids will wander around and poke at this and that aimlessly for a while before it happens. Two or three children start playing with each other, spurred by something or someone (it can't be determined ahead of time). Play can't be artificially forced because play involves pleasure, which is (sadly) immune to scheduling.

Games can be scheduled, and often are. You can start and stop a game at precise intervals. But games don't have to be pleasurable. You can play a game and hate yourself for playing it and wasting time and avoiding that which should be courageously faced and defeated. You can be addicted to a game and play the game until it kills you. A game is mechanical, sometimes pleasurable and sometimes not, but pleasure isn't a required condition. An injured but indomitable NFL linebacker, in almost unimaginable pain, is certainly "playing the game of football" when he takes to the field on Sunday, but his rationale trades temporary torture for the following week's paycheck. He doesn't like the game at that moment, indeed might well hate it, but he's going to play it even if it kills him.

For the critical-minded and pedantic, it's easy to poke holes in these definitions, just as it is with any two definitions encompassing a wide range of human activities. Yes, sometimes pure *play* has material consequences (you are given a tongue lashing for playing too long in the sultry dusk of a midsummer evening); yes, sometimes *games* can be productive (who can build a brick wall faster?). You can even come up with absurd edge cases and imagine a masochist experiencing a burst of pure pleasurable play while being whipped and actively coerced into fun by his beloved tormentor. These types of specific objections don't obviate the truth of general definitions. Dogs have four legs—except for Tripod, who lost one when he was a puppy. We don't throw up our hands in despair because the Platonic form of "Dog" now needs to include three-legged varieties; instead, we continue discuss, productively, the fact that dogs have four legs.

A further distinction should be made. It's perfectly sensible to talk about a computer playing a game a chess, in fact playing it so well that it defeats any and all humans on the planet, which is the current state-of-the-art. The computer does not know it is playing chess; it has no intention to play chess; it feels no pleasure in playing chess. Playing a game does not necessarily involve desire or will or even consciousness. When watching a low-order animal, such as an insect, behaving in ways that seem to indicate it is playing a game, we need not worry about whether the insect is entirely driven by evolutionary forces and does not "really know" it is playing a game. It doesn't have to understand that its behavior generates a different sort of reality, distinct from its standard experience, although this might still be the case. Playing a game can be an entirely mechanical exercise, driven by silicon or guided by evolutionary forces, which again aligns with everyday human experience. Many of us have found ourselves playing a game mechanically: dealing the next round of solitaire while thinking of other things, or guiding *Tetris* blocks distractedly, not fully aware of our fingers manipulating the keyboard.

Play often involves ad hoc rules, spontaneously generated and mutable, but it need not: you can play with a friend in a pool, splashing about, bounded by the special reality of water and sun. Play is the traditional domain of children and an occasional lucky adult who engages with the world in creative, open-ended ways and manages to glean pleasure from the process. Games, however, require rules; games require boundaries, intellectual or physical; games have a rigid structure.

We seem to have made some progress with these definitions, but there's a specter looming in the shadows. Ludwig Josef Johann Wittgenstein, one of the most famous philosophers of the twentieth century, published just one slender volume, *Tractatus Logico-Philosophicus*, during his twenty-year academic career at Cambridge. In this book he focused, at least in part, upon the important role played by *spiel*—i.e. games and/or play (the German word means both). Wittgenstein's point was relatively clear given the opaque nature of most of the rest of the book: *it's impossible to define what is or is not a game.* Wittgenstein did not mean that such a definition would be difficult to discover or extremely involved, he meant that, strictly speaking, no definition is possible for a term such as "game." Instead it's necessary to use a hermeneutic method, sometimes termed "Wittgenstein's ruler," that roughly states the following: sometimes, when measuring a table with a ruler, you are also measuring the ruler with the table.

This isn't meant to be an irritating koan, it refers to the fact that when we define something there is often an interplay between the definition and the thing being defined, with the definition being shaped by what we are defining. In other words, to ask "Is X a game?" involves some flexibility about what we understand "game" to mean. We might have come to the determination (as a culture) that playing solitaire *does* constitute a game, despite it being played without other human interaction. It might not have been considered a game a hundred years ago and instead have been called an "amusement" or "distraction," little different from knitting. But we don't currently consider solitaire as anything but the canonical example of a solitary game. In other words, repeatedly asking over time, "Is solitaire a game?" modified our understanding of the definition of "game"; these changes can broaden or shrink the definition, but the two are in flexible conversation. Any strict definition of "game" necessarily fails because it can't capture all things that might have once qualified or might in the future. The border between game and not game is forever in flux. I'm willing to accept Wittgenstein's objection as theoretically valid, but for our purposes the definitions in the above box are good enough.

CHILDISH PLAY AND MATURE GAMES

Speaking broadly, an adult game can be imagined as the formal, restricted evolution of childhood play, rigidly defining what had been open to change.

It's often difficult for an adult to engage in open, light-hearted play; I honestly don't remember the last time I experienced it. Were I to step outside and seek that feeling, running around the lawn, transforming a rake into a pole-arm and attempting to consciously coerce play into being, the result would be abject failure. Maybe I'm just out of practice, but it's probably more than that: I'm aware of myself attempting to circumvent my apathy even while I see myself from the outside acting in ways a stranger might deem absurd, if not downright insane. It's hard to get there from here. It's like trying to force yourself to fall in love with a woman because she seems like she should be the one—she's the perfect match, the inevitable end of years of searching . . . but you can't flip a switch and make it happen. Love doesn't work like that.

Games regularize behavior and give us socially acceptable, comprehensible, and highly proscribed links to the experience of childhood play. Through games adults may, and sometimes do, achieve an immersive experience of play every bit as deep as any child. But the desire to re-experience pleasurable play is not entirely innocent. The biological urge to play, operating through mechanical rule-based games, can often entrap the player without offering much in return.

Play is both creative and immersive, involving give-and-take between other participants and/or the environment. Games can be creative, highly so, but they can also be overwhelmingly passive. Lines of people sitting in rows at Las Vegas casinos, playing nickel slot machines for hours on end, are certainly playing a game of chance, however simple it is and however pointless it might be as a money-making venture, but there isn't any way to view this type of game as anything but extraordinary passive. They have, in a sense, been incorporated into the mechanical gears of the slot machine, a biological automaton existing only to move a lever up and down.

Why would anyone put themselves into this situation? Why do people play games, and sometimes spend the vast majority of their lives attempting to master a specific game? (Or, alternatively, shorten their lives in the boxing ring or by speeding down steep French mountains, relying on the strength and flexibility of incredibly thin bicycle tires that sometimes, tragically, explode?)

Because the root of all play is biological (infants play well before they have rudimentary understanding of language), investigators have turned to the animal kingdom to better understand the point of this apparently useless activity. A naive evolutionary hypotheses takes for granted the obvious benefit of strictly conserving energy at every opportunity. A family of foxes rolling around and play-biting each other, engaging in energetic chases, and leaping into the air simply for the fun of it seems to be indulging in a terrible waste of resources and will surely, given the passage of hundreds of thousands of years, experience a steady winnowing of play behavior as starvation during periods of inevitable hardship strikes playful fox families particularly hard. They used up their precious calories racing about, while a family of less-frequently playing foxes had more calories to spare, allowing them to survive. This is what often happens in other areas of animal behavior. It's a rare animal species that gets to waste significant portions of their time and energy on a useless activity and still manage to compete in the incredibly demanding evolutionary landscape.

In addition to the obvious caloric expenditure, animal play also occasionally causes serious injuries or becomes so distracting that predators are overlooked. I've seen this first hand in my yard, as two young squirrels chased each other to within a foot of my extremely lazy cat. Had the cat been lean and hungry, one of the squirrels would certainly have been killed.

The implication of this sort of unscientific, intuitive evolutionary argument is that play should have been extinguished long ago. But that's not what happened. Not only do a *few* animals play, *almost all* intelligent animals play, and the more scientists look at animal play the deeper it runs, descending the evolutionary tree from the great apes to the higher mammals to the lower mammals to the reptiles and even into the insects. It's baffling.

The commonsense hypothesis, which had seemed reasonable given evolution's incredibly stingy and tight control over resources in almost every other behavioral instance, fails when confronted by reality. Let us bow to observation and admit play must have advantages outweighing its many obvious disadvantages, or else it would have been winnowed by evolutionary forces. The basic questions become: *What are the evolutionary advantages to play? And why do humans play more games than any other species?*

THE UNEXPECTED POWER OF GAMES

As an indication of the fundamental power of games, observe the following slice of our modern world, as represented by a young South Korean couple:

> Kim Jae-beom told the police he wasn't sure what killed his daughter, and that "she was a premature baby from the beginning." But the cause of death determined by authorities was less vague: The baby had died of malnutrition as a result of her parent's online gaming addiction.
>
> So begins the tale of Kim and his wife, Kim Yun-jeong, a South Korean couple whose all-consuming video game habit led them to neglect their 3-month-old baby. When real life shockingly interrupted the gaming fantasy they'd been sucked into, the couple was actually caring for a virtual child in 6- to 12-hour online binges. She was a cooing and cherubic mini-avatar called Anima, which players earned after reaching a certain level in the game Prius.[1]

I don't want to cherry-pick a tragic example and make a general claim from a specific instance, but it's nevertheless instructive to think about what happened here. New parents, with their first child, feel an evolutionary impulse to care for the child—or at least feed it enough to keep it from starving. However, children are messy and difficult. To remove themselves from the demands of the real-world infant the couple turned to an alternative reality, created by a video game, but the game didn't function as an engine of pure distraction. They weren't spending their time playing *Dig Dug*; they were still engaged in a highly modified type of parenting. They essentially transferred their child-rearing impulses from the dirty real world into the pristine virtual world, choosing to maintain a cute clean baby avatar instead of a crying, defecating, and extremely demanding human infant.

The couple ended up playing parents instead of being parents; play, and the world of the video game, did not distract them from their responsibilities but enabled something more powerful: it created a *new and more convenient reality* into which to funnel their emotions and responsibilities.

I don't think anyone could reasonably claim that the urge to play games is, in general, stronger than the maternal impulse, or that this couple didn't suffer from an irrational, mutually reinforcing flight from reality. At the same time, I understand how it might have happened. The demands placed upon new parents are sometimes enough to make stable people crack; the effect upon the unstable can obviously lead to extreme results, which are not necessarily unique to this couple.[2]

This story tells us nothing about games being good or bad, or about the dangers or benefits of video games, or about the importance of leading a balanced life. None of that can be determined from a single point of evidence. What we *can* indisputably take from the event (and others like it) is the games can be *incredibly powerful*. You would think evolution would go out of its way to safeguard the safety of our gene-bearing children, using whatever tools were at hand. Maternal love, fatherly love, a baby's cuteness, our instinctive desire to keep these helpless needy creatures from harm, even if they are another parent's child—these impulses exist for good and obvious reasons.

Does play sidestep maternal and paternal evolutionary strictures, which in other contexts function as iron laws? Games are not something to be taken lightly; just because children play games doesn't mean that, for adults, games don't have unusual and unexpected power.

CHAPTER ONE

BIRDS DO IT, BEES DON'T DO IT, BUT SOME PIG–FACED TURTLES DO IT

Some nearly universal animal behavior makes intuitive sense. Sexual reproduction is the standard for animal species, excepting a small number of parthenogenetic outliers who are able to reproduce with an unfertilized egg (but these represent a vanishingly small fraction of the overall animal population). That humans share the basic elements of sexual reproduction with the salmon, even if the method of bringing the sperm and egg together is wildly different, doesn't strike anyone as particularly notable. Sexual reproduction has shown itself to be an incredibly effective way to transmit genes, facilitate natural selection through gene mixing, and enable the fundamental evolutionary function of propagating the species. Sexual reproduction is such a useful tool, and so successful from an evolutionary perspective, that it's no surprise to find it up and down the evolutionary tree, ranging from insects to reptiles to mammals. We view a beetle's sexual escapades as both unobjectionable and unsurprising.

It's hard to find other behavioral and biological universals covering a similar range of animal species. The laws of thermodynamics require, at minimum, energy intake greater than output, so you would expect that all animals eat or absorb nutrients, but even here incredibly rare exceptions exist. The Prometheus silk moth, after emerging from its cocoon, has only a few days to reproduce before dying of starvation (it lacks a mouth).[1] Animals require oxygen, either from air or water, except animals from a single phylum, the tiny *loricifera*. In 2010, three species of *loricifera* were discovered living two miles below the Mediterranean in a brine lake so supersaturated with salt that all oxygen was driven off—yet they were able to thrive. Most animals drink water, although paradoxically mammals in marine environments, such as dolphins, produce water internally from the metabolic breakdown of food and most can't be said to drink water during their lifetimes (although seals are sometimes seen eating snow, and manatees are drawn to estuaries for the fresh river water).

These are extreme exceptions. Almost all animals share the following common features: sexual reproduction and the need for food, water, and oxygen. These are fundamental. It seems wrong-headed, if not an outright categorical error, to add another to the list: *play*.

Play deserves to be on the list—after outlining some obvious limitations.

Play isn't exhibited by all or even most animals. Earthworms don't play, and if they did I wouldn't want to see it. There is a strict correlation between general intelligence and frequency, or likelihood, of play. As you move up the intelligence ladder from insect (rare examples of play), to reptile (occasional examples of play), to birds (extensive examples of play), to mammals (play is ubiquitous), the frequency of play increases, as well as its depth and complexity. Looking only at mammals, we find that mice play simple games, cats slightly more complicated games, dogs surprisingly sophisticated games, and when you get to the great apes the complexity of games explodes. There comes a point in the tree of life at which brainpower reaches a certain threshold, and at that point all animals play—they *must* play. It's as certain a result as the thermodynamic laws.

Robert Mitchell, conducting animal research in the 1990s, and paralleling the work of many investigators before and after him, categorized play types through strictly defined terms. What follows is his well-known four-level breakdown of animal play, ranging from the simple to the complex:[2]

Level	Design Process	Name of Play	Examples of Play
1a	Perceptual-motor coordination	Autotelic	Locomotor-rotational; cat object play.
		Schematic	Much play fighting, sexual play, escape play.
2a	Learning	Learned autotelic	Badger somersaulting and ice sliding; bonobo funny faces and eye-closing game; bird dropping pebble for sound.
2b		Teasing	Dog object keep-away; gorilla acting interested in infant to surprise mother
2c		Mimetic	Parrot vocalization; intentional play solicitation based on simulation
3	Intentional Simulation	Pretend	Chimpanzee bathing doll; rhesus monkey imitating child-carrying mother.
4	Intentional Communication of Simulation	Communicative Pretend	Rhesus monkeys simulating play fighting; human sarcasm and parody.

It's easy to make fun of the nomenclature (is it really necessary to call something *Learned autotelic*?), but Mitchell's schema is compelling if not definitive. Less sophisticated twentieth-century investigators would have appended another column to the table, explaining the functional or evolutionary benefits of each play type. For example, a chimpanzee "simulating the bathing of a doll" is a level 3 type of play (*intentional simulation*), and previous researchers would likely have explained the behavior by pointing to an obvious benefit: bathing a doll prepares a chimpanzee to bathe her actual baby. What could be more obvious?

It makes perfect sense—too much sense. Playful fighting between jackal babies was understood to be training for real battles later in life. Such an obvious inference hardly required investigation; play fighting enables the development of stronger bodies and more skilled combatants, and kicks off early the relentless social competition found in jackal packs. Cats batting at balls of threads improve paw-eye coordination, leading to better mousing. Dogs chasing each other work wonders on their respiratory and circulatory systems, as well as hone basic hunting skills.

The first researchers to carefully look into these obvious explanatory claims were often mystified by what they found.[3] Female chimpanzees who frequently bathed dolls did not actually become more successful mothers. Jackals raised in big families, with lots of play fighting, didn't fight better than jackals raised alone. Playing around with string doesn't hone a cat's mousing skills. Lastly, dogs chasing each other don't contribute to a recognizable change in their overall health: young dogs are already running around so much for various doggy reasons that the benefits of relatively infrequent games of chase get lost in the wash. While it's clear that some animal games produce direct benefits for some species, in the main these benefits are often 1) incredibly modest given the time and energy of the play involved, or 2) difficult or impossible to detect.

In other words, why do cats play with string when there isn't any direct, measurable benefit to their playing with string?

Robert Mitchell isn't a nineteenth-century, naive, common-sense behaviorist, and he essentially rejects the idea that animal play has any ultimate adaptive or functional aim. He argues that the reasons for animal play aren't hidden or too subtle for our crude yardsticks, but that such cause-and-effect doesn't exist. In Mitchell's view, "Play is intentionally directed towards ends, but is unlike other such activities in having 1) no end outside its own enactment, 2) a frivolous end or means, or 3) has an end different from its apparent end."[4]

This parallels ideas you might hear coming from the French postmodern crowd,[5] but given that Mitchell's definition is extremely clear and, at root, makes intuitive sense, it doesn't hide behind Derridean obfuscation. Essentially his claim is that *play has escaped function*. Perhaps in the murky evolutionary past play was *always* linked to improving some "useful skill" or facilitated survival in a subtle way—but no more. Mitchell is quite clear about the self-referential nature of play. The overall goal of a given act of play depends on specific goals defined by that act of play, and these goals are necessarily frivolous. Mitchell's severing of the functional cord lines up well with definitions for human play that I outlined in the introduction, and, if nothing else, leads us away from easy answers and simplistic assumptions.

A strict evolutionary biologist might consider Mitchell's claim to be inherently paradoxical. Given play's widespread distribution and persistence across long evolutionary time frames, play must—by definition—give some sort of functional advantage. Evolution is inherently parsimonious. It's a filter, a strict and unforgiving judge of usefulness. Play might tweak neurons or alter the brain in ways we won't ever be able to pinpoint. Play might subtly alter emotional responses, allowing for a more successful navigation of nature's bloody war zone. This is argument by definition, and it assumes evolution is so all-encompassing in its restrictions that there isn't any wiggle room. Play is functional because it exists; if play wasn't functional, animals would not play. QED.[6]

This is a comforting idea, as are all definitive dogmatic assertions (at least if you believe in them): The world isn't as chaotic or confusing as we think. Evolution has shown itself to be spectacularly fertile as a theory and has withstood endless scrutiny and rigorous investigation, so it makes sense to assert that play is somehow implicated in its mechanics. We don't know what play does, exactly, but at least we know why it exists—survival of the fittest.[7]

The problem with this claim as a claim is that it doesn't explain much. What is there about intelligence, in particular, that requires play? What is the minimum level of intelligence that necessarily gives rise to play, and what mechanism(s) is/are being facilitated by play? If play is so important, worth burning calories and upping the risk of possible injury or predation, why can't scientists point to some clear and specific universal benefit? It's as if evolution itself is taking part in the fun, playing peek-a-boo with play's function, but it's an extremely annoying game because animal play seems to be the only universal behavior resistant to empirical investigation. The behavior of bees in a hive, or of snapping shrimp within their host sponge, is perfectly explicable.[8] Soldiers bees creep through the hive, guard entrances, and fight intruders. The queen is feted, fed, and impregnated, producing eggs. Forager bees take part in strange dances, indicating a source of food in direction X at distance Y. Bee behavior has been intensively researched, and almost all bee behavior "makes sense" from a reproductive and energy harvesting perspective. Bees are incredibly successful. But they don't play. And it's only play that perversely hides its benefits. Is this because we haven't discovered the benefits—or is play not about a strict cost-to-benefit ratio but something else?

Could the very burden of consciousness, which might exist along some sort of sliding scale (mediated by intelligence), demand something like play in order to make the world bearable? Would a world bereft of play but filled with conscious beings at varying levels of self-awareness be indescribably more intolerable than it is already? The world is often excruciating enough to cause many of us to escape into distraction, drugs, cults, rigid ideology, or the ultimate renunciation: suicide. In which case, play's functional value is staring us straight in the face: it's one of the many things that allow us to exist in the world without constant torment.

We can conduct a thought experiment and envision a functional world emptied of various human and animal qualities: humor, beauty, play, empathy. We could *probably* get along without them; the functional role of beauty (to indicate health and youth in possible mates, to facilitate care for infants, etc.) could have been replaced by another sensation or visual cue. There wasn't an overt need for evolution to cook up the emotion we recognize as "recognition of the beautiful." At the very least, such an emotion need not have been so strong, and in some cases all-encompassing, as it can be. Yet it exists. A similar argument can be made for the baseline, healthy human physical experience; we could imagine another world where this baseline is not relative somatic quiescence but a low-grade ache or pain, only slightly moderated by activity or sleep. Pain would function as a constant spur, forcing us to get up, work, forage for food, construct a new shelter—any activity that slightly relieved the ongoing ache. But this, again, isn't what we find, and lack of the negative can be used as a data point if we believe the evolutionary hypothesis to describe most of our biological mechanisms.

The human tendency for laziness and procrastination must be as much an evolutionary advantage as color vision; our ability to exist without physical pain (barring injury or illness) is a feature, not an accidental by-product. Yet pain is an excellent spur; why not deploy it more insistently? Evolution has cleverly manacled pleasure with harsh constraints: exceedingly fast diminishing returns. We are not allowed to achieve a desired goal and have that pleasure linger at the same intensity throughout our lives; this clearly would cause us to stop striving. The rich get richer, but it's never enough; Don Juan works his way through a seemingly endless line of buxom countesses; the best athletes in the world train constantly to gain additional advantages, however small. This is explicable with standard evolutionary logic: satisfaction often breeds stagnation. But it does not explain why evolution eschews the negative axis and resists actively punishing us for sloth and instead embraces the far more pleasant alternative: hastening the degradation of our pleasures.

The answer might be that conscious, or even semiconscious, existence, which requires an immense sensory apparatus and extremely sensitive pain receptors, not to mention the ongoing burden of socially inflicted or self-inflicted emotional stress worming around our skulls, would be insupportable without 1) a relatively pain-free baseline and 2) some sort of positive, pleasurable, innately enjoyable options. Play fulfills the latter function. Yes, we can easily imagine a world completely free of games and anything like play. It seems like a pretty minor change, less extreme by far compared to a world without hearing or a world without color. But I think that's short-sighted. If you removed play and games, many people would be left with staggeringly little to interest or amuse them. How many happy memories of childhood are bound up in play and games and the give-and-take of the competitive contest? If play has no direct functional effect yet is a large part of making the world a place worth living in . . . that's as powerful a reason for its persistence as any.

But this is purely theoretical. I've made the claim that many animals play; let's look at a few canonical examples.

BIRDS AT PLAY, OR AT LEAST PLAYING A GAME

Many animals play in unexpected ways, and previously held assumptions about the inability of reptiles and other cold-blooded animals to play have been shown, again and again, to underestimate their fun-loving capabilities. In general, likelihood of animal play is a statistical feature, moving from unknown (amoebas, for example) to endemic (great apes). The fact that many lower-order animals don't play doesn't obviate the curious fact that all higher-order animals *must* play.

For a typical example of play from avians, let's turn to the willow warbler (*Phylloscopus trochilus*). This species is commonly known as the "fighting wren," for reasons soon to become clear. For these birds, the impulse to fight waxes as breeding season approaches, a process described in 1898 with prose that can't be bettered:

> . . . as the pairing time arrives . . . the willow warbler males fight continually and with no apparent cause—if not over the female, over a fly, a worm, a beetle, a place to perch, anything or nothing. It is just the same whether females are present or not, whether they enjoy absolute freedom or are in captivity, whether they have been taken a few hours ago or have lived in a cage for years. In short, they fight at all times and under all circumstances.[9]

This would initially appear as a readily understandable if overactive type of dominance behavior, triggered by the need to reproduce. What is most interesting is the structure of the bird's preferred competition:

> When free, they collect at an appointed spot; usually a moist elevation covered with short grass and about two metres in diameter is chosen for the arena, and is resorted to several times daily by a certain number of males. . . . The first arrival looks anxiously about for a second, but when he comes, should he prove not exactly fit, a third and fourth are awaited, and then the battle opens. Each having found his antagonist, they fall to, fly at each other, and fight vigorously till they are tired, when each returns to his place to rest and collect his strength for the next round. This goes on till they are exhausted and retire from the field, to return soon, however, in most cases. More than two never fight together, but if a good many are on the ground at once, as often happens, they fight in pairs, and cross one another in such marvellous leaps and bounds that a spectator at a little distance would think the birds were possessed of an evil spirit, or else gone crazy.[10]

I find this behavior remarkable. The fighting isn't triggered by a female wren's presence, nor does evidence indicate that particularly successful fighting wrens gain some sort of reproductive advantage—the females are not around to witness it, nor do male wrens voluntarily submit to more dominant/successful peers during mating competitions. From a reproductive standpoint it's a game without a reason.

Yet these birds can't resist the urge to play what we recognize as a fully realized game of arena combat. When free to roam, and when given the choice, these warblers identify a specific location for the contest (a "moist elevation with short grass about two meters in diameter") and communally observe a complicated set of rules. Fights are one-on-one or between two pairs of temporarily aligned birds but never more than a pair; the birds wait for an adequate opponent instead of attacking the weakest; the birds do not interfere with other fights; when needed, they take turns fighting. When exhausted, a warbler is not pecked to death but allowed to leave, recuperate, and return to the arena at a later time. However frenzied the competition, however hyped by an overabundance of what in male humans would be testosterone, *the rules of the game are sacrosanct*.

This might not seem like an unusual event in the animal world; lots of males compete in sham-fighting during mating season, which might or might not help their genes to pass to the next generation. But let's step back for a moment and consider what's happened: evolution created what is unmistakably a game and incorporated into it all the character-istics and complex rules associated with sophisticated competition. We don't need to hypothesize that the ancient Romans must have seen the "fighting wrens" doing their thing and been inspired to create their Coli-seums. It's a simple case of independent evolution, strictly biological in the case of the birds, but culturally mediated in the case of the Romans.

The same impulse driving the warbler drives us: fighting is baked into our DNA. Fighting is extremely dangerous, but fighting is also inherently exciting. Nobody passes a spontaneous street fight without stopping, and looking, and sometimes clucking in moral disapproval—even if they soon shout in sudden glee at the splendid distraction. Why not regularize the matter and banish chaos: you must fight in *this* area, at *this* time, using *these* weapons, under *these strict rules* (no eye gouging, no ganging up, and absolutely no killing of the wounded unless the emperor decrees it).

The point is not that a game for the fighting wrens developed through evolution, it's that the game is what humans would call entirely reasonable and *fair*. You aren't allowed to fight an obviously weaker opponent. You can't fight two against one. You can't traitorously turn on your fighting partner in the middle of the battle, hoping to produce an injury while they're distracted. You can't kill the wounded or exhausted. You have to take turns when you get to the area, and you must be polite, however violent your behavior when it's your time to fight.

I always thought nature a brutal abattoir where mother bears defend their cubs from attacks by father bears, and in those rare cases when a mother fails to halt a cub's death, she calmly ingests her child's corpse. That's nature at its most basic: kill or be killed and eat what you can.

But the game of the fighting wrens is backward in this view, or at least incomplete; it's likely that our very understanding of what constitutes a "fair fight" or a "fair competition" has its roots in evolutionary biology. The vast majority of humans cultures the world over generally agree on what constitutes a fair fight, and the fighting wrens certainly live up to these expectations. Is something fair not because a specific culture has decided it's fair, or even because it aligns with our philosophical or ethical notions, but because the notion of fairness has been developed to promote an obscure evolutionary advantage? Children go through a spontaneous and often tedious phase of overwrought justice-seeking, where their most common complaint is "It's not fair!" This might develop into little more than a rhetorical device as the child grows up, but it's clear to anyone raising children that, in addition to bouts of needless cruelty and unthinking egoism, the issue of *what is or is not fair* is sometimes paramount: children feel it deeply and innately.

The major question lingers: why did evolution produce in fighting wrens what appears to be, even to a rigorous skeptic, a Platonic instantiation of a chivalrous combat sport?

THE SAD TALE OF PIGFACE, AND HAPPIER TURTLES

Once upon a time there was a large turtle held in captivity at the National Zoo in Washington, DC. It was a *Trionyx triunguis*, more commonly known as an African soft-shell turtle, the lone surviving species of the genus *Trionyx*. Members of this species are heavy aquatic turtles, sometimes weighing two hundred pounds, and they can live for over fifty years. They are big beasts. Keepers at the zoo affectionately named their turtle

Pigface, for its typically "ugly" (to human eyes) head: wide, flat, smooth, and speckled, with an absurd bulbous-tipped protuberant nose. Things were going fine until Pigface was observed clawing his own neck and biting his stubby forelimbs—typical self-harming behavior often noted in captive birds and mammals but rarely witnessed in reptiles. Common sense suggested that the turtle, if the turtle was sophisticated enough to feel such emotions, was lonely, under-stimulated, and quite possibly depressed.[11]

Because Pigface's self-inflicted wounds were becoming infected and posed a serious hazard to his health, something had to be done. Researchers made the obvious move: they injected a little fun into Pigface's constrained world. They added different types of objects to his tank, hoping to improve Pigface's mood and lessen his injurious behavior. It worked, but in a limited way. Initially Pigface interacted and played with the new objects, and his self-harm behavior decreased. After a week or two, however, as the shiny objects lost their charm, his self-harm behavior began to ramp up again. This is perfectly explicable from an anthropomorphic point of view, as it's the same way humans respond to new stimuli. The stimuli result in immediate excitement, slow degradation of interest, and a return of the status quo. What was to be done?

Researchers decided to scramble Pigface's expectations: they removed all objects from the tank for a week before slowly reintroducing them, and followed up with another week of ascetic shock. This constant shakeup and alteration in the environment had the expected effect. Pigface managed to stabilize as environmental change, increasing or decreasing the complexity of the tank environment, was sufficient to save him from what seemed to be suicidal tendencies.

An animal behavior researcher, Gordon Burghardt, happened to hear about the turtle's plight and, curious about the apparently sophisticated consciousness it implied in a reptile—which were not generally thought capable of such subtle states—videotaped Pigface's interactions with various "play objects." These included an everyday brown basketball, a smaller orange basketball, a floating hoop, a submerged hose pumping fresh water into the tank, and a scattering of live fish. The researcher kept an eye on how often Pigface interacted with these objects, and the total was impressive: 31 percent of waking time. One of Pigface's favorite toys was a floating hoop that the turtle was able to bite, grasp, and temporarily submerge; when submerged, Pigface was able to swim through it while raking it with his claws.

The hoop was fun, but something else was even better. Pigface loved the feeling of fresh water flowing out of a hose. He would often place himself directly in front of the hose's outlet and adjust his head so that it was perfectly in line with the current. He would float there for hours as the water slipped over his head and around his body. Of course, *Trionyx* is a river turtle, and in its native habitat would constantly be navigating currents of wildly varying strengths and directions, so Pigface's love for the hose made a certain amount of sense: it's what he was used to feeling, or what he had evolved to respond to.

In the world of animal behavior things were getting exciting. Turtles were not supposed to act like this. Reptiles were not commonly thought to be a playful bunch, being deeply unsporting and (it was imagined) intellectually feeble. Pigface threw it all into doubt, and might have been the center of a more ambitious research project had not tragedy occurred, dispassionately reported but surely underrepresenting Burghardt's true feelings: "Pigface's recent death has precluded further study."[12]

That might have been the end of it except for other instances reported from other zoos and observations in captivity and in the wild. Pigface's play-like behavior might be explained as an artificial result of stress in captivity except that it wasn't: scuba divers have reported seeing green turtles, in the open ocean, identifying objects, singling them out, moving them around, and playing with them in similar ways.[13]

Crucially, a captive wood turtle (*Glyptemys insculpta*) was seen doing something that can't be viewed as anything other than play. This common North American turtle, found across the northern reaches of the East and Midwest, lived in a captive environment that included a large water source as well as an accessible angled board, one end of which was submerged. What happened might have been expected if the captive animal was an otter or fisher, but this was a turtle. He realized he could climb around to the raised end of the board and push himself onto the angled wood. At this point gravity took over, resulting in a sliding splash into the water pool below. Once discovered, the water slide became the turtle's favorite activity.[14] If this isn't a slam dunk proof of reptile play, you have to work really hard to avoid the obvious conclusion.

THE IRRESISTIBLE APPEAL OF SPACE [TO] GECKOS

The unmanned but not unpopulated Russian spacecraft *Bion-M No. 1* was shot into orbit on April 19, 2013, and carried a payload of forty-five mice, fifteen geckos, eight Mongolian gerbils, and various snails and fish. Sadly all of the gerbils and fish, and most of the mice, died during reentry due to equipment failure.

The trip wasn't entirely tragic, though. The *Pachydactylus* geckos (*pachy* = thick, *dactyl* = finger/toe, i.e. "thick toed" geckos) not only managed to survive the round trip but spent quite a bit of time during orbit exploring their weightless environment. In particular, one of the geckos managed to wriggle its way out of its restraining polyurethane collar during prelaunch—because of this and other details, I'm not convinced that the Russian engineers really had a firm grip on either animal health or their motor capabilities—and in the microgravity of the orbiting spacecraft nudged the floating collar with its snout. The collar slowly and majestically moved away. Another gecko, interested, nudged the collar back. Pretty soon they were all involved with the collar: exploring how it rotated in the air, pushing it around, poking their heads through the loop when correctly oriented, etc. Onboard cameras recorded the entire trip— do yourself a favor and watch the video highlights, culled by the Russian animal behavior specialists who later wrote a paper about it. Viewer discretion is advised; the gecko enclosure grows evermore dirty and chaotic as the space mission lengthens, and at one point meal worms (their food source) are seen chaotically wriggling and twisting in free-floating panic. The sight is intensely disturbing.[15]

Gordon Burghardt, who also documented Pigface's play, was inspired by the tale of the space geckos and began to study earthbound geckos for similar behavior. After hundreds of hours of observation, Burghardt came to the following conclusion: "Do geckos *play*? Probably not, but it is hard to know for certain."[16] What happened on the Russian spacecraft remains an incontrovertible evidence of gecko play, however. Investigators reviewed the entirety of the geckos' space vacation, and in 2015 were able to distinguish between times the geckos spent actively manipulating the loose, floating collar and times when they ignored it; apparently the geckos had to be in the right mood to play. Play wasn't a blind instinctive response for them, nor a result of stress. To put it in possibly the most boring way imaginable:

> Our data suggest that in a suitable habitat even adult small reptiles are capable of performing play behavior. Our results and those of Burghardt (2013) suggest that playfulness may be stimulated in orbital experiments by using an enriched environment.[17]

MORE, MORE, AND MORE

The academic view of animal play has been constantly expanding. People have long accepted that certain animals play and receive pleasure from the play. Anyone with a dog would find this claim obvious. The great apes, in particular, indulge in extremely complex forms of play, involving satire, mimicry, and cooperation. Until fairly recently, scientists assumed that only the higher mammals were capable of play—until they noticed other animals playing as well. Careful investigation has pushed the play-indulging species list outward. Only mammals play, except for those reptiles who also play. And don't forget the insects: some species of wasps play. And some fish—and so it goes. The percentage of mammals indulging in play behavior is far greater than in the reptile or insect world, but our knowledge of non-mammalian play is increasing across the board.

One major stumbling block for researchers is *pleasure*. Is Pigface the turtle feeling pleasure when he messes around with various objects? Or is he responding to blind evolutionary impulses? The lessening of self-harm seems to indicate that his behavior, if not pleasurable, certainly has stress-reducing benefits. Is our clever wood turtle, navigating his primitive water slide, actually experiencing joy in the activity, or is it a reminder or reenactment of his native behavior near rivers and streams? Do the fighting wrens enjoy their arena combats, or are they a result of impossible-to-resist mating-related insanity? Because we can't measure an animal's level of pleasure, or assume an animal under study is capable of pleasure, there's always room for doubt. A skeptic might say that all animals, including the great apes, are behaving in ways that we humans, simplistically anthropomorphizing the visible behavior, *assume* is pleasurable play. Nobody claims bees are great mathematicians despite finding a maximally efficient packing geometry (hexagons) for their honey stores. It's just evolution working blindly using trial-and-error.

Let's grant the skeptics their due. Let's say that most if not all animal play is mechanical—that is, it involves playing games rather than experiencing pleasurable play. For animals, play = mechanically playing a game. Except that even here there are clear exceptions to the rule.

GIGGLING AND WRESTLING RATS

Here is one last example arising from some of the most playful animals in the world: rats. Male rats have a special love of wrestling and have developed an complicated system for setting up an wrestling competition, determining when to start the grappling, and figuring out when a rat has lost (taps out). There even exist recognizable rat grappling techniques with various styles and holds. It's a heavily regulated and well-organized sport. This type of clarity ensures that there are few rat-wrestling injuries; pinning techniques are well-recognized, and the pinned rat gives up the contest without much of a struggle. In addition to competing in instances of this well-defined wrestling game, rats also recognize each game as forming part of an ongoing series of games. One game effects the next; the goal isn't to win the current game but to maximize overall pleasure in the sequence of games. Rats not only play by shortsighted rules, they take into account long-term meta-game variables.[18]

We know rats are capable of this sophisticated behavior because they carefully keep track of who's winning and losing. An alpha rat, a master of form and technique, who wins every competition through strength and skill, soon finds himself alone at the pinnacle of his sport. Other rats don't want to wrestle with him anymore. What's the point? The paragon always wins. What happens in the rat world as a result of this dominance is surprising but sensible—if we were talking about humans. The unbeatable expert starts to lose matches on purpose. With occasional losses other rats become inspired to rejoin the competition because, hey, maybe he's getting old or overconfident or has a previously unseen weakness. From the point of view of the wrestling master it makes sense to occasionally throw a fight but only if rats *enjoy* wrestling, which they certainly seem to do. It's better to engage in play than be excluded from play, even if your exclusion indicates your utter dominance.[19]

An additional fact might explain some of this otherwise confusing behavior. It's recently come to light that rats, when tickled, giggle.[20] It's not something I want to listen to, and I couldn't if I wanted to. A rat's laughter is ultrasonic—which is why nobody noticed it one hundred years ago. But observation confirmed what we expect to be true: rats laugh in appropriate circumstances, and their laughter maps directly onto what humans would call joy, or delight, or pleasure in success. There isn't any way to tell directly, of course, as a rat's consciousness is likely as profoundly strange as anything discovered by high-energy particle physics, but we do know at least one thing. After a dominating display of skill, the wrestling rat masters, even as their struggling opponents are pinned beneath their paws, do something absurdly human. If you have the right listening devices, tuned to just the right frequency, you can often hear them giggling.[21]

CHAPTER TWO

ALL WORK AND NO UNSTRUCTURED PLAY MAKES JANE WHINY

We know from animal studies and experiments that *some* of the time, for *some* species, and for *some* individual animals, play hones motor skills, improves predatory or escape ability, strengthens socializing and bonding, and so on. As we have seen there are so many exceptions to these broad rules that they don't qualify as rules but guidelines. The old problem returns: evolution shows us, again and again, that when a behavior becomes redundant or unnecessary it is swiftly weeded out. If play has an advantage for animal X, and a hundred thousand generations later animal Y, descended from X and inheriting X's play tendencies, still plays but *without* gaining X's advantages from the experience, play should eventually disappear for species Y. This happens all the time in extremely obvious ways: species that were once living under the bright sun but for whatever reason took to living exclusively in caves soon find their eyes diminishing and, over generations, the species slowly becomes blind. This is true parsimony; the small amount of energy required to keep eyeballs healthy is enough to separate poorly functioning eyeballs (using less energy) from really excellent ones (consuming more), leading to a slow degradation of the optic nerves and associated structures. You end up with blind fish cruising around dark pools, living quite well after minimizing their energy consumption. Conservation of this tiny energy delta (the difference between healthy and degraded eyes) is the difference between sight and blindness. Yet the outrageous, by comparison, energy and time demands of animal play continue to persist through the ages. You can see why scientists call it one of the great mysteries of the animal kingdom.[1]

We are sure of at least this much: the play urge has incredibly deep biological roots. The play urge is spontaneous. It doesn't need to be taught; infants engage in it as soon as they realize their limbs are part of their own bodies. Instead of looking for direct functional benefits to play, it might be more useful to tease out play's advantages by looking at what happens when *play is artificially removed or denied*. Take a bunch of fun-loving, roughhousing rats and raise them in an environment where all play is artificially halted. What sort of rats do you end up with at the end of the day?

The results are pretty clear. Play has significant effects that are, for the most part, only visible from the context of *play deprivation*. This is particularly true in social species such as rats and humans.

One reason that play's advantages are hidden is that play deprivation does not "produce a failure to develop species-typical behavior."[2] A rat raised in isolation still behaves as a rat and isn't immediately distinguishable from a rat raised with other rats and free to play. The rats, if placed in two solitary cages, are essentially indistinguishable. They are both relatively unhappy (confined to solitary) and busy doing unhappy rat-like things. When you inject a play-disadvantaged rat into a happy rat pack, however, the differences between the two rats begin to emerge. The rat raised without play has difficulty in social contexts. If you were to cut open these two rat brains, you would be able to spot a significant biological difference: solitary rats, or rats raised exclusively with adults and bereft of juvenile play, have a modified prefrontal cortex, a smaller subcortical striatum, and abnormal dendritic arborization—the ways their neurons form synaptic connections is noticeably different.[3]

These are significant neurological changes and result in observable behavioral changes: play-deprived rats have extremely poor executive functions compared to social rats. *Executive functions* is a catchall category describing a suite of neurological and regulatory control mechanisms including short-term memory, attention, emotional regulation, impulse control, and decision making. The category includes all the stuff that makes you a better or worse performer in social situations: Can you remember everyone's first name in the room? Are you too scattered to pay attention to your neighbor's tale of his burning shed? Are you able to regulate your emotions, control your impulses and desires, and judge correctly what would or would not be an appropriate action for an extremely specific social situation?

While these would seem to be relatively minor social advantages, let's remember what happens to a fish species transplanted to a dark cave. The tiny energy consumption required by healthy eyeballs is enough to result, in time, in utter blindness, as nonessential energy is conserved. Next, consider the difference between a well-functioning social rat and one with atrophied or poor social impulses. The more socially successful rats are higher on the social pecking order, have better reproductive results, enjoy better nutrition, feel less stress and in general enjoy happier and longer lives. This isn't a tiny energy delta we are talking about, it's a massive advantage that accrues and compounds over the lifetimes of both the well-adjusted rat and its offspring.

We might be nearing a defensible hypothesis. Play's visible effects are subtle because they occur, for the most part, in the brain of the playing animal; while it might be possible to inspect the brain and actually see some structural changes, this is not something most investigators are inclined to do by habit or training—assuming there is something to be seen, as in the case of rats. Experts also find it extremely difficult to tease apart the precise social hierarchy of a rat pack, even in a laboratory, much less distinguish between subtle social gradations. (The biggest winner and the most unfortunate loser are easy enough to determine, but could anyone distinguish the twelfth most socially successful rat and the thirteenth?) When you put these difficult-to-spot differences together with behavior that might have occurred years before animal researchers even got on the scene, you end up with something like what we currently find: play behavior apparently ruptured from functional effect. In other words it's hard to see the functional benefits of play because they occur invisibly (within the brain) and in behavior humans are temperamentally unsuited to recognize and categorize: the complex social context of a given species.

Humans are excellent intuitive detectives when decoding and recording human social interactions; however, it's not clear that humans are very good at determining the precise social hierarchy of, for example, a herd of gazelle. Even if investigators grant that gazelle have a complex social life (and it's not a given that most investigators believe this to be true), an exceedingly thorny problem remains: how to reliably get access to the gazelle's social data. It's far easier to assume these social organizations don't exist or are relatively simple, but for rats this is an illusion— they have an extremely complicated and fully realized social world. With social animals, proper socialization and the ability to maneuver through the social minefield is extraordinarily important. Play may have significant add-on effects, such as making the world a worthwhile place to continue to exist in, but even if play only upped one's social savvy the evolutionary effects would be noteworthy.

One of the most interesting results from this type of rat research is the fact that while adults do play with juvenile rats, this type of play is less frequent and less effective for later executive function development than peer-to-peer play. Young rats do best when they wrestle, chase, and play with others of the same age in an unstructured way. It's almost impossible to resist the temptation to extend these sorts of hypotheses to that most social of all animals, humans. Imagine that unstructured childhood play (free play) was proven to either increase or decrease social success later in life—given the extreme importance humans place upon social status and everything that goes along with it, wouldn't free play suddenly transform from an afterthought into something parents would facilitate for their children at every stage of their development? On the other hand, what might be the results if, as in our current society, free play is either discouraged (too much else going on) or not particularly free, i.e. highly supervised (limiting the benefits of rough-and-tumble, unstructured play)?

THE HELICOPTER PARENT HYPOTHESIS

The helicopter parent hypothesis is a tempting thesis (although not one I feel has yet been rigorously justified by science), and you could write a book or two about it and all the related issues. Many have, including:

- *Free-Range Kids: Giving Our Children the Freedom We Had Without Going Nuts with Worry*, by Lenore Skenazy.
- *The Coddling of the American Mind: How Good Intentions and Bad Ideas Are Setting Up a Generation for Failure*, by Greg Lukianoff and Jonathan Haidt.
- *Antifragile: Things That Gain from Disorder* by Nassim Nicholas Taleb.

The general thrust of these and other books in the genre is straightforward: "Good intentions" have driven most parents, social organizations, and educational systems into a quagmire of overly strict supervision, resulting in poor real-world outcomes. The claim is that from an early age most children in first-world nations, particularly those in North America, have extremely limited opportunities to engage in free, rough-and-tumble, and sometimes chaotic play during which feelings are hurt, bruises and bumps appear, and delight, anger, and frustration mix in a morass that the child must navigate both socially and emotionally. The results, from the perspective of these authors, are dire, and I'll quickly review the claims in each book.

Free-Range Kids: Giving Our Children the Freedom We Had Without Going Nuts with Worry

In this book, Lenore Skenazy notes the moral panic of the 1970s when a few high-profile incidents generated absurd amounts of worry about an exceedingly rare event: child abduction. The actual numbers indicate that, aside from the kidnapping of offspring by a disgruntled noncustodial

45

parent, child abductions are extremely unlikely. Due to this irrational fear, you run the risk of police involvement for allowing your ten year old to walk a mile home from school.[4] The effects of this panic upon free play are obvious: only thirty years ago, children often had the "run of the neighborhood" after school and would return home only in time for dinner, whereas today's children have little if any unsupervised time outside of the home.

The 1970s childhood experience sounds like something out of the middle ages, but many of my friends grew up this way, and I'm not an old man. The shifts in child-rearing and play opportunities since that time have been seismic, leading one to wonder about their long-term effects. For Skenazy the results are obvious: children suffer from a deficit of confidence, individualism, responsibility, and the sort of growth (sometimes painful, sometimes scary, sometimes thrilling) that is generated through unfettered interaction with the real world, as well as with the social world as mediated by play and games. Lack of unstructured play and freedom, including the freedom to be bored and the obligation to moderate that boredom through self-directed activities, have resulted in a generation lacking in emotional resilience. Constant supervision inculcates dependency. An overly strict focus upon physical safety unnecessarily downplays the robust nature of children and teaches that the modern American world, which is the most safe and humane society ever to exist in the bloody and barbarous history of humanity, is full of child predators and omnipresent threats of grave physical harm. It's certainly not a place to wander about in and explore without an adult guiding and shaping and controlling the action.

The Coddling of the American Mind: How Good Intentions and Bad Ideas Are Setting Up a Generation for Failure

Greg Lukianoff and Jonathan Haidt take the broad thesis of generational "coddling" (i.e. constant supervision by parents and institutions) as a given and point, as partial evidence of the result, to what is happening on college campuses with the current generation of students. One of the most telling changes is the apparently instinctive move by the students, out of choice and habit, toward purely administrative solutions to any and all problems, particularly those of a personal nature. In the 1960s and 1970s, students broadly resisted any effort by college administrators to tell them what to do or what to think, and they actively discouraged bureaucratic meddling in student affairs even if things got messy. And in the 1960s they got messy to a degree unheard of nowadays. Armed student protesters occasionally took over buildings, such as the AAS (Afro-American Society) occupation of Willard Straight Hall in 1969 on the Cornell campus.[5] While police massed in downtown Ithaca the administration raced to defuse the situation, which would have surely ended in bloodshed had the police stormed the building as was their plan. After thirty hours the students agreed to peacefully end the occupation, and a picture of them ("Campus Guns") leaving the building armed with rifles, shotguns, and bandoleers lined with bullets won Steve Starr the Pulitzer prize for spot news photography, in great part due to the shock value of the absurd contrast between an assumed idyllic university atmosphere and its current violent reality.

Sometimes the overt conflict between students and administration turned deadly; the famous 1970 Kent State shootings saw the Ohio National Guard called to the campus to "restore order" and fire upon peaceful antiwar student protesters, killing four and wounding nine. There isn't any need to continue citing examples; the general point is that in the 1960s and 1970s, in an atmosphere of justified societal unrest, college students were at the forefront of active protest. Not all of it was either moral or ethical, and most of it was illegal and likely counterproductive, but there were significant victories claimed amidst the chaos. If nothing else, the students organized in response to legitimate grievances related to both local and national problems and took matters into their own hands—for good or ill.

During this time period, students wanted to control their own lives;

if there was a problem they dealt with it either on an individual level or through student-run organizations, self-organized protests, etc. This set the tone for the general state of campus life for the rest of the twentieth century: universities consisted of professors and students working together in limpid agreement, messy conflict, or bland apathy, with the ultimate goal of producing well-educated and well-rounded graduates. Layered on top was a light sprinkling of administrative personnel, whose job was to keep the lights on, the toilets cleaned, and to ensure that rare events (extreme protests, violent acts, crime) did not spiral out of control. It was a thoroughly hands-off environment.

What do we have now? Haidt makes the following claims: starting in roughly 2005, accelerating in 2010, and showing no signs of slowing down, the expectations of a new generation of students diverged from those of the past. These student's instinctively turn to bureaucratic solutions, something Haidt terms *moral dependency*: when something uncomfortable happens on campus, however slight, and however minor the offense (intended or not), the natural impulse of the students is to run to a moral arbiter. Bias committees are formed, counseling services offered, security teams beefed up, and endless layers of investigative inquiry produced in response to any and every slight. The helicopter parenting model has essentially been carried on from grammar school, through high school, and has been formalized at the university.

The result on the educational outcome has been pretty obvious.

According to a new report from the New England Center for Investigating Reporting, "The number of non-academic administrative and professional employees at US colleges and universities has more than doubled in the last 25 years."[6] Meanwhile, full-time tenured faculty positions are at the lowest rate in twenty-five years, while the prevalence of adjunct professors—part-time, nontenured professors—is at its highest. In fact, according to the American Association of University Professors, "more than three of every four (76 percent) of instructional staff positions are filled on a 'contingent basis,' meaning without tenure."[7]

It's impossible to expand the university bureaucratic system at such a high rate and have enough money left over for those doing the teaching and research. The fact that three-quarters of current professors are not tenured, and do not have any chance of gaining tenure, is a shocking and under-appreciated statistic. One result of this growing imbalance is that the remaining tenured professors are often overwhelmed by graduate student responsibilities, advisory roles, and conducting and publishing their own research. This doesn't represent a degradation of higher education; it's essentially the end of what, twenty years ago, was the norm: most undergraduate classes being taught by fully tenured faculty. While many adjunct professors are good teachers, they are working at an extreme disadvantage. Adjuncts typically make between $2,000 and $5,000 dollars per course in a semester;[8] attempting to teach enough courses to generate a functional salary isn't fair to them nor their students. (It goes without saying that adjunct professors receive few, if any, supplemental benefits.)

Stories about homeless adjunct professors busy teaching yet forced to sleep in their cars unfortunately abound;[9] the crushing weight of student loan debt for these professors is doubly destructive, given the paucity of opportunities for many with graduate degrees. The obvious solution for such an economic quandary is hard to avoid: get out when you can. The best and brightest are no longer working in academia, and those who do are getting the short end of the stick by any measure. The dedication of many adjuncts is used as a manipulative lever to reduce salaries down to, and in many cases below, the poverty line.

In addition to the deleterious educational effects of a swelling administrative staff, we should warily consider the basic generative priority embedded in any bureaucracy: a desire to continue or (if possible) expand its size and reach moving into the future. Bureaucracies of any type are notoriously difficult to steer and even more difficult to shrink: there are few examples of bureaucracies solving a problem, recognizing that the problem has been solved, and voluntarily disbanding their administrative apparatus. It's unlikely that university administrative power centers will easily concede that students don't require quite as much oversight as they currently have and that their fundamental goal is a solution looking for a problem. The current incentives lead to the opposite conclusion: the problems on campus are real and increasing. Declaring victory would result in a diminution of power and (in the extreme case) loss of employment. It's likely that the recent wave of administrative hiring will continue unabated, offset by more and more classes being taught by adjunct professors or graduate students.[10]

Why do universities require so much administration? In part it's due to increasing reporting demands for Title IX and other state and federal regulations, but a chunk exists to service perceived student needs. If "helicopter parenting" is going to exist on campus it will require a huge number of support staff. What's driving this increase?

Haidt is explicit about the cause: lack of free play during childhood due to incredibly intrusive supervisory interventions in public school and the broader culture as a whole have created a student body that demands, and expects, a large and powerful administrative presence. In Haidt's view there are increasingly few times when children are free, even at recess, to play in unstructured ways, to make mistakes and rectify them independently, to succeed or fail at delicate social maneuverings during heated arguments or debates, to defeat an enemy or in turn be defeated and realize, upon defeat, that the game isn't over. One loss does not lose the war nor crush the losing combatant. You just have to adjust your tactics and try again the next day.

Antifragile: Things That Gain from Disorder

Nassim Nicholas Taleb's *Antifragile* expands the general theme of good-intended but flawed parenting behavior. Any rational parent knows that saying yes to all of your child's demands produces terrible results in the long term. You need to cause your child short-term suffering every day, in many facets of their lives. You drive them to school despite their tears, deny them a much-craved third episode of a favorite television show, and fail to fully appreciate the importance of a concert or event, nixing attending due to the cost or energy (and time) required to satisfy it. Children feel these conflicts are the most important things in the history of the world, but parents don't usually experience serious moral quandaries about denying them. We might feel bad about it for a bit, but we know, deep down, that the weak answer (always giving in) exacerbates the problem and generates profoundly unhelpful power dynamics. What we are counting on, and know to be true, is that children are essentially robust; they are not fragile.

Coddling isn't necessary, it's counterproductive. Taleb makes the point that children, adults, and various systems and organizations not only continue to function in the face of conflict but actually refine and improve themselves because of conflict, maximizing their operational strength. A strong army is a veteran army. Removing conflict from the world stifles growth and reduces strength.

A simple analogy from medicine is entirely appropriate. Doctors used to think that a severe knee injury was something to be treated with kid gloves. The knee is a large, messy, and relatively poorly engineered joint, which is subject to large amounts of daily stress. After surgery doctors imagined that such a complicated structure required rest and rigorous immobilization. If you felt pain when attempting to use your knee weeks or months after surgery, doctors suggested you wait until the knee pain decreased. Yet rehabilitation results under this scheme were poor. It turned out that a better solution wasn't to coddle the knee but work it as soon as possible. Painful rehabilitation was the rule; the knee healed better when it was manipulated as soon as possible, however painful the process. (Hip replacement surgery is the same; patients are tasked with putting weight on the joints sometimes the same day as the surgery). It's not fun. It hurts. But it's the only way to get the knee fully functional again. Knees are robust and not only handle stress but require it for full growth and recovery. Patients who fail to push themselves through the inevitable pain end up with far worse clinical results.

THE RESULTS OF UNSTRUCTURED PLAY, AND THE INEVITABLE EXPANSION OF PERCEIVED HARM

Haidt agrees with Taleb's basic thesis and confidently makes the next logical step: the coddling of children, high school kids, and college students isn't necessary. Worse, it's counterproductive. If you are offended by something somebody says, the solution is to talk to them about it, get into an argument, exchange views, make your point, and do your best. Don't immediately run an administrator and lodge an (increasingly) anonymous complaint. The long-term effects of this sort of moral dependency (counting on bureaucracy to enforce every slight) is a repudiation of independence and is profoundly unhelpful as a long-term strategy for dealing with the world. It reduces the social cost of trivial, false, or incoherent claims to an absolute minimum and incentivizes those most willing to look for offense whenever possible, allowing them to report perceived misbehavior with a clear sense of moral rectitude.

The reason for this is clear: offense is personal and holy. It's hard to imagine a situation on college campuses where it's acceptable to say, "I'm sorry you are offended but your offense isn't that important and you might want to ask yourself if your offense is delusional." Offense is a foot soldier in the broader social battle between those in power (the privileged, as marked by race and gender and sexual orientation) and those without power (the unprivileged, marked by race and gender and sexual orientation). Offense is a way the unprivileged fix the world, change societal norms, and inform those in power that what they are doing isn't right and won't be tolerated. Offense is an act of courage, of protest, and carries the moral weight of the oppressed rising up against the oppressors. A student taking offense at something they hear or see is a sacred event: it's often unacceptable to question the validity or importance of the actual offense, nor the intent of the perceived offender.

If the social drawbacks to being continually offended have been reduced in the current climate, and when reporting such offenses offers clear emotional and social advantages, is it any wonder that campuses seem overrun by racial animosity, gender violence, hatred for marginalized people, and who knows what else—this despite American campuses being, according to every crime statistic available, some of the safest places humans have ever constructed in our brief existence on this planet?[11]

The social and psychological benefits of *moral outrage* have been extensively studied and don't simply include the well-known and obvious device of "virtue signaling" (taking offense to show you are aware of a specific issue and are actively attempting to call it out). More subtly it's also been found that "Outrage driven by moral identity concerns serves to compensate for the threat of personal or collective immorality . . . and the cognitive dissonance that it might elicit. . . . [It] expose[s] a link between guilt and self-serving expressions of outrage that reflect a kind of 'moral hypocrisy,' or at least a non-moral form of anger with a moral facade."[12]

In recent studies, the degree and intensity of moral outrage was found to be linked to one's own perception of social or cultural guilt. For example, if you sew your own clothing and buy your fabric locally from a throwback corner store weaver, your level of moral outrage against companies using sweatshop workers in China to crank out American clothing is relatively low. However, if you shop for clothing at discount stores you'll have a much higher level of moral outrage against this type of exploitation. Why the disparity in outrage? It's emotionally useful. Displaying strong moral outrage diminishes one's own sense of guilt and culpability: the more guilt the louder and more strident the outrage. As a coping mechanism, researchers have found it functions relatively well—at the cost of being utterly hypocritical. It also helps the person being outraged convince themselves that they remain a "Good Person" despite making absolutely no changes to their actual behavior, such as refusing to buy sweatshop-generated clothing. *That* might be slightly inconvenient.

If nothing else, modern research on the increasing prevalence and stridency of moral outrage should lead everyone, at the very minimum, to be suspicious of those complaining the loudest. They might have genuine grievances that deserve to be publicly aired, but moral outrage is often generated by a mix of impulses, a fair number of them self-serving and the majority completely severed from any true connection with the source of the presumed outrage. In other words, moral outrage still functions socially and emotionally even if the outrage results from presumed (but nonexistent) offense giving.

None of these authors support bullying or hateful discriminatory behavior leading to prolonged suffering or violence, but these types of clear-cut and extreme instances of prejudice are vanishingly small in the ongoing and expanding litany of reported triggers, verbal aggressions, and other activities that produce, in some way, "uncomfortable environments" on campus. The mere presence of a deeply held but diametrically opposed opinion is often enough to cause offense and generate administrative reporting. The effect upon students and professors is well-documented and ongoing;[13] syllabi are scrubbed of any topic that might cause mild discomfort to the most sensitive or paranoid students. This represents a serious lack of courage and moral fortitude on the part of professors, but it's somewhat understandable; in the hothouse environment of top-ranked college campuses failure to toe the line on increasingly extreme pedagogical strictures[14] generate immediate and debilitating charges of racism, transphobia, misogyny, etc. Careers can, and do, come to an end from extremely minor or nonexistent student-driven reporting of offenses.[15] But the effects upon students is equally dire; a large and recent study (2017) showed that, "Among those 1,250 students, a majority have censored their viewpoint during classroom discussions."[16] These are not racist ideologues worried about being socially ostracized; many simply have an opinion not openly shared by their peers. The line between imperfect adherence to dogma and other/enemy status is exceedingly thin, and many students gladly trade silence for social acceptance.

Many extreme examples of overly fragile triggering can be found; my favorite comes from Emory University, where somebody scrawled

"TRUMP 2016" in chalk at various places around campus, igniting controversy from the alleged assault. Protest groups were formed and (of course)
the administration was called in to fix things. The college president deigned
to talk to the offended group and reported the following, "During our conversation, they voiced their genuine concern and pain in the face of this
perceived intimidation. After meeting with our students, I cannot dismiss
their expression of feelings and concern as motivated only by political preference or oversensitivity. Instead, the students with whom I spoke heard a
message, not about political process or candidate choice, but instead about
values regarding diversity and respect that clash with Emory's own."[17]

The key phrase here is "perceived intimidation." This doesn't have
anything to do with a Republican student thumbing his or her nose at the
candidate overwhelmingly preferred by campus culture. There isn't any
way to determine the motives of the writer given the two-word message.
What's important is the message's effect, and the effect is *based on feelings*.
Because it was felt to represent some form of intimidation, it was some
form of intimidation, requiring intervention by no less than the university president.

Emory has detailed guidelines outlining acceptable locations and
methods for student chalking. However, after tracking down the guidelines, I think that the president (and those who removed the chalk mark-
ings) were in violation of their own stated policy, although I might very
well be wrong. I suggest you look it over if you want a deep dive into
tangled legalese, but it seems to me that protest (chalking) that does not
actively hinder the passage of students upon various walkways, or otherwise disturb their studies (because of sound or other environmental
effects), is explicitly allowed regardless of protest content.[18]

This is truly a tempest in a teapot; that chalked graffiti urging students to vote for Trump resulted in protests and counterprotests and
heavy-handed multilayer administrative efforts is a signal that, at the very
least, more important issues are being avoided by such rigorous attention
to the trivial.

There is room for hope. The tale of Emory's "TRUMP" chalking scandal ended with an extremely sensible and sober report,[19] generated by a student senate committee with input from various professors, which explained in great detail that the "TRUMP" chalking (and other related incidents) were wholly protected and supported examples of free expression completely in line with campus policy. Emory University has made it clear that objections to such trivialities are absurd. Yet protests continue.

Are the cause-and-effect theories promulgated by Haidt and related authors, blaming lack of unstructured childhood play for college-age emotional fragility and eager offense taking, plausible or correct? I'm formally agnostic but somewhat suspicious. The overwhelming number of college students in public universities around the nation manage to get through four years of classes without being exposed to any of this type of absurdity. You hear stories from Yale and Emory, Evergreen and Brown, but these are prestigious or extremely liberal schools with relatively high public visibility; when two Yale professors get shouted down by a mob of confused but aggressive students for failure to correctly respond to the extremely important topic of bureaucratic regulation of student Halloween costumes it immediately goes viral on YouTube. Something happens at Harvard or UC-Berkeley and it's all the chattering classes talk about for a week or two. For those who get all their information from mainstream media or "hot take" news or podcasts, it might look like the campuses are melting down, but these schools represent only a tiny fraction of the overall student population, and any incidents involve an even smaller percentage of relatively extreme students.[20] Is anyone going to report about a relatively tranquil year at Elmira College in Upstate New York? Selection bias in the age of YouTube is extremely strong.

Yet it's clear that *something* is happening; the Emory example probably wouldn't have occurred ten or twenty years ago—parties claiming deep internal injury from everyday political chalkings would have been laughed off the campus, not given a meeting with the president. And it's not enough to say that most schools don't suffer from such problems; it's surely not coincidental that the most prestigious schools, with the most expensive tuitions and largest endowments, are the ones at the forefront of intense student-led finger-pointing and gleeful offense-taking. The general rule is this: the more privileged the student population the more likely it is that you will witness extreme "coddling" events. The fact that Yale and Harvard are at the forefront of some of the most extreme cases is disturbing, as these universities not only represent the vanguard but generate a disproportionate percentage of difference makers in business, culture, and academia. If North Carolina State avoids this sort of trouble but it infects the top fifty schools in the country—that's no joke, and it's something to take seriously.

SOMETHING IS UP

The atmosphere on university campuses has obviously changed to some extent, but it's not clear what these publicized offense-taking events really mean. Do they represent a fundamental transformation of our culture? Or are they simply tantrums by well-meaning proto-adults living in such safe environments that there isn't anything else, locally, to protest about? That's my first layer of doubt, but even more dubious is the claim that lack of childhood free play has brought about moral dependency and victimization-embracing in (some small group of) college students at (some small group of) prestigious campuses. This *might* be true, but my suspicion about the claim is based partly on my sense that the explanation is extremely easy, and it flatters those making such judgments. Coddling is the thread running through it all: coddling in childhood, coddling with supervised play, coddling in increasingly structured high schools, and coddling by administratively enabled parental universities. Granted, this might be one of the times when a straightforward, simple reason explains a complex behavior, but it's important to remember how rarely this actually occurs in the real world.

An alternative explanation might be just as significant as the lack of unstructured play, enhancing whatever extreme victimization behavior students currently exhibit. Just as there is often no social penalty for extreme triggering or offense-taking on the part of students within the current student cultural moment, and because reporting such incidents is largely taken to be a sign of progressive activism, there is a clear and obvious monetary incentive[21] for those within the university administration to view college campuses as increasingly dangerous and problematic territory for disadvantaged students. We know from economic theory, history, and common sense that incentives need to be correctly aligned to ensure that organizations don't run off the rails (extremely poor incentive structures cause the vast majority of Wall Street bad behavior, for instance).[22]

The newest development in the quest for ultimate safety involves "unconscious bias," which is defined by the University of California at San Francisco as follows:

> Unconscious biases are social stereotypes about certain groups of people that individuals form outside their own conscious awareness. Everyone holds unconscious beliefs about various social and identity groups, and these biases stem from one's tendency to organize social worlds by categorizing. Unconscious bias is far more prevalent than conscious prejudice and often incompatible with one's conscious values. Certain scenarios can activate unconscious attitudes and beliefs. For example, biases may be more prevalent when multi-tasking or working under time pressure.[23]

This claim, widely accepted by many business groups and universities around the United States, is based on the Implicit Association Test (IAT), which in 1998 claimed to be able to ferret out "implicit bias" in those taking the test.[24] The test has been widely criticized in the decades since; the test is not reliably replicable (taking the test multiple times results in widely disparate results), but there has been an aggressive and earnest desire to inject the test results into business and/or education institutions in order to rectify the perceived bias. The problems with the test are multiform, as Jesse Singal explains:

> A pile of scholarly work, some of it published in top psychology jour-
> nals and most of it ignored by the media, suggests that the IAT falls far
> short of the quality-control standards normally expected of psycholog-
> ical instruments. The IAT, this research suggests, is a noisy, unreliable
> measure that correlates far too weakly with any real-world outcomes to
> be used to predict individuals' behavior—even the test's creators have
> now admitted as such. . . . What all these numbers mean is that there
> doesn't appear to be any published evidence that the race IAT has test-
> retest reliability that is close to acceptable for real-world evaluation.[25]

A meta-analysis of 494 IAT-based studies, released in 2017, indicates that, "Many procedures changed explicit bias, but to a smaller degree than they changed implicit bias. We found no evidence of change in behavior. Finally, changes in implicit bias did not mediate changes in explicit bias or behavior. Our findings suggest that changes in measured implicit bias are possible, but those changes do not necessarily translate into changes in explicit bias or behavior."[26] Large result sets from the business commu-nity in Silicon Valley (Google, Facebook, Pinterest) that mandated anti-implicit bias training in the last few years, show conclusively that they have no effect; other studies have even shown that IAT testing decreases interracial communication and leads to *worse* community outcomes.[27]

Let's grant as true the following large assumptions: implicit bias actu-ally exists and reliably maps onto unconscious gender or racial prejudice, and this bias does influence real-world behavior. What is the role of a uni-versity or a business in mucking about with people's unconscious thought processes? The most sophisticated psychologists in the world make no bones about their inability to understand and reliably modify "uncon-scious impulses and thoughts," or even agree if these structures are avail-able for manipulation.[28] The underlying hubris of those promoting the "implicit bias" cure is breathtaking.

While most people working with the IAT are well-intentioned, and view the test as a real-world tool for making society a better and less prejudiced place, a flawed tool clumsily wielded (which has been shown to have absolutely no real long-term effect on behavior) must be viewed not as a solution to a problem but as a method to extend the boundaries of that problem. To state the case in the most extreme way possible: if a hardened racist teaches at a predominantly African-American college for twenty years and is widely viewed as an excellent teacher, and has on record absolutely no prejudicial interactions with African-Americans during the course of a long career (i.e. no complaints at all), is this a problem to be rectified? This isn't unconscious bias we are talking about; this is deep-felt *conscious* bias, which in this example has no effect upon a professor's ability to teach, guide, and help students proposer. In this instance the work/home split is complete; what this hypothetical professor believes in the safety of his basement is entirely private and split from his rigorously self-imposed and entirely equal behavior on campus. It's hard to argue that this teacher should be fired for private beliefs having no work effect (assuming such a thing is even possible).

Move from this extreme to the issues the IAT is intended to address: somebody has some sort of implicit (unconscious) bias about something or other, but this bias (if it exists) has no discernable effect upon behavior. Unless you make the difficult argument that such bias will *inevitably ooze outward* into harmful actions toward someone at some point—again, what's the problem? I'm not saying it can't happen, or that methods to tamp down these unconscious biases (should they really exist and be capable of being pinpointed) might not be useful in the future in some way, but there is little evidence that we know what we are doing in this realm. Ham-fisted do-gooderism almost inevitably generates blowback worse than the potential benefits of the well-meaning fix. Suicide prevention billboard campaigns, for example, can have a deleterious effect upon vulnerable teenagers, making them "less likely to endorse help-seeking strategies."[29]

Part of my objection to the use of IAT as a tool of social improvement is linked not just to the science showing the IAT to be worthless as a behavior modification tool but to the general expansion of bias training in universities. Wilfrid Laurier University, now famous for another extremely small but illustrative conflict, the Lindsay Shepherd recording and its aftermath, recently held an event, the e(RACE)r Summit, which explored "Race and Racism on Canadian University Campuses" and offered solutions for rectifying these types of issues. As a base for their position, the following was asserted:

> Step 1: Take responsibility: Do not believe that the racial climate on campus is okay when the community has indicated that it is not.

Notably absent from the report is evidence of systemic racism or criminal sexual assaults. While data for Canadian universities is difficult to find, unlike data for American schools where campus crime statistics must be gathered and released due to the Clery Act (1990), the CBC (Canadian Broadcasting Company) News did a survey in 2015 of eighty-seven universities and reported the results.[30] Wilfrid Laurier University has the following sexual assault numbers per year: 2010, one assault, 2011, five assaults, 2012, three assaults, 2013, zero assaults. For a school with 17,000 students these are remarkably low totals; while even a single sexual assault is of course both a crime and a moral abomination, there isn't any way to view these numbers as anything other than incredibly hopeful. If we take these numbers at face value, it's unlikely that, in the history of the world, there were many places safer from potential sexual assaults than Wilfrid Laurier University in 2013—unless it was the University of Ottawa (42,000 students), which had one reported assault that year.

It is a well-recognized problem that sexual assaults are underreported (the generally accepted estimate says that only 20 percent of sexual assaults are reported), but even if you multiplied by ten the totals of reported university sexual assaults the results remain astonishingly low—far lower than among the general public. Yet the CBC report was taken as evidence of a larger problem: "Overall, experts say the number of sexual assaults reported to Canadian post-secondary schools is surprisingly low, and an indication that they are doing a *poor job of encouraging students to come forward*."[31] Lack of widespread assault becomes evidence of nothing more than lack of sufficient crime reporting: "'I find [the numbers] laughingly low,' says Lee Lakeman with the Vancouver Rape Relief and Women's Shelter and a leading voice on the issue of violence against women. 'It's just not that possible that they're that low. I can get more reports of sexual assault by walking across the street on a campus [and asking students directly].'"[32]

The Association of Universities and Colleges of Canada wrote a response objecting to the CBC survey, taking them to task for reporting *more assaults than actually occur*: ". . . by inflating rates by 10,000 students, CBC *overstates* the incidence of sexual assault on campuses."[33] According to those with the best information, who are in daily contact with the university students under discussion, and who must by law be involved when police are called onto campus, the actual rates are *lower* than those presented by CBC. How can this be possible when Lee Lakeman claims to be able to generate reports of sexual assault from a high percentage of students she talks to?

A large chunk of the problem is that "sexual assault" has vastly different meanings from an administrative and legal perspective than it does in the current university climate. Concept creep, whereby ideas or words with an agreed-upon definition expand to colonize new territory, have extended the idea of harm to microaggressions and other forms of "verbal violence," and vastly broadened the definition of sexual assault, which now includes offenses such as unwanted kissing or groping—again, this isn't a defense of such actions, but they are distinct from what most of us think of as sexual assault, and a case can be made that watering down terminology to such an extent lessens the moral and cultural severity of the more violent (traditional) understanding of sexual assault. In a similar way, completely consensual, energetically engaged, and emotionally rewarding drunken sex between two besotted (both meanings) and enthusiastic partners has been redefined as rape for failing to adhere to one axiomatic claim: one cannot give consent when drunk. In such a case, both participants are equally guilty of rape and could be expelled from a university for such an activity. These "drunk sex = rape" guidelines are obviously intended to stop predatory (typically but not always) male behavior when confronted with a drunk or incapacitated female, and it seems callous or absurd to object to such strictures if they stop even one case of rape. (This is a widely heard justification.)

This is an extreme position regarding intoxication; incapacitation is one thing, drunk or tipsy is another. Why cannot one give consent when drunk, or at least take responsibility for decisions made when drunk? Can one be charged with murder if the crime is committed when drunk? (Yes). In what other contexts is being drunk (a bit, a little, or extremely) an excuse for not being able to make rational choices? Our drunk driving laws are quite explicit on this point: even if you are completely wasted, you need to be able to make sensible decisions, such as "I'd better not drive, I'm lit." Attempts to explain to the judge that you were too drunk to realize you shouldn't drive will see you in jail before you finish the sentence.

The enshrined freedoms of Americans allow us to do all sorts of dangerous and unhelpful things that can result in death or social unrest, but the fact that these are the occasional outcomes don't inspire us to clamp down upon individual choice.[34] Balance is important: how far is too far to take our laws, regulations, and cultural strictures? At what point is the truly horrendous classical understanding of sexual assault/rape blanched by being associated with an activity whose definition depends upon administrative parsing of ability to consent? There is something deeply problematic with defining fully consensual nonviolent sexual activity as rape. At the very least, it makes the truly vile and violent rapists feel a lot better about themselves. *Slate* published an excellent review of this issue from a woman's point of view (it was originally hosted in their DoubleXX section), and discusses how cut-and-dry laws regarding alcohol and sexual consent, administratively enforced by colleges and universities, inevitably founder when confronted by messy reality.[35]

The endless expansion of definitions of harm and the embrace of victimhood do seem linked to a general failing of the current generation: a reflexive turn toward authority, which is a strict requirement for the rise of microaggressions on campus. The reasons for this flowering have been calmly and convincingly argued by Bradley Campbell and Jason Manning in their paper "Microaggression and Moral Cultures":

> In the settings such as those that generate microaggression catalogs, though, where offenders are oppressors and victims are the oppressed, it also raises the moral status of the victims. This only increases the incentive to publicize grievances, and it means aggrieved parties are especially likely to highlight their identity as victims, emphasizing their own suffering and innocence. Their adversaries are privileged and blameworthy, but they themselves are pitiable and blameless. To the extent that others take their side, they accept this characterization of the conflict, but their adversaries and their partisans might portray the conflict in the opposite terms. This can give rise to what is called "competitive victimhood," with both sides arguing that it is they and not their adversaries who have suffered the most and are most deserving of help or most justified in retribution. . . . A culture of victimhood is one characterized by concern with status and sensitivity to slight combined with a heavy reliance on third parties. People are intolerant of insults, even if unintentional, and react by bringing them to the attention of authorities or to the public at large. Domination is the main form of deviance, and victimization a way of attracting sympathy, so rather than emphasize either their strength or inner worth, the aggrieved emphasize their oppression and social marginalization.[36]

The entire article is worth reading in full, and the author's conclusions appear, upon reflection, obvious in hindsight: "Microaggression complaints and other specimens of victimhood occur in atomized and diverse settings that are *fairly egalitarian* except for the presence of *strong and stable authority*. In these settings behaviors that jeopardize equality or demean minority cultures are rare and those that occur mostly minor, but in this context even minor offenses—or perceived offenses—cause much anguish."[37]

In other words, the rise of microaggressions is a response not to a horrific university culture teeming with violence, prejudice, and intractable bias; it arises, rather, from a culture so serene and safe that the only possible offenses to be had are those of the micro variety. Similarly, the concept of innate bias is only possible in a climate where *overt* bias has been thoroughly discredited and appears with increasing rarity, forcing bias enablers to turn to a new, and apparently limitless, domain of festering evil: the unconscious mind.

These facts by themselves aren't enough to create the current problem: the role of a "strong and stable authority" (in the words of Campbell and Manning) is crucial. Without the presence of the real administrative power of the $20 million dollar yearly budget of UC Berkeley's Division of Equity and Inclusion, there wouldn't be any way for relatively (or entirely) trivial slights to become publicized and actionable. The problem isn't so much hypersensitive play-deprived students but a victimhood culture melded with authority, arising from a bloated and ever-increasing university administration. The real losers are 1) the students, who are poorly served by this bureaucracy and its promulgation of victimhood, 2) professors, who not only live in fear of student-led reporting of potential slights but actively scrub syllabi of "controversial topics," 3) the educational quality of the overall institution ($20 million a year could fund a large number of *tenured* faculty), and 4) everyone. Ten years ago, Republicans were enthusiastic about the value of a college education; as of 2017, a majority felt that a college education actively harms America. Education budget cuts by Republican-led state legislators are now the rule, not the exception. Nobody is winning: not students, not professors, and not the public at large. Well, that's not quite true. University equity and inclusion departments are expanding at a frightening rate; top salaries often exceed $230,000 a year (at least at UC Berkeley). It's a nice gig if you can get it. But it's worth asking a question: If you do end up working in one of these offense-enabling administrative divisions, how likely is it that you'll ever find on-campus bias and prejudice to be diminishing instead of posing a large, burgeoning, and ever-present danger to the student body's very existence?

PLAY IS FUNDAMENTAL

For all I or anyone knows, authors such as Lenore Skenazy, Greg Lukianoff, Jonathan Haidt, and Nassim Nicholas Taleb are right in pointing to our radically altered childhood play experience in order to explain our increasing culture of victimhood. People seem to be slowly waking up to the concept that play is crucially important, and, while we still don't know many of the details, play exists deep in our DNA, deeper than many experts previously suspected. It's one of the primal forces animating both animals and humans. Yet the modern world has a way of talking about play that presumes it to be innately childish, and *playing a game* isn't seen as serious activity. This type of cultural disdain functions to obscure the importance of play's biological primacy.

Whatever purpose play has in the animal kingdom is exponentially true for humans, the most social of all animal species. Play is serious. Play is fundamental. Play creeps up the evolutionary tree from dark roots, expanding as it moves upward, infiltrating the major branches, waxing as it winds toward the sun, prominently conquering the mammalian line and surging in power across interstices, gaining additional strength in the primates before exploding in power as it reaches the great apes. Humans, at the tip of the evolutionary tree, representing the pinnacle of the animal kingdom's complexity, have bitten most deeply from the forbidden fruit. The average time spent playing games, as well as the general complexity of play, reaches its apex with our species. Humans are not the strongest animals in the world, nor the fastest, nor the quickest to breed. In very few areas do humans actually best all other animals, with two clear exceptions: general intelligence and *time spent playing games*.

CHAPTER THREE

MASSIVE SIZE IS MASSIVE

In the fall of 2017, the dry, somewhat stultifying, but engagingly accurate Bureau of Labor Statistics finally posted data for 2016.[1] The results are eye-opening. Americans spend more money on entertainment than they do on health insurance, gasoline, education, or clothing. Americans spend roughly the same amount on entertainment as they do going out to eat. But the *entertainment* category is broad: entertainment includes pretty much anything that's voluntary and supposed to be fun, including overpriced desert music festivals, mind-bogglingly silly (from an aesthetic sense) modern art displays, awe-inspiring Arvo Pärt concerts, etc. This report doesn't really give me what I'm looking for; there's no *games* subcategory. Nor does it capture the secondary economic market for play-related activities, such as the highly relevant water-ski manufacturing sector.

The 2017 "global games market" only tracks money spent specifically on video games, and it puts the US total spent at $30 billion (2016 came in at $25 billion, giving the market an astonishing 20 percent growth rate).[2] This is significant, about one-fifth as big as the economic output of America's farms ($130 billion). The amount averages out to $100 per year per American adult spent solely on video games. Even this data point is far too narrow, though, capturing only a fraction of the actual total spent on games and game-related activities.

The exact amount is difficult to estimate, but the overall slice of the American economy involved in game production, game distribution, game advertising, game technology, and direct game-related activity is vast. It includes, but is not limited to, preparing food for huge football-obsessed crowds in university stadiums; arranging Las Vegas gambling vacations, involving planes and taxis and hotel bookings; televised hockey, requiring exorbitant pre- and post-production overhead; e-sport competitions for video games such as *Overwatch*, which have global tournaments and rabid fans; development of cheap and durable basketballs, which feel like leather but can be produced for less than a dollar apiece; coach and training staff salaries at all levels of competition above pee-wee; hangers-on who go by the name of ESPN and the United States Tennis Association—all these and a million offshoots constitute the American Game Economy, growing at four times the rate of the GDP, a juggernaut continuing to gain momentum and speed.

The American professional sports market is worth $70 billion,[3] but this estimate doesn't include indirect economic activity, which at minimum doubles the total to $140 billion. The outdoor sports economy is somewhere in the neighborhood of $887 billion,[4] Americans gambling lost $116 billion in 2016 (this only includes direct legal losses),[5] video games (alone) $30 billion[6]—and there's plenty still missing in this rough-and-ready estimate. The board-game/hobby-game market, worth over $1.4 billion[7] in the United States and Canada, is growing between 20 percent and 40 percent annually in what's being called the "Golden Age of Board Gaming."[8] More people are playing more board games and the types of games being played have expanded exponentially. *Settlers of Catan*, for example, was first released in Germany in 1995 and managed to attract a small but vocal following in the United States. A translated English version soon appeared, but the board game wasn't thought to be a good fit for the American market. The game takes a while to set up using a clever randomized board, and the action is both strategic, tactical, and social (part of the game involves haggling, trading resource cards, and occasionally deep rhetorical ploys). The typical audience for such a game is college-aged board gamers and D&D players, who had significant overlap in their communities. Thirty years ago that would have been the end of the story: a cult game, much admired, but with little penetration into the broader culture.

That's not what has happened, however. *Settlers of Catan* is now the fifth-most popular game in the history of the world after chess, *Stratego*, *Monopoly* and *Risk*.[9] It's also a far better game by many standards: it involves multiple players; it's relatively easy to learn; it's faster to complete from start to finish; it's never the same game twice given that the board is constructed using three random steps; it's far more socially engaging as the rules require player-to-player talk and wheeling/dealing in every turn; and it's vastly more rewarding from a strategic sense. It takes flexibility to become a really good *Settlers of Catan* player. You can't just decide upon and attempt to maximize a specific strategy because that strategy won't be appropriate for all board configurations or ongoing development patterns. Like the recent upswing in role playing games, which is inspiring articles such as "When Did Dungeons & Dragons Become Cool?"[10] board games have crept outside their niche and colonized a huge swath of culture, which is probably a good thing. If people are playing more games than ever they might as well be playing *Settlers of Catan*, interact with actual humans, participate in relatively complicated strategic decision making, and remove themselves from dank self-imposed basements.

Even this preliminary and incomplete financial summary creeps toward $1.5 trillion, and it still misses huge swaths of the game economy. An extremely conservative estimate puts the total of American play/game economic activity at $2 trillion, or one-ninth of the American economic output.[11] It's not as big as health care ($3.4 trillion),[12] but it's growing faster than health care spending. This segment of the economy currently exceeds the yearly economic output of India and is in a state of frenzied expansion.

It's a remarkable monetary total but more pressing from a cultural point of view is the amount of *time and energy* dedicated to play, sports, and games. Let's look at the big time sinks first.

It's actually quite difficult to find information about the average time Americans spend playing video games. Basic research supplies few easy answers despite this being a relatively common query. What's going on is entirely logical: industry surveys take pains *not to ask this question*, and the reason is pretty obvious. For decades, a similar statistic plagued the television industry. The gaming industry doesn't want a critical media tracking how much time is being "wasted" playing this or that game, so they don't ask. Fortunately, the government does want to know, and it tracks the results year by year. The totals are revealing.

In 2016, Americans who play games report playing them an average of 2.41 hours a day (men) and 1.85 hours a day (women), resulting in an overall average of 2.15 hours a day.[13] Television watching comes in at 3.45 hours, and "computer use for leisure, excluding games" totals 1.51 hours. These totals can't be blindly summed; obviously most people are incapable, from a time perspective, of spending almost seven hours a day staring at screens at home. These are averages over the population, and the categories surely overlap. Some Americans don't play games at all; others watch no television; a few don't have a computer. But it's possible to look at past reports and chart what activities are decreasing or increasing, given that there are twenty-four hours in a day, which offer a limited amount of relatively free time. If gaming and "computer use for leisure" are seeing high percentage increases every year (and they are), something else has to be diminishing. The categories affected most by the increase in gaming are "socializing (seven-minute daily decrease since 2003), reading (four-minute decrease), and arts and entertainment, not including TV (two-minute decrease)."[14] These might look like small numbers, but they are true averages across the entire population; a four-minute decrease in time spent reading represents a huge number of people who no longer read anywhere near as much as they used to, and who previously pulled up the average for the majority who read very little or never.

One of the most interesting statistics is that men and women are quickly converging in their gaming habits, with "a larger increase in gaming time among women (58 percent) than there has [been] among men (50 percent) since 2003."[15] There exist significant differences in time spent playing games by age. One of the most disturbing trends was reported by Ana Swanson in the *Washington Post*: "Young men without college degrees have replaced 75 percent of the time they used to spend working with time on the computer, mostly playing video games, according to the study, which is based on the Census Bureau's time-use surveys. Before the recession, from 2004 to 2007, young, unemployed men without college degrees were spending 3.4 hours per week playing video games. By 2011 to 2014, that time had shot up to 8.6 hours per week on average."[16] Again, this is a true average; lots of unemployed men without college degrees don't play many games at all, or have no access to them, which means the group playing games play *a lot* to pull the average up to 8.6 hours a week.

Game-playing demographics are difficult to interpret due to lack of detailed data, but surveys continue to show a massive increase in dedicated gaming in America (as of 2016):

- 63 percent of US households surveyed include at least one frequent gamer.
- 65 percent of homes own a video-game-playing device, while 48 percent own "a dedicated game console."
- The average guy who plays games is 35; the average woman is 44.
- The average gamer has been playing video games for 13 years.[17]

We have more disturbing data about our use of mobile devices: Americans are up to an astonishing average of five hours per day,[18] an increase of 69 percent from the previous year, most of it coming from use of social networks such as Facebook and Twitter. Gaming only comes in at 11 percent of this five-hour total, but that's a full thirty minutes of mobile gaming per day for the average American, from a source that wasn't widely available five or ten years ago. Games are now available at all times and are everywhere you happen to be. This represents a seismic change in game-playing habits.

Taken along with the entertainment sector (writ large) and the $3.4 trillion dollar healthcare sector, at least half of our national economy is consumed with entertaining us or keeping us healthy—both worthy goals, but requiring a vast expenditure of resources not being used elsewhere.

A massive yet subterranean transformation of our gaming habits has already occurred, a fact easy to overlook but made explicit by a simple question: What made more money way back in 2014, a) video games or b) the combined might of the Hollywood movie-making machine added to that of the American recorded music industry?

From a PR perspective it's not close; movies and music suck up an inordinate amount of airtime, but from a financial perspective video games had them soundly beat. Given the ongoing and constant year-over-year rate of increase for video-game sales, by the end of 2018 video games will have left all other forms of profitable entertainment completely in the dust. But even these numbers and totals fall short of accounting for the real time and energy people put into games, which is hinted at by what we currently see on YouTube. Everyone is playing more games than ever before on mobile devices, dedicated gaming systems, laptops, and every other electronic device under the sun, but this still fails to capture the inroads gaming has made into our everyday lives. To help illustrate this change I'll turn to YouTube, which has seen unbelievable growth: "The *Wall Street Journal* reports that the online video platform has seen a 10-fold increase in viewership over the past five years, due in part to the use of artificial intelligence to predict user preferences and keep people tuned in."[19] Americans watch around 1.5 billion hours of hours of television per month, and YouTube is currently at 1 billion hours per month and has a growth rate that television can't match. YouTube is poised to overtake television as the most-viewed media platform in the United States and the world.

What are people watching on YouTube?

YOUTUBE INCENTIVIZING BLANDNESS

Some might find this a surprise, but it's incredibly common for people to watch other people playing games on YouTube, and sometimes even to watch people watching people playing games on YouTube (i.e. a You-Tuber making a video of him/herself watching another YouTuber playing a game and commenting on the action). This might seem strange: what can possibly be gained from watching another person playing a game? I thought the whole point of games was that they were, at least minimally, interactive. Passively watching another person playing a computer game feels like an extremely degraded television game show; you are not even watching other humans competing against each other to win prizes, you are watching a single person (typically) playing against a bloodless computer. You might imagine this to be a niche YouTube category, like antique radio repair videos[20] and the like, but you would be, simply put, wrong. YouTube game channels are some of the mightiest on the platform.

The most popular (most subscribed) channel on all of YouTube is PewDiePie (Pewds), who reigns supreme with over 60 million subscribers as of March 2018.[21] Begun as a pure gaming channel it's morphed into broader comedy in recent years, but PewDiePie still plays a lot of computer games, records himself playing them, and narrates his experiences and reactions to the game. Recent videos included a *Cuphead*[22] "Let's Play"[23] that somewhat shocked me. *Cuphead* is one of the most creative games I have seen in at least a decade. It is a visually stunning reimagining of early Mickey Mouse/Popeye cartoons, with the early film style rigorously maintained (skipped frames, simulated optical distortions, and music straight out of 1929), but transformed by the game into a run-and-gun sidescroller. It's an extremely strange and compelling graphical presentation.

Cuphead, the eponymous hero, is a mischievous finger-shooting bipedal creature with a cup for a head, and he's pitted against a large number of amazingly flexible, rubbery enemies, who rise from the ground as a demonic carrot wielding a hypnotic cone of death, or appear as oversized smiling frogs with huge boxing gloves capable of generating a bazooka-type missile of pure glove-shaped energy, or pop out of a lake as a purple-haired (purple-snaked) medusa surrounded by electric eels who gives a disturbing (because fanged) come-hither look from beneath her slithery tresses. We watch PewDiePie attempt to progress through the levels, watch him fail (the game is extremely difficult until you get used to the controls and gameplay), and in turn we fail to smile at PewDiePie's running joke, after every death, that, "He's never died while playing any video game ever."[24]

Because the game is incredibly visually entertaining, PewDiePie's *Cuphead* videos are far more rewarding than they have any right to be; PewDiePie is essentially leveraging the visual sophistication of the game designers to generate relatively high-end content at rock-bottom production costs. The three or four *Cuphead* game play videos PewDiePie has produced have racked up, as of March 2018, over 16 million views; the cost to PewDiePie for making them is only the price of the game ($20 or so), and I suppose the daily amortized cost of his recording equipment and studio. By any standard it's a wonderful business proposition; a million-view video on YouTube (should it not be demonetized for having advertising-adverse content) brings in widely variable amounts of money (estimates range from $400 to $8,000 US dollars),[25] but even if it's on the extremely low end of the range, $500, that's at least $8,000 dollars for 16 million views, and is surely far higher given PewDiePie's sponsorship and promotional opportunities due to his status as the number-one YouTube channel in the world. The videos themselves are roughly fifteen minutes long and do require editing and sound correction before being uploaded, but in general PewDiePie is in an extremely enviable situation. His overall 2017 earnings were down from a 2016 height of $15 million and came in at only $12 million, due to an advertising controversy surrounding satire gone a bit haywire, but he's not hurting *that* much.[26]

Demonetization, the bugaboo for all YouTube content creators, is the name of the process used by YouTube for lowering the percentage of ad revenue paid to YouTube creators or, alternatively, making a video entirely unavailable for ad revenue. In other words you don't get paid for a demonetized (ad-free) video no matter how many people watch it. While this is clearly not an issue of censorship (anyone can upload whatever non-pornographic, non-obscene, and non-copyrighted material they want), it does cause serious ripples in the YouTube economy. The idea is this: advertisers don't want to be associated with certain types of videos. It would look bad, extremely bad, if a large multinational company ran an ad on a video that openly proselytized for a return of slavery and white racial domination of the planet. The company running the ad would, in fact, be supporting the content creator directly with advertising revenue. To get around this obviously problematic business outcome YouTube uses various algorithmic methods to guide advertisers to relatively "safe" or at least appropriate YouTube content.

Somebody selling a new type of golf club wants to advertise on videos watched by male sports enthusiasts. Somebody selling a new type of cyber defense system wants to sell to middle managers the world over. YouTube's job is to align advertisers with a specific audience and ensure that advertisers don't end up in a messy public controversy by showing up on politically charged videos or any video with a chance of containing any controversial content. You might think Alphabet (the parent company of YouTube and Google) capable of making extremely fine and granular determinations about video content. It's quite possible to run videos through voice recognition software and parse not only the overt content but the emotional content as well. This doesn't seem to be happening. YouTube's algorithm is simplistic, and has caused endless trouble for YouTube creators.

One example will suffice: an extremely uncontroversial video about woodworking and guitar restoration was famously demonetized minutes after the video was uploaded.[27] This was extremely puzzling to the content creator, who had never experienced demonetization before. After various unhelpful emails were exchanged with the mostly automated YouTube resolution system, no clear reason was supplied for the action. The YouTube creator was left in the dark about the mystery and asked for help from his viewers. The answer was so obvious he had completely overlooked it. The video description included a short explanation of the guitar restoration tips being documented on video, which included clamping wood, gluing various bits together, repairing electrical components using wire strippers and soldering irons, cleaning up chemical residue, applying shellac, and after it was all dry doing some heavy buffing with decreasing values of sandpaper and/or liquid polish. Did you spot the problem? "Wire stripper"— clearly this isn't a video that advertisers want to be associated with. It involves a *stripper*. An extremely basic YouTube banned word list had been triggered, resulting in instant demonetization. This is the opposite of artificial intelligence; it's artificial stupidity. I'm not the only one connecting the dots by any means; YouTube-focused message boards are full of similar stories and complaints, of which the following post is typical:

> The demonetization issue stems from videos being rejected for being even able to play ads, which most YouTubers who do it professionally are reliant on because even with Patreon it's still the norm for most revenue to come from ads. The YouTube Purge that we're going through is seeing entire genres of video makers demonetized, from gaming channels to political discussion ones (regardless of political leaning or how radical/moderate they are), and what's worst is that things are so broken that some (such as Razorfist) have confirmed it has nothing to do with content (he uploaded a private video that was just footage of his room and him saying random words and it was demonetized), while others have found that videos allowing unskippable ads will stay up but the same video [with] skippable ads will be demonetized (ShortFatOtaku).
>
> *To put it simply, Google has taken the well-known fact that the people it has running the site have no idea what the hell they're doing and ramped it up to levels never seen before. Expect the CEO and many others in the management to be removed by the shareholders in the next 12 months.*[28]

While the guitar-repair YouTube video kerfuffle is a trivial example, the demonetization algorithm has had significant real-world effects for YouTube content creators. While YouTube creators can upload whatever they want, if they want to get paid for what they upload they must be *extremely* careful.

YouTube's demonetization policy is extremely broad and includes the following language:

> Controversial issues and sensitive events: Video content that features or focuses on sensitive topics or events including, but not limited to, war, political conflicts, terrorism or extremism, death and tragedies, sexual abuse, even if graphic imagery is not shown, is generally not eligible for ads. For example, videos about recent tragedies, even if presented for news or documentary purposes, may not be eligible for advertising given the subject matter.[29]

The problem is clear. "Sensitive topics" can be flagged, as well as discussions related to "political conflicts." As a result, many YouTube creators are having their entire back catalogue of content demonetized, essentially destroying their ability to function as profitable YouTube creators. Dave Rubin, for example, a middle-of-the-road, gay, happily married, Libertarian-leaning free-speech advocate had this occur in late 2017 because many of his interview subjects discussed current events and topical, sometimes hot-button issues.[30] YouTube obviously has the right as a private company to enact such policies and justify them on an ad-revenue basis following demands from advertisers, but the language used in the policy is extremely troublesome: what important events are there to talk about that can't be viewed as "controversial" or "sensitive" to some group or another, particularly in our enthusiastically offense-taking cultural moment? And free-speech advocates aren't the only ones who are getting dinged; the staunchly left-wing news commentary program *The Young Turks* recently had a large swath of its content demonetized for the same reasons (discussion of current events and various political topics).[31]

The capitalist argument goes like this: if you don't like YouTube go elsewhere. There are many other sites that allow you to upload videos and create communities of fans and viewers. Of course YouTube is the biggest, and nothing else really comes close, but in the long run the idea is that the market will correct for any overreach on the part of YouTube and drive demonetized channels to Patreon[32] or other systems of support. This might eventually occur. In the meantime, the world of YouTube has been rattled and is busy adapting to the newly implemented demonetization rules.

You can't really blame YouTube. Their explicit and overt goal is to make money, not ensure that content providers who are busy swearing, making dirty jokes, and talking about pretty much any "political positions" under the sun continue to receive ad revenue. YouTube can't make money without being extremely strict in response to advertisers who want a 100 percent guarantee that their ads won't run on a video addressing any controversial topic whatsoever. For a potential advertiser it's not worth it. A single advertisement run on a video that discusses the idea that affirmative action *might possibly* be more detrimental than helpful could generate huge and long-lasting brand blowback, making such a risk impossible to justify. All it would take to generate controversy is a screen capture, an inflamed posting on Facebook, and you have yourself the start of a PR nightmare.

Incentives drive humans. If YouTube won't pay ad revenue to creators who discuss "controversial issues and sensitive events," pretty soon they won't get many creators discussing "controversial issues and sensitive events." It's actually quite difficult to generate engaging content with such severe restrictions. You can't talk about politics, you can't talk about any aspect of any culture war, you can't talk about your views on the economy or (likely) healthcare, and you certainly can't talk about religion. There is one obvious thing you can talk about to your heart's content without much fear of demonetization, particularly given the coveted audience range of your probable audience: games, movies, television, music, and pop culture in general. These are extremely safe topics, with obviously wide audience interest, but even here there are problems.

Movie clips are rigorously copyrighted, and this copyright is strictly enforced; the same goes for music (more than few seconds will have your video removed from YouTube for violation of fair use); and television stills are in the same boat. It's fun and sometimes exciting to talk about a movie you just saw, and to review the latest blood-and-guts television extravaganza, but as a visual product you're left with talking heads over a background of still images, if that. The one exception to this list is games; game companies are thrilled to have YouTubers play and publicize their games as much as possible, and they eagerly send free early-release copies to the top five hundred YouTube game channels, along with generous goodie bags and other forms of quasi-bribery.[33] More to the point, any modern game is tens if not hundreds of hours long—enough content for dozens of videos if the game is particularly good (fun to play and watch being played) or particularly bad (fun to slag on and find glitches/hack). Everything is in perfect alignment here, particularly post-demonetization.

"Let's Play" videos are extremely safe for advertisers. They hit a very desirable target audience, feature free-to-use audio and video content of nearly unlimited length and variability, and slot in effortlessly to the huge public appetite for anything game-related. But their popularity stems from other reasons as well. "Let's Play" videos are not just cheap to produce and visually rewarding, they offer the chance for YouTube creators to connect with their audience in a direct, unfettered, and unscripted way by means of the game itself. For many viewers, these videos are emotionally satisfying to watch, but to really understand that fact I had to interview the eleven-year-old daughter of my cousin, who is, if not a YouTube fanatic, at least a fan.

"MINECRAFT IS LOVE. MINECRAFT IS LIFE."

These are the first two sentences of LDShadowLady's (aka Lizzy Shadow's) YouTube channel description.[34] Her introductory video has 10 million views; she has over 3.5 million subscribers; she started her channel in January 2010 and has uploaded well over a thousand videos as of March 2018. She's twenty-five years old, dyes her hair wildly different neon colors depending on her whim or inspiration, and is traditionally pretty in a wide-eyed, smiley, bubbly sort of way. She lives near Liverpool, England, or used to, and makes no attempt to moderate her accent for her global audience—it's one of her most attractive features. As her channel description indicates, she's best-known as a player of *Minecraft*, and it's *Minecraft* that my interview subject, Frederica, loves.

I was sitting in her family's living room as she bounced on the couch, and I tried to understand what made watching LDShadowLady's videos so appealing for her, while attempting not to feel irredeemably middle-aged. I won't include the wandering conversation word-for-word because the words floated over a wide variety of topics only tangentially related to my initial question, but the answers, when they arrived, were often quite sophisticated and revealing. I have included relevant parts of the answers in full.

[Who is LDShadowLady? Why do you like her channel?]
LDShadowLady (Lizzy)'s channel is awesome because it's incredibly fun to watch because she's really engaging, and funny, and has a cool *Minecraft* world. She recently got engaged to her boyfriend Joel [who also has a *Minecraft* YouTube channel, SmallishBeans] and I hope they get married soon.
[How many hours per week do you spend watching people playing games?]
I don't know. I spend about one and-a-half hours each day ... so that would be about um ... something like ten hours a week maybe. Almost a full day.

[Do you only watch people playing games that you have played yourself?]

No, I haven't played most of the games that they are playing, but my favorite is definitely LDShadowLady. She only plays *Minecraft* and she has a group of friends she plays *Minecraft* with. I also play *Minecraft* but I got all my knowledge about *Minecraft* from watching her. I would know literally nothing if I did not watch her channel.

[Is it mostly just entertainment for you or are you watching it to learn more about the game?]

She's a person and she has her own ideas and things she's good at that I'm not good at. So you can see the stuff she is good at when you watch her.

[Why are you watching gaming videos instead of videos of people going through a jungle or metal detecting or whatever? What's more appealing about watching a gaming video compared to all the other things people are doing?]

I mean, gaming is a thing that I am into and I like, and if you liked watching people going through the jungle you would watch people going through the jungle. But I just personally like to watch people playing games because I like games.

[But you have all kinds of interests, why narrow it down to games?]

Well, that's the one that has the most demand on YouTube, a lot of YouTubers have gaming videos with really good equipment because they're so popular.

[What personal relationship do you feel you have with LDShadowLady? When you are watching her are you laughing with her, or laughing at her? Do you want her to be happy?]

I know in my heart that she could be like a really mean person in real life. She could be an awful person and just putting up an act for the channel. But I feel like she's a nice person and I know she doesn't know who I am but I know who she is a little bit—what color her hair is, what animals she is into, stuff like that.

[So you feel she is genuine, and not an actor?]

I believe so. I could be wrong but I highly doubt it.

[Let's think about her life. She's around twenty-five let's say, and let's imagine her life. What she does all day is play Minecraft and talk to her friends and go to YouTube conventions and sell merch. As a life do you think that's something that's worth emulating?]

Well, she's just a normal person; she also goes on hikes in the woods and goes to museums. Her life is not centered around gaming. It's her career to play video games.

[I mean, compared to another twenty-five–year-old, who is doing research into nematodes or lizards, or a twenty-five–year-old who's busy trying to help develop some new medical procedure or something like that. Because she's doing YouTube gaming videos, she's not doing other things that she might be doing.]

I think maybe being a scientist or doctor would probably be the more ethical choice, but I think that if you don't want to be those things and you like X and you think you will be really good at X then just do it.

[I'm not trying to put you on the spot, but as a society if we have a lot of people turning to gaming, is that something that is a worthwhile use of everyone's time? Can we ask if it's reasonable for so many people to be doing so much gaming-related stuff?]

I mean . . . probably not a good thing . . . I know a lot of people watching gaming YouTubers start up a channel, you know, get a thousand subscribers, have rich parents, buy a lot of equipment . . . but don't make very good videos . . . and eventually their interest kinda peters out. I think it's OK to have a few gaming YouTubers, that's fine, but they have work hard to make it big.

[You think it's a good thing LDShadowLady is making videos because you would rather watch her than watch TV, right?]

Yes. Because on TV they are actors and with YouTube it's just her and her life, and she tells little stories about what happened yesterday and what her cat and dog did, and it's her. It's not all scripted.

[So even though it's her playing a virtual game it's more real than fake actors trying to pretend they are dealing with the real world?]

Yeah.

[Would you rather watch LDShadowLady or watch a new movie that
came out?]

Well, it pretty much depends on the movie, but most of the time I
would prefer to watch Lizzy.

[Is it normal among your cohorts and peers for people to watch these
types of channels?]

Yeah, I know when I started watching her I told my best friend about
her and she started watching her and she's a big fan too. When I go
to school we talk about her together and other kids know who she
is and are fans too. She's, like, a popular person that a lot of people
know about. There's a kid I knew last year, he's a boy, and him and
his sister were also big fans.

[Does it feel natural for you to watch people playing games on
YouTube?]

I guess since I was raised in a civilization where it doesn't seem weird to
anyone it doesn't seem weird to me either.

This interview should cause anguish in Hollywood at the very least,
as the youngest generation has increasingly less patience for scripted
entertainment, in particular scripted "reality television." Why bother
with the simulacrum when it's trivially easy to find actual "reality television" on YouTube (or at least something that appears more legitimate)?
Most interesting from my perspective is the fact that my interview subject
is watching a lot of gaming videos because they are so readily available
and popular on YouTube, with YouTubers creating plenty of content and
helping to create the appearance of a demand for it. Humans are tribal
creatures; this is a trivial but true proposition. Link interest with avail-
ability and what you get is an explosion of game-related content, feeding
the beast. Crucially, this type of game-related but not explicit game-
playing behavior is extremely difficult to capture from a statistical point
of view. Were you to give Frederica a survey and attempt to gauge the
time she spends playing games you might get a very small number—some
weeks it's less than an hour. But if you expand your question to include

game-related events, game-related activities, and game-related conversations, the total number would be shocking. It would include not only the time she spends watching YouTube gaming videos but the time she spends talking to her friends about it, talking to her parents about it, and thinking about it. It's not an exaggeration to say that for Frederica games are the central focus of her time and mental energy. While Frederica is one data point, not a reliable sign of societal change, we do have broad supporting statistics from YouTube and time-use surveys for the claim that Frederica is less an exception than the rule for the youngest members of our society.

Psychologist Brent Conrad, looking just at young children in 2017, writes, "The time spent with on-screen media dramatically increases from the toddler to preschool to school-age years. Children under two have a screen time average of 53 minutes per day. This increases to almost two and a half hours per day among two to four year old and almost three hours for kids in the five to eight year old range . . . children under eight spend an average of 25 minutes per day playing video games."[35] And older children play more games than younger ones: "By the age of 21, the average child will have spent 10,000 hours playing video games. The average 8–12 year old plays video games for 13 hours per week."[36] Note that the younger children already play more video games than their older peers did when they were the same age; experts expect game-playing and screen time averages to continue to rise.[37]

Games in general, and video games in particular, are a massive economic force in the modern American economy, but they have an even greater impact upon our increasingly narrow slivers of free time. Games are not like an expensive car that, when bought, represents the end of the major time investment (choosing the right model and financing the purchase/saving up for the purchase in advance). Games represent an active and ongoing use of our time, and because of this it's not sensible to ask if games are "good" or "bad," or if they impact children and adults in ways that are aggressively negative or positive, because playing a game, or watching a gaming YouTube video, or reading a message board about cheat codes and technical game strategies, removes the time spent on the activity from our use forever. The question isn't a black-or-white "Are we playing too many games?" The question should be, "Because we are playing so many games, what are we not doing in the meantime, and is this a long-term benefit or harm?"

This isn't a question anyone really wants to ask because it's not possible to definitively determine the answer. Maybe you would be doing something worse than playing a game if you were not playing a game. Or maybe you would be doing something far more rewarding. All anyone can do is make an educated guess. But it seems increasingly likely as games gain ground that more worthwhile activities will be pushed to the sidelines, if only for lack of time or energy.

CHAPTER FOUR
ANATOMY OF A BESTSELLER

I bring this up not in a lame postmodern spirit of "writing about what I am writing about" or in an attempt to make myself look clever (which I feel is at the root of much postmodern fiction and posturing) but to clearly distinguish between a book written honestly, attempting to fairly represent all sides of an issue, from one carefully constructed and narrowly targeted for maximal cultural impact—the truth be damned. I'm attempting the former.

However, if you don't want to know more about why this book is structured as it is and the methodology behind it, skip to the next chapter. It's not necessary to know more about this book's origins than the following: I believe both in objective reality and some version of universal truth, and this book attempts to respect both as it investigates the subject at hand. If you are willing to accept my word on it and move on to the next chapter, *Thank You*. You should also feel free to stick around; there is a lot of interesting and scandalous rubbish discussed.

I have played games most of my life; I grew up with an Atari 800 computer system, delved into *Dungeons & Dragons* as a teen, still enjoy and follow professional chess, and remember many happy hours playing absurdly complicated war games with college friends (I'm looking at you *Squad Leader*). I've played sports, still enjoy monthly poker games, and find the luck-free, diceless, and entirely psychological sparring of Avalon Hill's *Diplomacy* endlessly fascinating.[1] When attempting to get something unpleasant accomplished my default mode is to turn it into a game, tricking myself (when it works) into viewing the challenge as a step toward a greater goal within a broader game reality. I've played arcade games, handheld games, modern video games, and Unix-based text-only roguelike RPGs. It's part of my extended family culture during get-togethers to break out the *Scrabble* board, pull out *Rummikub*, or rustle around in a dark closet looking for a pack of cards. I play *Settlers of Catan* with my two daughters, *Ticket to Ride* when I can talk them into it, and informal tee-ball in the yard, with the runs scored carefully tallied. My wife and I used to play an early form of internet chess together, even before we were formally dating; the program allowed one-line chat messages to ping back and forth, which were occasionally thrilling. I'm not a game addict nor am I a professional, but it's likely I have played and enjoyed far more games than the average American.

This highly defensive tally is a rhetorical gambit offered in advance to assuage those who might think me, like my father, deeply uninterested in games or actively disparaging of them. That's simply not the case. My impulse in thinking about games, researching games, and ultimately deciding to write a book about games was neither moralistic nor condemnatory. The spur was the simple observation that games are everywhere; they have crept into and colonized a major slice of the population, even those who were previously immune to gaming's charm (middle-aged women, professional businessmen, philosophy professors). The size of the American economy taken up with games, broadly understood, has been spiking over the last few years, and it consumes an astonishing percentage of American's GNP. The growth of gaming is an underreported and slightly shocking fact of modern life—well worth investigating.

That was the cause; the book you are reading is the result. The method of its construction is rigorously and tediously old-fashioned. I conducted research, talked to people, read scientific and popular literature on the subject, gathered evidence, listened to those who think games can heal the world as well as those convinced games are leading to our destruction, thought about the issues involved, bounced ideas off collaborators and friends, and came to various conclusions, which I then wrote about.

It's trivially true and utterly trite to claim that I'm not being *perfectly* fair to the immensely huge subject of play and games; yes, I have my own take on the issue, and I can't escape my own prejudices (however large or small), nor can I escape my upbringing, my culture, or any of the rest of it. I'm not unaware of my own limitations, and I have attempted at every step to remove my self-imposed blinders. I have little interest in polemics, which are rigorously and self-consciously one-sided; I don't own a game company nor have any financial interest in anything game-related; neither, luckily, do games in our culture have a long history of emotional or ethical baggage to contend with. It's difficult to sit down and write a book about transgender issues, for example, without warning bells going off for anyone even slightly interested in the topic. Games aren't like that; writing about games is more like writing about the history of infinity and discussing Cantor's proof showing that different infinities have different sizes. You can argue about what Cantor did or didn't accomplish, but it doesn't usually get emotional. Because of this, it's *relatively* easy to be impartial about games.

The impartial approach is one method of conceiving and writing a book, and the assumption undergirding it is that if you enter into such a project with an open mind, and attempt to self-regulate and limit the bubbling up of personal prejudice or unwarranted assumptions, the result will be both more useful to the reader and closer to the ultimate truth of the matter. (I'm aware that sounds incredibly staid and old fashioned.) I actually want to *get at the truth*, as much as that goal is achievable, and I'm using a method that has been shown, historically, to be vastly more successful than any other.

One last defensive screed before plunging forward. A common attack against somebody proclaiming they are searching for the truth, particularly somebody who has already confessed to being in some way prejudiced or influenced by culture or limited because of their innate human weaknesses and manifest social blinders and all the rest ... anyone showing any sign of weakness, indicating less than 100 percent ability to view a topic in a purely rational manner, gets the following take down: *Well buddy, that's just your opinion.*

The long form of this objection, as represented by some parts of academia, goes something like this:

> It's naive to search for the truth because there isn't *a* truth, there are *many* truths. You have already admitted that you can't be wholly objective, that you view the world through the lens of your life, that in constructing an artificial form such as a book you take the messy world and constrict and limit it in ways *you* select and *you* choose. It's cherry picking all the way down. Just be honest about it. You're not writing a book about the truth of a subject, you're writing the book you want to write, truth be damned.

This type of argument pops up all the time, in many domains. Less than 100 percent purity opens the door to infinite abuse. From the world of literary criticism, for example: it's uncontroversial and obvious to state that any text, such as Poe's "The Masque of the Red Death," can be read in an infinite numbers of ways. Given this assertion, some claim, therefore, that there isn't any "real" or "true" or canonical interpretation of the story, or even a reading more reasonable or cogent than any other. An entire branch of literary theory has developed whose axiomatic assertion is that since a text is infinitely interpretable it's infinitely malleable, guided primarily by the reader's personal history, background, culture, privilege, location in the power structure, current psychological state, etc.[2] The text either has no meaning or contains all meanings. You can essentially argue whatever you want about it: Poe was writing about rainbow-maned Unicorns fighting over beer sponsorship deals and hey, that's just as valid an interpretation as one concerned with the ultimate futility of human power when pitted against nature and/or death. Yes, the first reading is patently insane and feels like a straw man and the second is rather trivially obvious, but for a certain strain of theorists they have the same truth value. Why? The purity of interpretation has been punctured; there is no 100 percent legitimate interpretation and, therefore, no reason to privilege one person's take over another's: the barn doors have been thrown open wide. Actual interpretive implementations are yet another instance of power at work: what makes a given interpretation resonate with the public is the result of the machinations of the powerful and privileged asserting their interpretive dominance over all others. Make of anything what you will and enforce your view of its meaning it if you can manage it.

Let's step back from the overheated brink and state the obvious: some interpretations are absurd, some less so, some even less so, etc. It's a messy business, sorting out these possibilities on a graduated scale. What makes one reading absurd depends upon culture, chronology, and personal/shared experiences, but that doesn't invalidate ordered rankings. Stuff may float and shift around, the exact placement of the rungs are fuzzy, but it's clear that interpretations of Poe's story involving rainbow-maned unicorns are high on the ladder of crazy, and a reading based on plague-fear is pretty low. You don't need purity to put stuff in a rough order. You can acknowledge limitations without being completely undermined by them, particularly if you are aware of them in the first place.

Let's be adults and reject absolute purity and instead accept the fact that as flawed humans we can still a) recognize some if not all of our flaws, b) work to limit the effect of those flaws, and c) engage in a system of inquiry that does not limit input, data, analysis, and alternative viewpoints but seeks to maximize them. The old way is still the best way: get interested in a topic, do a lot of research, and write about it.

That's how I thought things were done.

Until I realized it's very much *not* how things are done.

HOW (SOME) THINGS ARE DONE

After much investigation, reading, and soul-searching, I've decided you can throw most nonfiction into three big bins. They consist of the following broad types:

- **Polemic**

    The author deeply believes in a given subject, makes this clear from the start, and writes a book attempting to convince the reader to agree. Political hagiographies fall into this category: books about Reagan written by former Reagan appointees, or books about Obama by former Obama appointees. You know what you are getting going in. There isn't any real expectation of even-handed fairness; the goal is to be convincing and entertaining.

- **Explanatory**

    The author is deeply interested in a given subject, makes this clear from the start, and writes a book about the subject attempting to educate the reader about it in an entertaining and relatively fair-minded way. Examples include anything written by Stephen Jay Gould, Michael Lewis, etc.

- **Targeted**

    The author may or may not be truly interested in the given subject, and this isn't clear from the start. The book is written with an eye toward popularity, sales, and cultural impact. While polemical, the style is unemotional and crucially quasi-scientific. While apparently explanatory, the book obfuscates and panders to prejudice and irrational preconceptions. Appearance of contrarianism a bonus. Example include: All of Malcolm Gladwell's works, Steven Johnson's *Everything Bad Is Good for You*, and the most cringe-inducing title of the last twenty years, *SuperBetter: The Power of Living Gamefully*, by Jane McGonigal.

I'm going to look closely at some of these books in order to give a sense of what my book is attempting to do and, more specifically, what I'm attempting *not to do*.

NOTHING'S GOOD AND (PRETTY MUCH) EVERYTHING'S BAD WITH STEVEN JOHNSON'S *EVERYTHING BAD IS GOOD FOR YOU*

Steven Johnson is a bestselling author and an early web pioneer who leaped enthusiastically into the digital world when the internet started to become mainstream. He created the first exclusively online magazine (*Feed*, 1995–2001), became a contributing editor for *Wired*, and ended up writing a string of bestselling nonfiction books, finding early success with *Everything Bad Is Good for You: How Today's Popular Culture Is Actually Making Us Smarter* (2005).

In his most recent work, *Wonderland: How Play Made the Modern World* (2016), Johnson argues that it's play, rather than science, driving technological progress and innovation. Even to book reviewers without much historical training the book comes off as unconvincing,[3] with a thesis that's hard to take seriously. At least the book includes interesting historical details and doesn't flatter our worst prejudices, merely our broad desires: play is fun and natural so by all means keep playing, and remember that while playing you're contributing to the ongoing technological advancement of our species in a limited way (though not as much as Johnson claims).

But to really get a grip on where Johnson is coming from as a thinker it's crucial to look at *Everything Bad Is Good for You* and assess how the book holds up ten years after publication.

Everything Bad Is Good for You has led an active post-publication life, accepted by some academics but wholeheartedly embraced by the digerati. Marc Prensky, American educational specialist and author, takes the thesis of the book as a given: "Digital technology is making us smarter. Steven Johnson has documented this in *Everything Bad Is Good For You* (2005), in which he argues that the new technologies associated with contemporary popular culture, from video games to the Internet to television and film, make far more cognitive demands on us than did past forms, thus increasing our capabilities in a wide variety of cognitive tasks.

As Johnson puts it, 'Today's popular culture may not be showing us the righteous path. But it is making us smarter.'"[4] Richard Van Eck claimed as early as 2006 that digital game-based learning is now fully mainstream and broadly accepted thanks to the explanatory power of books like *Everything Bad Is Good for You*, plus the simple fact that, "digital gaming is a $10 billion per year industry, and in 2004, nearly as many digital games were sold as there are people in the United States (248 million games vs. 293.6 million residents)."[5]

Tom Chatfield, British broadcaster and technology philosopher, has this to say: "Since the book's [Steven Johnson's *Everything Bad is Good for You*] publication in 2005, Johnson's argument in favour of what he labels the 'Sleeper curve'—the steadily increasing intellectual sophistication of modern popular culture—has become something of a shibboleth for futurologists. . . . Malcolm Gladwell writing in the New Yorker, [said] the book was a delightful piece of 'brain candy.'"[6]

Since it's already been mentioned, Malcolm Gladwell's enthusiastic review[7] of *Everything Bad Is Good for You* sums up the "obvious wisdom" for a certain type of technology-besotted enthusiast. Gladwell's review is incorporated and recounted by another book review in the *MIT Technology Review*: "The basic premise of the book is nothing new to the digerati: living in a world of integrated media and popular culture has made us smarter because we have to manage a dizzying array of information being thrust at us from every direction. . . . Even Gladwell's long synopsis [the *New Yorker* book review] about video games, which Johnson correctly argues are one of the primary stimulators in our information development, is likely to strike the digerati as basic."[8]

The technology and popular culture author Nicolas Carr sums up the zeitgeist: "Some popular-science writers draw on [a few scientific studies] as evidence that the heavy use of digital media—not just video games, but web-surfing, texting, online multitasking, and so forth—actually makes us 'smarter'. The ur-text here is Steven Johnson's 2005 book *Everything Bad Is Good for You*."[9]

WHAT DOES THE BOOK ACTUALLY CLAIM?

The core of Johnson's argument in *Everything Bad Is Good For You* involves the Flynn effect, an increase of roughly three points per decade in the average American's IQ score. James R. Flynn reviewed IQ data and research and noted that this increase started in 1930 and continues to the present day. Johnson takes it as a given that higher IQ test results represent an increase in general intelligence rather than improved test-taking skills or other explanations—despite some countervailing evidence, such as the average SAT score dropping over the last five years (does this indicate a decrease in general intelligence?).[10]

What might explain the Flynn effect? Johnson's answer is a combination of video-game playing and increasingly complicated television shows. Johnson repeats his assertion throughout the book while resolutely refusing to supply any scientific evidence that popular culture was the *exclusive* (or even partial) driver of the Flynn effect. In any case, the chronology of his account fails to line up; video games could not possibly account for any IQ increase from 1930 until roughly 1990 given that a) no video games existed for most of that period, and b) they were only played by a tiny fraction of the population even after they did arise. The same can be said of "more complicated" television programming, which Johnson asserts achieved broad popularity in the 1990s and beyond.

Basic math shows that 60 percent of the Flynn effect occurred before the advent of electronic media. To account for this, Johnson should take pains to show that the mysterious force (or forces) driving the Flynn effect, which might include better nutrition and/or education, abruptly stopped working in 1990 and were thereafter entirely supplanted by the benefits generated by video games/television. This is nowhere done.

The main reason Johnson imagines video games to be beneficial, unlike passively watching bad and uncomplicated 1950s television, is that video games require *input*: decision-making by the human player. Johnson explicitly disregards the quality of the decisions being made—

saving Zelda from the Dragon after tracking down a glowing crystal, requiring thirty minutes of relentless button mashing, is just one of his many examples. In Johnson's view, the most important requirement is rapid-fire decision making—this is the key to video games' mental benefits. Johnson presents the reader with "decision trees" arising from video games, featuring relatively complicated and widely branching structures showing that *yes*, decisions must be made when playing a video game and that these decisions in sequence create a branching, tree-like structure when graphed.

Even if some video games are as deep and intricate as Johnson believes, involving multifaceted, ongoing, nontrivial decision-making, he never feels the need to show that these types of games are the ones the public is actually playing (99 percent of people might be addicted to *Pong*). That's another big problem.

In any case, his entire theory collapses when you consider a real-life basketball game.

Imagine playing five on five at the local gym. You get the ball from out of bounds and start bringing it up the court. Your brain is doing a thousand things at the same time: scanning the court, dribbling the ball, moving your feet, motioning with a hand for more movement under the basket, yelling out a play, catching somebody's eye in preparation for a pass, keeping the defender's grimy paws away from your dribble . . . The decisions multiply and branch into the future and past: angle a drive toward the tall defender or the shorter, speedier player? Pass the ball, try to turn the corner, rotate and back in, or give up the ball? Launch it? Should you heckle your defender? What do you know about him? Is he safe to heckle or will it make him angry and a more tenacious defender, or will it make him angry and a worse defender?

A "decision tree" consisting of one minute of on-court basketball is almost impossible to conceive; every player is making calculated or instantaneous decisions in reaction to the flow of players, the ball bouncing off the rim, the position of the opponents and teammates, the score of the game, the social game-within-the-game as players attempt to show up the showboat or prove their worth to a friend . . . It should be obvious to everyone that if pure decision-making is what increases intelligence, the *last thing* you want to do is sit in front of a video game, remove all possibility of direct social interaction from your world, and slow to a crippled crawl the fluid dynamism of synchronous engagement, and instead break the steady flow of "real experience" into discrete, game-designed sequences of static decisions. A fantasy role-playing game might require input every second or two (click button A or B). Playing basketball merges the physical, mental, and social worlds, requiring continuous decision-making along a vast spectrum of complexity.

There isn't any comparison.

Even if Johnson's unproven theory is correct and decision-making is the key to increased IQ, common sense would urge precisely the opposite of his conclusion. Video games are manifestly worse decision-making generators than almost anything else you can do in the "real world."

Johnson's circular logic is exemplified by his recounting of the story of Troy Stolle, a construction worker who loved playing the fantasy game *Ultima Online*, and who "spent six months doing nothing but [virtual] smithing. He clicked on hillsides to mine ore, headed to the forge to click the ore into ingots, clicked again to turn the ingots into weapons and armor."[11]

Stolle worked construction full time but spent much of his free time slowly improving his online avatar's smithing skills. Johnson admits that what Stolle was doing was "finger numbingly repetitive work with 'hammer' and 'anvil,'" but when Stolle says he *enjoys* what he is doing, Johnson is inspired to dig a bit deeper. Having fun isn't enough. It's question begging. Johnson wants to get to the root of it: *Why* does Stolle enjoy playing the game? Johnson waves the flag of neuroscience around a bit before claiming that Stolle and other gamers enjoy the gaming activity because "it taps into the brain's natural reward circuitry."[12]

As an explanation this is embarrassing; it's nothing more than an obfuscatory method of leveraging science's cultural power to make the unsurprising claim that "people have fun playing games that they find fun." Neuroscience is reduced to restating the obvious: "tapping into reward circuitry" = "somebody likes something." The only reason Johnson phrases it like this is that it's rhetorically effective.

Johnson also explicitly concedes that the *content* of games doesn't matter because even he couldn't make the extravagant claim that they are intellectually challenging. Most video games have incredibly simple or non-existent content. Despite all this, games are somehow making us smarter, and their very emptiness opens the door to the related claim that mind-numbing, repetitive, virtual *Ultima Online* "mining" is just as good as any other game activity, virtual or real. As an argument it's completely incoherent, but more worryingly Johnson completely ignores *opportunity cost*.

It might be true that Troy Stolle learned a bit about a few details of in-game mechanics by virtual mining five hours a night for six months—but what was he not doing in the meantime? That's the real loss. Thirty years ago, before the advent of the internet, Stolle would have been playing poker with his friends or trying to find a date or tinkering in his garage with a lathe or motorcycle or reading a book or listening to the radio. It's not that video games are, in themselves, generally noneducational; it's that highly immersive, reductive time sinks such as video games limit growth by closing off other avenues of deeper enlightenment.

I can't imagine anyone making the argument that the Stolle who played *Ultima Online* heavily for two years, mindlessly clicking on buttons to mine virtual metals, is a better human being than an alternative timeline Stolle who never played *Ultima Online* and instead did anything else (barring a crime spree). At the very least, Johnson should have to tackle this argument and show that playing *Ultima Online* improved brain functioning to such a degree that its benefits likely outweighed the benefits of anything else Stolle might have done in the real world—a complicated claim Johnson never considers, much less addresses.

A BESTSELLER AT ANY COST

How can a book like this be written, much less become a bestseller? Not everything in Johnson's *Everything Bad Is Good for You* is wrong or in complete conflict with science and common sense, but much of it is. How did it ever get off the ground and convince casual readers it wasn't complete bunk? Part of the reason is that Johnson's got a trick up his sleeve. It's a basic trick, but it's a really good one.

Johnson asserts things that are radically in conflict with what we *suspect to be true*, but they are crucially things we desperately *want to be true*. That's how faux contrarianism works. Somebody writes a diet book claiming that doughnuts and cake are good for you. It's a radical idea; it's clearly out-of-the-mainstream. Perhaps it's an original thinker at work? No. It's just somebody telling you something you want to be true but isn't, and in the case of doughnuts you know, deep down, it's bunk.

True contrarianism posits that the truth is sometimes misaligned with the mass of popular thought and something that occasionally needs to be corrected by an outsider championing an unusual theory. On the other hand, faux contrarianism isn't concerned with the truth, only with pandering to desirable but false impulses.

With this in mind, it's easy to spot the thematic thrust of the book, and it goes something like this:

> Guess what? You were taught that watching TV was bad for you, but it's not! You thought video games were bad for you, but they're not! TV shows like *Hill Street Blues* and *The Sopranos* are so much better and more complicated than previous TV shows that the increased intellectual challenge they represent spur your brain into growth. Watching them is educational! When playing video games you are busy making all kinds of decisions, and your brain grows! Lemme tell you, it's great! Keep watching TV and keep playing video games!

Does Johnson actually believe that video games directly explain the Flynn effect and are one of the major causes of humanity's apparent intelligence increase? He might, but we can't be totally sure. If Johnson doesn't believe it, how could he have come up with such an obviously absurd theory? This is where it gets ugly.

Johnson is personally invested in technology and defending its place in the world. He made a lot of money due to his prominent role in the early internet; he is an enthusiastic booster of everything new, be it (back in the day) *MySpace* or *Facebook* or *Twitter*. He's a dyed-in-the-wool rah-rah technological utopian. He believes technology provides benefits and if there are drawbacks . . . well, that's a big IF. IF there *are* drawbacks they are overwhelmed by benefits. It might be the case that Johnson is so deep in his technological bubble that he thinks the argument presented in *Everything Bad Is Good for You* sensible, or reasonable, or worth making, despite a complete lack of evidence. To be fair, it probably feels right to him.

The ultimate question reduces to this: Who is the conman and who is the mark?

They might be the same person. My feeling is that Johnson isn't an out-and-out grifter who knows he's talking bunk and doesn't care. He's at least half-deluded himself; blinkered; unable to see outside the confines of his mutually reinforcing techno-world and its techno-babble. Everyone he knows and interviews is wildly successful and typically has technology to thank for their place in the pecking order. It would be unnatural for Johnson to step back and look at things with a more jaundiced eye. Unnatural, but not impossible. That's on him; it's his weakness as a thinker, not a writer.[13]

The other way to look at *Everything Bad Is Good for You* is as a pure manifestation of a targeted nonfiction book. Unfortunately, *Everything Bad Is Good for You* has all the hallmarks of a cynically structured and artificial production aimed at flattering its audience and exploring an apparently contrarian position. In other words Johnson wrote a fictional nonfiction book with an eye to maximizing sales and increasing its cultural impact. Truth of content was secondary. Hey, there's nothing wrong with wanting to write a bestseller. It's great to have written a bestseller. The issue is how you get there. Some people want to believe that in America it's money that counts not how you get the money: try telling that to a Nevada brothel magnate, squeezing every drop of profit he can from his ever-changing stable of workaday prostitutes. He doesn't hold his head high in the community. How you get there matters, both to society and one's own sense of integrity.

A targeted bestselling scheme requires an aggressive thesis that is a) something the general public wants to be told is true, b) something that can be told is true in a way that seems scientific (by citing a study or two) even if it makes little more than superficial scientific sense, and c) something that appears to be contrarian while at the same time *strengthening the status quo*. And crucially, from my point of view, d) something in which truth, honesty, plain speaking, and straightforward argumentation can be casually jettisoned. It's really not about that. It's about "telling a good story."

I can say with complete assurance that I would not take credit for Johnson's nonfiction monstrosity unless I later revealed the book to be satirical, a commentary on the general lack of critical thinking in the publishing industry and the book review process. This is not because I don't like money or am "better" morally than Johnson or a million other authors. The truth is that I am inured to the draw of bestselling status because it's not something I ever expected to achieve nor, honestly, care much about. It's easy to be an idealist about stuff that doesn't matter to you; the hard part is applying the same principals to heart-felt issues where doing the easy thing, the wrong thing, is incredibly rewarding and feels completely justified.

To sum: I don't care enough to be hypocritical or I might be doing the same thing. But I can't really work myself up into mortgaging everything for a possible bestseller, and I certainly can't, by self-imposed will, force myself into believing what is obviously absurd. Bereft of any concrete link to "reality," *Everything Bad Is Good for You* is destined to become a bit of cultural fluff, the sort of thing an academic, in fifty years, reads with amusement and adds as a footnote to a study of technological blindness. You can't really learn anything from it outside of the cultural moment allowing it to take shape. You can't really understand the world better from having read it. Truth be told, reading this type of nonfiction *actively obscures the reality of the world*, leaving you deeper in fiction than ever before.

This book isn't written with an eye to cosseting or placating the reader. If you don't like what's written you don't like what's written: I'm not trying to con you by pretending that whatever you happen to believe in makes sense, much less that it's scientifically rigorous. It might be, but then again it might not be.

We live in an age of the "big con." Anyone with passing knowledge of Mexican-funded border walls is fully aware that things can be promised with rhetorical flair and demonstrable power without having an accompanying expectation of the promise being delivered.[14] Certain "sophisticated" defenders might argue that *the result* is beside the point: the power of the message weighs more than the actuality, or lack of actuality, of the claims being made. This method of debate certainly works and can generate impressive results, but it's the time-honored and once-derided province of the snake-oil salesman. It's rhetoric, devoid of content, and entirely nongenerative.

I'm old fashioned. I'm not a proselytizer. I don't hate or love games. I'm not trying to flatter anyone (not even myself) or make you feel better about what you are or are not doing with your gaming rig at two o'clock on a Thursday morning. But let's talk about it honestly, okay?

CHAPTER FIVE

CANDY CRUSH(ING) THE COMPETITION, AND HARPOONING WHALES

"God bless ye," he seemed to half sob and half shout. "God bless ye, men. Steward! go draw the great measure of grog. But what's this long face about, Mr. Starbuck; wilt thou not chase the white whale? art not game for Moby Dick?"
— Captain Ahab, in Herman Melville's *Moby-Dick; or, The Whale*, chapter 36

Fish: A weak or inexperienced player.
Shark: An aggressive player who feasts on fish.
Whale: A huge, juicy player who spends and loses massive amounts of money. The target of many harpoons.

HATE-PLAYING *CANDY CRUSH*

Candy Crush and its suite of spinoffs (*Candy Crush Saga, Candy Crush Soda Saga, Candy Crush Jelly Saga*, and likely more to come[1]) are the most popular, profitable, and despised games in the world.[2] This paradox (most played / most hated) gets to the core of *Candy Crush*'s contradictory appeal. From one perspective *Candy Crush* surely qualifies as a great game: it's simple and easy to learn; it's engaging and rewarding as levels are cleared and the player advances to simulated applause and light shows; it features bright clean graphics and a well-designed sound-scape. The problem isn't playing the game—it's putting the game down.

San Francisco native Emilee Pham supplies us with a canonical version of the problem faced and expressed by millions of players: "The moment I wake up I immediately turn on my phone, not to check for text messages or my email, but to play *Candy Crush*. Before my class starts, I am seen playing *Candy Crush*. At parties, I sneak in *Candy Crush* while talking to friends and strangers. And before I go to bed, I take up all my lives in *Candy Crush*. I am THAT addicted to *Candy Crush*, and that, my friends, is the biggest reason as to why I hate *Candy Crush* with a burning passion."[3]

Candy Crush is so enthralling it even trips up English Members of Parliament: "A Tory MP has issued something approaching an apology after being caught playing *Candy Crush Saga* for three hours during a Commons Committee hearing [on pensions]. . . . Mr. Mills said he would 'try not to do it again in the future' by way of an apology."[4] Note that he didn't promise not to do it; just that he would try. We wish him luck.

This type of deep engagement would seem to explain *Candy Crush*'s overwhelming success as a game: isn't it a good thing when players can't put down your product? Isn't this behavior the defining attribute of a quality game, supplying players with a gaming experience so fun and ful-filling they can't, or won't, stop playing? Yes and no.

It matters a lot whether *Candy Crush* is entertaining. The problem is that for many players it's not. *Candy Crush* is best described as a highly addictive virtual interaction hugely distracting from the "real world" yet strangely unfun: "Psychologist Jenny Taitz . . . [notes] that [*Candy Crush*] addicts can suffer from long-term stress, potential sleep loss and a diminished sense of accomplishment, especially if gamers are ditching responsibilities to plug in. 'I've never met someone who says, "I feel really great about myself, I just reached an all-time high on *Candy Crush*."'"[5]

Candy Crush players sense there is something nefarious going on behind the scenes and quickly come to resent the game. Everyone agrees that the first hour of *Candy Crush* is amusing as the levels fly by—it's a light and tasty confection. Soon the levels get more difficult, clearing them becomes a challenge, and at some point the fight to progress becomes explicit: it's a naked struggle. Yet players continue to forge ahead. What had been amusing becomes mechanical, a means to an end. The desire to proceed overwhelms any semblance of fun. Finishing a level is the reason to play no matter how long it takes—or how much it ends up costing.

The emotional backlash against *Candy Crush* comes from its players,[6] but more serious ethical charges arise from another direction entirely: professional game developers and neuroscientists like Ramin Shokrizade,[7] who see past *Candy Crush*'s sweet exterior into its rotten core. For scientists like Ramin, *Candy Crush* was built from the ground up to manipulate gamers into spending money on the game—that's the bottom line, and it tells the whole story, concern for profit controlling design and gameplay decisions both large and small.

From Ramin's perspective:

> The human body is a machine that is wired to do certain things in response to certain stimuli. These mechanisms have kept us alive for thousands of years. If they were not there we would have become extinct. In order to control a human you just have to learn what these hard wired "choices" are, and develop stimuli to trigger them in the right combination and sequence to get the organism to do what you want them to do. Start by putting them into a virtual reality (and you don't need "VR" to do this), so that they are disconnected from "real space," and make sure to put a lot of things in that space that make them feel good and that they trust. You can pull them pretty far down the rabbit hole before they realize what's going on. Clearly some people are more alert than others, but I would say that if you gave me the right team I could make a game that could control almost anyone in virtual space.
>
> It's just science. Used against people. For money.[8]

This seems a bit extreme; surely *Candy Crush* isn't a purely cynical product, offering up scientifically calibrated stimuli tapping into mechanical human responses leading to an almost irresistible uptick to in-game product purchases. I initially resisted the theory on the basis of common human decency—who would make a game that's both addictive and unfun simply to make money?

A few days later, I reconsidered the claim and realized that such a scheme is a perfectly viable business model, particularly when the results can total billions in profit. How would it be possible to prove such a theory about this or any other video game? My method of investigation was to look at the game design decisions that went into *Candy Crush* and ask if they were all, nearly without exception, manipulative toward a single goal—getting the customer to spend money?

To get to the root of the problem, I analyzed the game mechanics, researched where *Candy Crush* came from, and looked at which previous games had inspired its creation. To my surprise, *Candy Crush* has a complex origin story . . . it goes all the way back to the invention of the first mechanical slot machine in the dusty chaos of the unsettled West.

CANDY CRUSH ORIGINS

Candy Crush is a "match three" game[9] that, according to usage data, was downloaded a shocking half-billion times during the first year of its launch (2012)—an almost unbelievable figure. The Atari 2600 video-game console, the first to be taken up en masse for home use, was a global sensation in the 1980s, and its most popular cartridge game, *PacMan*, managed somewhere in the neighborhood of seven million sold over a decade and a half. The Nintendo Entertainment system beat out Atari in the late 80s and 90s, and sold 40 million *Super Mario Bros.* games during that time. More refined and powerful consoles followed, with games such as *Grand Theft Auto 4* doing spectacularly well, with over 60 million games sold.

These are stunningly successful games, yet they pale in comparison to the numbers *Minecraft* put up over the last decade across a broad range of consoles, mobile devices, and computer systems (Windows, Linux, etc.): at least 100 million sold. Yet all of these taken together fail to come close to *Candy Crush*, standing comfortably at peak popularity with over a 2.7 billion downloaded as of November 2017 (and still increasing). The only game anywhere near this absurd total is *Tetris*, which was first released in 1984 for the PC market and subsequently spread to every device possible. It is estimated to have been installed somewhere in the range of 495 million times over nearly twenty-five years. *Candy Crush*, by comparison, first appeared in April 2012.

Candy Crush and its rush of imitators represent a shift in the world of gaming—a product with extremely modest graphical and computational requirements capable of being deployed on low-powered, internet-connected devices of all types. Despite its simple mechanics and primitive graphics, *Candy Crush* managed to become the most profitable release in the history of video games, proving that complex and graphically rewarding gameplay is not a necessary precondition to making big money, nor is such an investment necessarily a wise business move. Why spend $50 million on a fleet of 3-D designers and programmers when you can pump out a successful game app for a few million (at most) and have a good shot at profits exceeding those of bigger, fancier, and far more expensive game productions?

What's going on here? Is *Candy Crush* a good example of capitalism at work, where companies fight against each other in the free market attempting to create the best games, and thereafter reap the rewards for a masterpiece that sells in the millions and generates profits beyond their wildest dreams?

The short answer: No. As we have seen, *Candy Crush* is well known for generating a negative backlash among users almost equal in intensity to their initial enthusiasm for the game—it's far from the most "fun" game out there. Professional game designers are shocked by the simplicity of *Candy Crush*, the lack of player choice and gameplay options, the paucity of creativity in its visual or mechanical features, and the repetitive and unrelenting nature of the game itself. *Candy Crush* could have been created twenty years ago and it would have run smoothly on any console of the period, requiring nothing more than bright and colorful single-screen graphics, a reasonably efficient sound processor, and an extremely simple input mechanism.

Compared to immersive 3-D games such as *Red Dead Redemption* (2010), requiring a huge staff of designers, programmers, and sound editors, as well as powerful computers to create and play it, *Candy Crush* is a throwback, something so simple it could have been put together by a small team working quickly and efficiently over the course of a few months.

What's the reason for its success? To understand, we must look at the car economy and visit Las Vegas.

THE GOOD OLD DAYS

There was a time before *Candy Crush* when video-game development appeared to be following the well-trodden economic path of, say, automobiles. In a glutted market cars span the range of possibilities: shoddy or well-built, featuring a powerful or weak engine, sporting a luxurious interior or one stripped of everything but the bare necessities. Marketing and advertising manipulate consumers as much as they can, but for the most part well-made and reliable cars sold at a reasonable price do exceptionally well, and badly made cars with a poor reputation for quality control tend to fail and drop out of the market, regardless of advertising or brand appeal. The long-term effect of this capitalistic evolution can be seen all around us: exceptionally safe cars, escalating minimum acceptable equipment levels, and astonishing mechanical and electrical sophistication. This is a success story as far as product development goes; there are plenty of global automobile manufacturers, relatively low market entrance barriers given the possible profits at stake, and a broad understanding that automobiles are both useful and necessary. In a situation where most people in North America regard car ownership as a birthright, the market will be glutted with possibilities and extraordinarily diverse options. There is a car, jeep, van, truck, or three-wheeled aberration catering to almost any whim. Throw in hybrid and electric cars and the scope of choice is truly vast.

Before *Candy Crush* a list of the top twenty bestselling video games of all time had everything we might expect from bestselling games or bestselling products in other categories. Many were early to market and hugely engaging (*Tetris*); others made the best of the current technology and featured gameplay that remains engrossing to this day (*Donkey Kong*). Faster computers and more powerful graphic rendering spawned immersive 3-D games and the first of many genre-busting *Grand Theft Auto* releases. *Minecraft* gave users unparalleled freedom to indulge their creativity by building virtual environments in a virtual world, and it became a global hit. These are the bestsellers, and their success stories align with our general expectations. Original and immensely fun games become sensations and have an extremely long shelf life. How else would the system work?

As it turns out there's another way of making a game, and it doesn't depend on product quality. To understand how this economic scheme operates we must turn our attention to gambling—in particular, Las Vegas.

HOW LAS VEGAS SEES THE WORLD

Let's imagine the operation of a simplified Las Vegas casino. Our hypothetical casino, Grandioso, receives two thousand tourists a day, which sounds like a lot of useful foot traffic. The tourists arrive at Grandioso, look around, enjoy free drinks, purchase the discounted food, make themselves a nuisance to the many waitresses and bartenders hired to staff the premises, gamble a bit, consume electricity, make a mess in the bathrooms, and require a mammoth operation to temporarily house them in relative comfort. Let's assume each tourist loses, on average, $50—some lose big, some small, and some improbably win small, or even more rarely win big. At the end of the day, the casino has "made" $100,000 dollars off the influx of tourists, which sounds pretty nice for a day's work, until the casino subtracts its labor, food, alcohol, security, and facility costs. The net take might well be negative.

On the other hand, if each tourist loses $500, far higher than any actual Las Vegas casino average, Grandioso pulls in a cool million per day. After all costs are subtracted, Grandioso might be $500,000 in the black on this most improbable of good days. How can Grandioso further maximize returns? To increase its profit margin Grandioso might attempt to lure in more tourists, increasing their daily take through sheer volume, but this requires investing in advertising and support staff, and when the extra tourists arrive they come at a fixed cost: more alcohol, more food, and more people to process. Increasing the number of tourists isn't the most efficient way to increase profit. What is? Attack the high rollers, those with a lot of money, who love to win but more importantly can be counted on, in the long term, *to lose big*.

A single high roller losing $100,000 to the casino represents a windfall that's nearly pure profit. It takes almost no infrastructure to "host" a single high roller. Imagine a group of high rollers, twenty or thirty in number, who lose $50,000 every time they come to town. A casino would be crazy to do anything besides focus upon these types of gamblers, and that's exactly what they do. All casinos have special gambling areas requiring a high minimum bet, and these areas are significantly nicer than those open to the low-spending masses. The waitresses dress better and are more attractive, and the alcohol is middle-of-the-range instead of bottom-of-the-barrel. One gets a whiff of Monte Carlo—not much, but a whiff. The place feels like an exclusive club, but the key to entry is just money. It's not *that* exclusive.

All casinos understandably lavish great care upon high rollers: they are comped free rooms, receive exclusive treatment, and occasionally are granted free airfare to and from their houses. From a casino's perspective the average gambler doesn't need to contribute much; if what they lose, in aggregate, is sufficient to pay for the day's operational expenses, that's enough. The real money comes from the big losers, known throughout the industry as whales. Twenty whales a day might average out to a few million dollars of pure profit.

Everyone loves whales. Car companies also target whales, with heavily promoted branding and advertising occasionally sufficient to convince people to pay far more for a car than it's worth. Extremely expensive cars, such as Bentleys, probably exist in another category entirely. The purchaser of a Bentley probably doesn't believe that the car is really worth, on a mechanical level, what they are paying (prices start at $180,000). The value of these types of cars is found more in social signaling than as an accurate representation of material value, and some might claim that, overall, they still represent fair value. It's hard to duplicate the impact of rolling up to your golf club in a new $2.5 million dollar Bugatti Chiron; those who are impressed by such overt displays of wealth might be extremely useful in one way or another. It's not a pretty way to get things done, but it might work for some people, making the actual cost of the Bugatti inconsequential if it helps you get elected to a coveted spot on the Board of Directors.

Regardless, it's still the case in the car industry that the most money is made from selling a lot of cars to the average consumer, all of whom require a car to lead a normal life and vastly outnumber those in the high-end car market. Targeting whales is a useful strategy for niche markets such as luxury cars or custom-made, extravagantly expensive but nearly useless (because dangerously overpowered) motorcycles, but the big boys chasing billions concentrate on mass sales (Toyota, Ford, and General Motors, for example). It's how we expect the market to function.

Most of the attention is paid to the mass of average buyers; the upper and lower ends of the market have a much smaller customer base and are tended to by smaller and more specific builds. We imagine the same sort of market functioning for most products we purchase: dishwashers, lawn mowers, and computers. The large middle is where most of the competition occurs, spurring positive feature creep and improving overall efficiencies at a lower cost to consumers. A laptop purchased today is both half the cost and twice as powerful as one available five years ago; it's ten times as powerful as a laptop available ten years ago; it puts all the early 1990s models to shame at a fraction of the price. This is an evolving, ever-improving market, marred only by the development of "planned obsolescence," which is a natural result of market forces busy at work. The very cheapest products have this type of obsolescence built in, but should you move up a bit (not a lot) you can moderate its effect and get longer-lasting products at slightly higher prices. In general the more you are willing to pay the longer a product will last and the better the long-term outcome. (Granted, this is a broad claim, and I've certainly experienced the opposite.)

The system isn't perfect because perfection is not what makes the most money in a system driven by profit. That said, it's a better system than anything else humans have come up with, and it's been the major driver for global poverty reduction over the last thirty years[10] (the rate of "absolute poverty" was 44 percent in 1981; by 2015 it was close to 10 percent).[11] We in the West are stuck with capitalism whether we like it or not, and often denigrate it in knee-jerk fashion,[12] but if you were to ask a modern Chinese or Indian person their take on modern capitalistic economic developments, the typical answer, given current conditions compared to historical ones, would be enthusiastic.

LEARNING FROM THE CASINOS

Many of the developers in the mobile casual (i.e. women-focused games such as Candy Crush[13]) are actually straight from the casino industry . . . These companies are aiming at

*people who have problems with compulsive behavior, the same
marks/whales the casino industry aims at. Having come from
a neuroscience background, I would say these people actually
have physiological handicaps, and these companies are preying
on handicapped people vulnerable to their methodologies.
Children also have the same problems, and while these games
do have a lot of children playing them, King.com lawyers
called me personally to make sure I did not say publicly that
they are intentionally targeting children.*

—Ramin Shokrizade[14]

Casinos are not subtle, because decades of real-life experimentation with gamblers has proven, conclusively, that subtlety doesn't pay.

Everyone is familiar with the most egregious types of emotional and psychological manipulation perpetrated by casinos, yet few object. We have become culturally deadened to the dubious ethics behind such tactics, which are often viewed as quaint throwbacks—relatively harmless given their exceedingly obvious intent. Casinos serve free alcohol within their domain, which is both legal (remarkable) and excruciatingly transparent as a method for befuddling gamblers, since befuddled gamblers make far worse decisions than the unbefuddled.

Similarly, high rollers (aka "whales"), those coddling a winning streak, and the very rare and lucky few who manage to win big from the scientifically calibrated slot machines, are immediately comped an expensive suite at the casino, free of charge,[15] for the unmistakable purpose of keeping the person, and their winnings, trapped in the casino overnight. The only way to escape a casino with a positive cash flow is to ride a short-term bubble and leave before it's pricked; the longer anyone stays in a casino, however sophisticated or clever they might be, the more the casino wins. The odds are always stacked against the players, the games are not fair, and the entire enterprise exists to pander to a gambler's love of gambling and take their money. If anyone has fun it's a byproduct, not a feature.

In addition to these overt manipulative haymakers are thousands of more refined design decisions defining the entirety of a casino's look and feel and its effect upon the gambler. Bill Friedman's *Designing Casinos to Dominate the Competition* (2000) is six hundred pages of close examination of every aspect of a casino's architectural and interior design with one goal in mind: "The analysis of player preference . . . is both objective and quantitative. . . . The only relevant considerations for casino designs are these: What percentage of visitors gamble? What percentage return to gamble? Nothing else matters."[16]

Friedman represents old-school casino design, and in his casino designs there are no windows (to exclude the outside world), no clocks (allowing players to lose track of time), and absolutely no calm or peaceful corners in which to relax[17] (stress and confusion clouds the mind, resulting in worse decision-making, ergo more gambling). Function takes precedent over form. The most glaring example of this single-minded focus are the hideous carpets found in Friedman-designed casinos, there for a single purpose:

> Not only is the ugliness of most casino carpets totally deliberate, it's actually the result of elaborate market-research tests, designed to find the patterns and colors most *displeasing* to the human eye! . . . The reasons? For one, the somewhat intense colors and busy patterns amplify players' excitement as they enter the casino and prepare to play. For another, wildly patterned carpets are such an assault on the visual that they (subliminally) discourage people from looking down and encourage them to look up—at the machines and table games. Along with the lack of clocks and windows, the "dizzy" floor designs also help with the process of generally disorienting you, so you lose track of time—and, with luck, of how much money you're losing and where the exits are.[18]

In these sorts of places everything is done rationally; as soon as a design change is made, the gambling effects associated with the change are reviewed, and the answer to the following question determines whether the change is retained: Did profits increase or decrease? The final design is a testimony to short-term evolutionary capitalism, with Friedman devotees playing the part of nature, tweaking the color scheme, adding pleasing scents to the slots area, or moving the slot machines a few feet closer to the loudest location in the casino in an unceasing attempt to drag an additional dollar or two from the pockets of their "guests." Within the Friedman rubric—the modifications allowed given his objectives—he found success. Friedman-designed casinos made more money than their more staid peers. They never rated high in anyone's rating of the "best" or "most fun" places to visit in Las Vegas, but their owners were more than happy with the tradeoff. The bottom line was all that mattered.

There is a megalomaniac edge to Friedman's profit-at-all-costs design theory. Each small tweak he championed might, in a vacuum, make sense, and not noticeably damage the overall atmosphere of the casino, but when taken as an overarching methodology and strung together one after another the result is a monstrous mishmash. For once the culprit is not design by committee but design by a relentless focus on human psychological weakness—the goal is to alter behavior using the most manipulative environment ever built by mankind.[19]

Friedman was the loudest cheerleader for his personal style of design, which rose to dominance in the 1990s and reached its zenith in the middle of the next decade—but it can't be said that gambling on the strip boomed after his methods were widely adopted. Overall, casino revenue was flat[20] and dropped slowly through the first decade of the twenty-first century (yearly local economic fluctuations proved relatively immune to national up- and downturns). If Friedman's designs were moderately successful for those casinos implementing his ideas their increased profitability (compared to their peers) was a result of extracting more value from the current crop of gamblers rather than increasing the size of the gambling public. Friedman was milking the same herd, just a bit more vigorously.

Unfortunately—at least for Las Vegas boosters—after tasting what the new casinos had to offer, tourists returning from the strip increasingly felt disgruntled and abused. The total number of visitors to the city flat-lined early in the twenty-first century,[21] and many long-term residents were shocked by occasional years of *negative* growth. It was hard to hide the truth, even to the most gullible: a James Bond casino experience was perhaps too much to be expected, but how about something moderately fun and relaxing that at the same time wasn't an aesthetic horror show? Glamorous Las Vegas (if it ever existed) now felt little different from a rough carnival shakedown. Casinos spent nearly no money hiding what they truly were since this had been shown, in the short term, to have no negative effect on the bottom line. The future was too far away to worry about.

How does one kill the goose producing all those golden eggs? Stress the goose to such a degree that eggs stop coming out. Las Vegas was stuck in the mud, and everyone wondered what was going on. Critics, always happy to censure Friedman's design choices on an aesthetic level, began to question whether these tone-deaf money extraction machines might be linked to the larger issue of slumping Las Vegas growth. Was a maniacal short-term focus on profits, relentlessly squeezing every drop of profit from the limited gambling public, really the best way to sustain long-term health?

Some began to imagine an alternative: a relaxing and enjoyable experience in casinos. Expanding the number of gamblers would be vastly more profitable (and sustainable) than continuing to grind down the current supply. How could this be done given the general stasis? Something new had to arise.

Real-estate mogul Steve Wynn's Las Vegas casino, Bellagio, opened in 1998, and it was the first major casino to explicitly reject the stylistic status quo. Bellagio not only had fountains and windows, it had a conservatory and botanical gardens, as well as the Bellagio Gallery of Fine Art, with rotating exhibitions mixing its own collection with works on loan from museums around the world. It was open to the public with titles such as "Classic Contemporary: Lichtenstein, Warhol, & Friends" and "Faberge:

Treasures From the Kremlin." Bellagio hosts a two-star Michelin restaurant (*Picasso*), and supplies tourists with many reasons to enter the casino for reasons *other* than gambling. Given the Las Vegas doldrums, Bellagio was more than a breath of fresh air: its bright and appealing interior design (its "elegant interiors [were] inspired by the style of northern Italy and southern France"[22]) made it obvious to everyone that this was far more than a dark, dirty den of gambling. People responded. The Bellagio has been a fabulous success, and a direct rejection of Friedman's "profit at all costs" design manipulations. There is another way, and possibly a better way to achieve long-term profits and growth: make the customers happy while taking their money.

SLOT MACHINES AND *TETRIS*

Slot machines make up the majority of every major Las Vegas casino's profits, a little-known fact that has been true for nearly a hundred years. In the popular imagination, slot machines (slots) are generally regarded as a lure for suckers, given that "serious gamblers" play poker or blackjack. The continued success of slots is understandable since playing a slot machine is safe from an interpersonal standpoint: you don't have to interact with other players, fight against them for chips, and deal with their superstitions and emotional outbursts. The rules are relatively straightforward. You can plunk yourself down with a bucket of coins and play for a few minutes or hours, depending on your luck.

Slot machines are all about luck. There is no skill involved; no special methods; no way to increase or decrease your chance of winning. Not only are modern slot machines computer-controlled, they are also dynamic; slot odds can be changed on the fly, remotely. It's not true that the odds of winning at a given machine are stable throughout the day. In the long run, yes, slots are capped in Nevada at 75 percent, and must by law return a minimum of 75 percent of the money paid into them over time. Every dollar spent on slots returns twenty-five cents profit for the casino. As with any gambling game there is high variation: some players win and win big, but computers find it trivial to balance these large losses against constant short-term gains. No casino ever went broke from slot machines. This is a case where more is always better.

Slots developed from a simple desire to automate poker. In 1891, the Brooklyn manufacturer Sittman and Pitt developed the first slot machine based on values derived from the familiar card deck. It featured five spinning drums, the same number as the most popular poker game of the day, five card draw, and each drum contained fifty possible card values (ace of diamonds, eight of clubs, two of hearts, etc.). The player pulled a lever, spinning five drums, and if, when the spinning stopped, a reasonably strong poker hand was revealed, the player won a token giving them access to—something. Two of a kind might be worth a free beer; three of a kind a comped meal; a full house a shave and haircut. Prizes were supplied by the establishment owning the machines, and varied widely from location to location.

Slot machines were an immediate hit, but their complexity posed a problem for operators. Because there were a large number of "good," and thus "winning," poker hands, the result of any given pull on the lever was difficult to calculate, which made it impossible for the machine to automatically distribute sensible rewards—too much or too little might be won. Calculating all the possibilities wasn't feasible from a technological standpoint given the gear-and-spring operation of early slots. A few years later, Charles Fey (based in San Francisco) took the unruly poker slot apparatus and simplified it. Instead of five spinning drums, his had three. Instead of fifty possible values for each drum, his had five. The total number of possible combinations resulting from a pull plummeted to five cubed, or 125. This was low enough to make an automated payout scheme feasible, which could be adjusted by operators to be more or less generous. Fey's version of slots, and those who copied it, was so successful it quickly dominated the market, driving out the older, more complicated models that required human supervision of winnings.

Slots' rapid evolution is an interesting example of a complicated and interesting game, a five-drum poker machine using fifty card values per drum, being immediately superseded by a less interesting and simpler game, with three drums featuring five symbols each. This drive toward simplicity was technological and cultural—not everyone knew poker hand values—but most importantly it was fiscal. It was possible to set up Fey's machine in a corner and not look at it again until the end of the day, when it could be opened and the day's take removed. Rewards based on food or other prizes had been replaced by coins. Fey's version was clearly and unmistakably a gambling machine, with money going in and (sometimes) money coming out.

An early offshoot of Fey's simplified slots was called a "trade stimulator," designed to do exactly what the name suggested: stimulate trade in a confectionery or general store. These were small machines, easily accessible, placed on the counter within view of both adults and children. Customers were offered the opportunity, for a penny or two, to pull a lever and possibly win more than a penny's worth of goods. Candy-based prizes allowed such machines to evade prosecution under antigambling laws, since no cash was directly won. One of the most popular of these slot machines rewarded players with fruit-flavored chewing gum, and used pictures of the various fruit flavors as symbols on the drums—three cherries might result in a free stick of cherry-flavored gum, for example. The familiar cherry and melon symbols on many modern slot machines are directly derived from these candy-counter trade stimulators. The otherwise inexplicable BAR symbol seems to derive from an image of gum packets (a prize to be won) on early trade stimulators, although the history of its origin is somewhat muddy.

What happened with slot machines was a case of reverse development: the initial invention proved to be more complex than its eventual replacement, which simplified the game and made it easier to implement and sell.

This was only possible from an economic standpoint because the simplification did not affect (and might have augmented) the true purpose and lure of the machine: gambling, and the rush of a gambling reward. It wasn't the only time when technical simplification occurred in a product's development—the same thing happened with video games.

Tetris is *Candy Crush*'s more sophisticated forerunner and ultimate progenitor, despite being more than two decades old. Both games are single-screen, level-based games involving symbols that fall from the top of the screen and pile up below. The user is required to clear the level by somehow getting rid of the stuff falling from above; this is accomplished by filling a row (*Tetris*), or by selecting a symbol to switch places with an adjacent symbol, creating a triple and causing the symbols to disappear and leave the space open for more falling symbols (*Candy Crush*). Levels are won by removing a certain number of rows (*Tetris*) or triples (*Candy Crush*), generating a new level exactly the same as the old but with the difficulty ramped up.[23]

In *Tetris*, relatively wide rows with twelve or more columns are filled by falling pieces that the player rotates in four directions and slots into empty spaces; when a row is entirely filled it disappears, giving the player a little more room to operate. As levels progress the pieces fall more rapidly and eventually stack to the top of the screen, overwhelming the player and ending the game. You can't win *Tetris*; it's always a matter of getting to a higher level and achieving a better score. *Tetris* a mix of luck and skill, with skill predominating. The falling pieces are randomly determined, and after one appears a skilled player has many opportunities to make good or bad moves by moving and rotating it.

An expert *Tetris* player will make consistently high scores compared to a novice. Any given piece can be slotted into twelve columns[24] and rotated in any of four ways, giving forty-eight possible human moves for a falling piece. A computer attempting to "look ahead" and figure out possible board combinations will be overwhelmed by rapidly mounting complexity; three falling pieces generate 48^3 (already over 100,000) possible results, with every additional piece adding another power to the exponent.[25] This is computationally unfeasible even on modern super-computers and forced the game designers to have the falling pieces determined randomly. Should they attempt to customize or alter the types of pieces falling from the sky to make a level easier or more difficult, the results would probably be the opposite of that which was intended. Humans would be able to spot these tendencies and, because of the huge variability in possible moves, leverage the nonrandom nature of the game-play to make the game easier, not harder. If you have played long enough to recognize a game's static tendencies you can use it against the game. It's far better for the game designers to make it completely random and let the dice fall where they may.

As we have seen, the inspiration for the initial invention of slot machines, an automatic way to play poker, was quickly simplified into a "match three" slot machine, the modern term for any type of puzzle game where the player attempts to match three or more symbols in a row. Similarly, *Candy Crush* took its wildly successful predecessor, *Tetris*, and reduced it to bare bones: twelve columns became nine, and human input ranging from dozens of possible moves involving piece rotation and movement were reduced to one or two matching options. In *Candy Crush*, the most a player is allowed to do, in fact their only way of interacting with the game, is to decide which triple among the possible triples should be created by switching two adjacent symbols—if there are any matches to be found. Unlike *Tetris*, the entire playfield of *Candy Crush* is filled with symbols, and it's the player's job to point out and select possible "triples" existing in the current configuration. This requires a certain amount of skill, since matching one triple instead of another sometimes simplifies matching in the future as the triple is removed and more symbols "fall" to take their place, possibly causing a domino effect of further matching leading to more matching. But since it's unknown what symbols are going to fall from the sky following any match, players must make decisions about the future with wildly incomplete information.

It's not clear, in the long run, how much player skill actually matters with *Candy Crush*, particularly at higher levels. There's so much chaos involved that insufficient information interferes with logical decision-making. If *Tetris* is 90 percent skill and 10 percent luck, *Candy Crush*, past the first dozen levels, at least tilts the other direction: 10 percent skill and 90 percent luck, with luck becoming an ever-more-important factor the higher the levels rise.[26]

It's important to note that, unlike *Tetris*, *Candy Crush* is capable of calculating both the current board configuration and how the board might look after dropping new candy from the top of the screen following any match. In any given *Candy Crush* level there are only a handful of possible human moves, making it easy for the game, running on what was, fifteen years ago, a supercomputer, to calculate all possible options available to a human player at any given moment and predict what can and can't be achieved for a given set of input in response to best play.

Tetris is a fair game, meaning that the computer does not punish the player by sending down impossible sequences of pieces during a critical point on a given level; it is rigorously random. *Candy Crush* neither promises nor does it deliver random and fair gameplay.[27] This is one of *Candy Crush*'s most subtle "improvements" compared to *Tetris*: because of its overall simplicity and lack of dynamic user input it's trivially easy for *Candy Crush* to peek into the future and change its difficulty on the fly, sending down blocks of candy that make life easier or more difficult for the player no matter how well he or she plays. The game can make clearing a level trivial by generating useful clumps of candy, allowing players to make moves freeing up a lot of space, or alternatively create situations where there are no good moves and few or no way to clear the level. At no point are these adjustments visible or made explicit to the user.

Dynamically changing a game's difficulty during play can be a useful technique for improving the overall game experience. It is common for games to scale according to the perceived skill and sophistication of the current player. *Resident Evil 4*, released in 2005, famously employed an invisible "difficulty scale" that rated the player on various abilities and adjusted enemies attacks/behavior based on the skill of the player. There isn't any moral or ethical reason for a game to be strictly and rigorously random; *Candy Crush* never promises such a thing, and it's unreasonable to expect it. It's just another tool available for game designers the world over; what matters is how the tool is used.

Where does this leave us? As we have seen, most casinos are now savvy enough to maximize both short- and long-term profits using every psychological manipulation known to mankind. Slot machines keep players reasonably happy and feeding the beast. *Tetris* comes from another place entirely. It was created in 1984 by a Russian game designer working on relatively primitive computers that only had, initially, ASCII (text) graphics. It became a bestseller due to its incredibly fun gameplay and unique look and feel—at the time, it played like no other contemporary game.

That leaves the question: why is *Candy Crush* so popular? Answer: *Candy Crush* is a Frankensteinian hybrid, taking the most addictive aspects of the games that came before it and putting them to work beneath the surface of a polished and superficially appealing product. The result is a remarkable and highly cynical game, which jettisoned gameplay, originality, and fairness to such a degree that the resulting product can barely be called a game (many don't consider it one),[28] and can barely be called fun (many current players, even while playing, admit they aren't having fun). *Candy Crush* has the repetitive, randomly rewarding appeal of slot machines, down to the very symbols used in the game; simplicity born from minimizing *Tetris* and its similarly complex spinoffs, and gameplay micromanaged to a degree fully as obsessive as Friedman's casinos with their ugly carpets and stressful atmosphere, focusing solely on extracting money from the player.

THE (DE)EVOLUTION OF GAMES

Mechanical Game:

Poker Machine (Match 5) → Slot Machines (Match 3) → Trade
   Stimulator (Match 3)
Result: Slot machines embedded in a casino with environmental
   design maximizing manipulation/profit.

Video Game:

Slot Machines → *Tetris* (Match 9) → *Candy Crush* (Match 3)
Result: *Candy Crush* embedded in a free-to-play design based
   upon casino forebears and neuroscience for maximizing
   manipulation/profit.

Candy Crush is delivered to players free of charge. Unlike old-school shareware, which supplied the full program and allowed you to donate money to
the programmer if you wanted to, *Candy Crush*'s free release was key to its
initial popularity.[29] It did not ask for money up front. Spending money on
Candy Crush was always the result of gameplay choices, called in-app purchases, not payment for the game as a whole. This development was crucial.

While hugely successful, *Candy Crush* has, like Friedman's casinos,
a cloying and ultimately unsatisfying effect upon the player, however
enthusiastic they might be at first. It's hard not to sense, at some level, the
overt manipulation going on; to feel as if the game is not as fun nor as
rewarding as the time spent playing it; to walk away from a session more
disgruntled and stressed than before playing it—and this isn't surprising.
It's what *Candy Crush* was designed to make you feel.[30] *Candy Crush* is
a sophisticated instrument targeting well-known human psychological

weaknesses and brutally leveraging them for profit. It was designed to be the most manipulative and addictive game ever produced, and by all accounts it's succeeded beyond its creator's wildest dreams.

OLD SCHOOL CAPITALISM

Video games, unlike cars, are neither necessary nor, apparently, capable of targeting whales. How could they? If a game costs $40 it costs $40 for everyone involved, regardless of income and regardless of advertising. There are no "prestige" video games, no insanely expensive upgrades or options.[31] It might be the case that a rich person would be willing to pay far more for a desired game, since it represents a trivial outlay of their total income, but there wasn't thought to be any way to monetize this discrepancy. Video games were at an economic standstill until the internet arrived. Everyone got the same game, pretty much, at the same price, pretty much. The price of the game had to be targeted to the masses, which put an end to Bugatti-style pricing.

Candy Crush was at the forefront of an innovative gaming model turning all of this on its head. *Candy Crush* is not only capable of targeting whales, whales were the inspiration for its development and mechanics. This new model was made possible because the internet allowed something completely new to arise: free game distribution. You no longer have to pay for a game. It's being given away for free. How's that for a new money-making venture? I would have loved to have been in that meeting—it sounds like a really bad way to make money. But let's consider the long-term consequences.

What if instead of selling a game you offer it to everyone who wants it? The idea is to get as many potential customers in the door as possible. Thinking back on our casino discussion, it's an ingenious solution: open the gates wide and let every tourist under the sun enter the building. Unlike a casino, a video game requires no overhead—downloads cost no more for one person than a million. Everyone's able to participate. A casino has to deal with actual people doing dirty, messy things in their place of business, and every customer comes with an overhead cost. The virtual world of gaming is totally exempt from such concerns.

It's only when people start to play *Candy Crush* and get engrossed that the game publisher offers various in-game purchase options allowing for upgrading or buying more lives or ending a level early or purchasing a special item. Crucially, *Candy Crush* is a solitary game. You aren't competing against other players who might object to your spending money for an artificial advantage. The question of fairness is inexorably bound up with competition between players. In a solitary game you are competing against the computer, and it's a purely personal decision to pay a bit for some sort of advantage. Idealistic players claim that such purchases are an affront to the purity of the game; the goal is to beat the game without help, not depend upon monetary crutches to make up for lack of skill. But this isn't a fraught decision for most people. They just want to have fun, and if paying a little more ups the fun factor then that's what they'll do. The game itself was free, after all, so the money a player didn't spend on buying it is "virtual profits." That's always easier to spend.

Everyone who fails to spend money on *Candy Crush* is by definition *not* a whale. Those who spend a little are minnows, those who spend a bit more are dolphins, and those who spend a lot, in excess of $50 over the lifetime of the game, are whales. These are the true targets, and *Candy Crush* puts a glowing bull's-eye on their iPhone or laptop.

It's not possible to play the original version of *Candy Crush* and "win" (i.e. finish all the levels) without spending a dime. The original version of the game had a "river bridge" that you could only pass by paying a small amount of money. Later versions, such as *Candy Crush Saga*, can be played to the end without spending money, and people claim to have done so. But this is operating the game in a way unintended by the developers, and doing so requires a huge investment in time. Anyone who actually finishes the game in this way likely considers themselves an addict, or at least heavily invested, given the huge time requirement involved and the paucity of the reward.

It's true that most people *don't* spend any money on *Candy Crush Saga* and voluntarily stop playing at some point—usually out of frustration. According to its maker, King, only 3 percent of *Candy Crush* players actually utilize in-game purchases, which seems like an incredibly low percentage and a terrible business model. But if a game is downloaded 2.73 billion times,[32] 3 percent is eighty-one million nine hundred thousand paying users—yes, that's over eighty million. If each contributes a dollar at some point in the game's life, King realizes huge profits given the simplicity of the game and the speed at which it was designed and created. But let's remember a crucial point: these 3 percent are not your average players. They are the players willing to spend money to get an in-game benefit and have shown themselves to be susceptible to pressure. Some of them are minnows, and some are dolphins, but some of them are veritable whales. Many spend far more than one dollar over the lifetime of the game and as they play, getting deeper into the game, the greater the temptation grows to spend more and more to get past the increasingly difficult levels. Some end up spending huge amounts of money playing what looks to be, on the outside, a "free game."

Candy Crush is the biggest casino on the planet, and as we shall see the whales have been scientifically targeted for harpooning.

EXTRACTING PROFIT: WHEN A GAME PLAYS YOU

It is difficult, in theory, to get consumers to pay for something they have been given for free . . . but clearly it's not impossible. Imagine purchasing a bare-bones but fully functional car for nothing more than the cost of local taxes. The purchase requires you to enter into a strict contract that states that all modifications to the car must be done by certain licensed dealerships—nothing can be modified at home or by third-party mechanics.

You also can't sell the car; if you stop driving it a certain number of miles per week, you have to return it to the car manufacturer in good condition or pay a big fine. This would seem to be an insane way to make money and a terrible way to sell cars. It is possible, however, to see a path to monetization allowing the car company to stay in business. What is needed is a method to extract income from the thousands of people who took up the "free car" offer. The question is the same as that facing game companies distributing "free games." How to make money from something that costs nothing to own?

In our example the car manufacturer would surely have stripped the free car of any and all amenities, including speakers, cruise control, air conditioning, heating… sure, the car's legal and works, but it's brutally uncomfortable: the seats are hard, there's no easy way to regulate the cabin temperature, there's no way to listen to music, etc. Taking the car to a licensed dealership reveals the bad news: air conditioning costs $5K, a music system $2k, new seats $3k, etc. Getting the "free" car up to normal American standards will cost, ultimately, at least as much if not more than other cars in its price range.

Yes, there will be a few hardy consumers who stick it out and drive the free car in sweltering heat and withstand unbearable discomfort, but soon consumers will discover they are being forced to spend a lot of money on their once-free car and are locked into using licensed dealerships for the upgrades. The result of this scheme might be short-term gain for the car company, but in the long-term customers will be furious. Selling air conditioning for $5k is nothing less than a shakedown; consumers paying for it will certainly hold a grudge against the company, making its long-term prospects dim. It doesn't matter that the initial car was free and that the consumer has already benefited from driving it; giving away something with significant design flaws baked into the product is a maddening way to operate, and will always be seen as such and rejected by consumers—which is probably why there are no car companies operating in this fashion.

The economic problem isn't how cars are sold and upgraded; there isn't any reason to think profits from upgrades to freely given cars are going to be better or worse, in the long term, than profits from cars sold in full, up front. Both have benefits and drawbacks: selling a car conventionally ensures an immediate fixed profit, while car upgrading leaves undetermined the profit made from any given car, which might exceed the initial cost many times over (or fall below). The issue isn't fiscal, it's emotional. You can't strong-arm people into buying air conditioning by roasting them during the summer. It's too crass a method. Nobody will forgive such a scheme because the company appears doubly responsible, both creating the cause of the discomfort (no A/C in the car initially), as well as the pain of the remedy (an expensive A/C installation). Blatant manipulation such as this is universally despised.

What's needed is a paradigm shift: the car company needs to supply reasonably comfortable "free cars" from the get go. These cars are still basic but now include A/C and comfortable seats and a stripped-down music system. The car company might pipe in ads when the driver enters the car, offering upgrade opportunities. Sure, the car drives reasonably well, but what if you could get a slightly improved carburetor for better fuel mileage and power? What about enhanced speakers and a USB port for your phone? How about side airbags and a better suspension? This is, emotionally, a far better way to proceed. It's not reasonable that a free car will have the best suspension in the world right off the bat. Sure it works, and it's safe, but given that the car was free . . . there's obviously room for improvement. There isn't any overt manipulation going on here; consumers will upgrade from a fully functioning if basic car to a slightly better one without rancor. They are not getting their arm overtly twisted; they are choosing to make a basic car a bit more refined. It's their choice, not something forced upon them by the car company's decision to make them suffer.

This scheme's drawback is the fact that any car that's reasonably comfortable and reasonably well-outfitted (regardless of build quality) gives a huge incentive to consumers to content themselves the useful free product and spend no money now or in the future. Forcing them to upgrade out of discomfort is rank manipulation, but without such painful stimuli how can the car company get consumers to spend? It's a stalemate predicated on universal human resistance to emotional blackmail.

There's a way around this dead end. Try something called "reward removal." This is how it works in our free car thought experiment: instead of a bare-bones version of the free car, customers are instead initially given an upgraded model with a much more powerful and responsive engine. This engine will magically downgrade in a month to the standard model, but getting access to a better engine for a month is an explicit bonus and not something the consumer views as normal—it's presented as a one-time, unexpected benefit. The consumer knows the engine is going to downgrade in a month but is grateful they get a month with more power. Time passes, the consumer drives the car around the block, and a month later some special engine parts burn away and the souped-up engine reverts back to its vanilla and humdrum version. What used to get 200 horsepower now gets 80. What had been a thrilling ride is transformed into a slow-to-accelerate chore. The difference between having an engine upgrade and not having one is stark, but the blame for the current level of unhappiness is not placed on the shoulders of the car company—in fact, the car company gave the consumer a free taste of bliss *without having to do so*. Any anger related to the poorly performing standard engine is transferred from the car company to the consumer since only the consumer has a way to fix the problem: pay to upgrade the engine. If the car is slow and unfun to drive it's the fault of the stingy driver, not the car company.

This is a nifty bit of psychological jujitsu because in both cases the car company is causing the consumer to suffer—yet the blame, in the second case, is shifted and obfuscated. It's too difficult to pierce the car company's intentions given that the facts are hidden. Did the car company supply an upgrade for a month only to create pain when it was taken away? How could a consumer prove such intent, even to themselves?

When the car company distributes cars without A/C in the heat of the summer the intent is clear: it's supposed to hurt. Can removing a more powerful engine be put in the same category? Doesn't that sound like complaining? Did you expect a free engine upgrade for a full decade? How fair is that in a free car after all? It's similar to what cable companies do when they offer you a free month of some new service, only to take it away after thirty days. This is a far less painful event: the status quo has been reinstated. Missing a few channels isn't too bad. When our hypothetical engine is downgraded, what had been a reasonable driving experience turns into something slightly (or very) painful, yet the blame doesn't fall upon the car manufacturer.

Reward removal is immensely powerful because it allows consumers to fully experience that which they will later have to pay to enjoy without any of the emotional drawbacks associated with having it torn away. A particularly clear example of this can be found in *Puzzle and Dragons* (from GungHo Online Entertainment), a free video game for those ten years old and older. It obviously includes optional in-game purchases. As Ramin Shokrizade puts it, "*Puzzle and Dragons* uses this technique [reward removal] at the end of each dungeon in the form of an inventory cap. The player is given a number of 'eggs' as rewards, the contents of which have to be held in inventory. If your small inventory space is exceeded . . . those eggs are taken from you unless you spend to increase your inventory space. Brilliant!"[33]

This is a wonderful example because it makes no sense for a video game to have a limited inventory: the computers and phones running the game are capable of handling an almost infinite number of digital eggs and their contents given modern storage sizes and processing speeds. If limiting the number of eggs is necessary to ensure game balance, why allow the inventory to be increased by spending, which tilts the game toward spenders, ruining fairness? The default inventory size is an artificial limit, imposed by the game in order to remove rewards (eggs) from players who earned them—again, unless players choose to pay for an expanded inventory. To see the absurd unfairness of this requires the player to escape the virtual world constructed by the game, where the rules are rigid and must be accepted to engage with the game, and look at the issue rationally and without emotional engagement. This is difficult for most humans to do in the best of circumstances, resulting in most players being stuck in the *Puzzle and Dragons* world, watching their fought-for and valuable eggs being taken away due to their own—well, what? Stinginess? If you want to keep your reward, you might as well pay two dollars for a bigger inventory. Makes sense, right?

Reward removal is just one of many manipulations used by *Candy Crush* to get its players to purchase in-game products, and the deeper you get into the game the nastier it gets.

THE MECHANICS OF
VIDEO-GAME MANIPULATION

When my wife first picked up *Candy Crush* and started to play it she was, like myself, entirely ignorant of how it had been constructed and who was responsible for its creation. When I asked her for her impression of the hypothetical game designer, she posited, given the relative simplicity of the game, a single hardworking individual who was probably as shocked as anyone by the global hit *Candy Crush* had become. It seemed like such a sweet game, pleasing to look at, easy to learn, with engaging sound effects and light shows and dazzling end-of-level fireworks—entirely cute and harmless. She was wrong on every count but it's not her fault: why *wouldn't* she imagine these things to be true? Unwittingly, she was going up against a professional and highly educated team of cognitive psychologists, grizzled marketers, and a profit-at-all-costs corporation. In retrospect, she didn't stand a chance.

Ramin Shokrizade put it this way when we last spoke:

Every aspect of these games [*Candy Crush* and its imitators] is scientifically designed to boost spending or engagement. As I showed the 2014 ICPEN (International Consumer Protection & Enforcement Network) in Panama, even the use of color is very important. I showed them *Marvel Super Hero Squad* (a Disney product), including the tutorial where children were instructed on how to use the microtransaction store, and how to use/spin the roulette wheel. Large companies are working very hard to indoctrinate small children into a gambling lifestyle through franchises that their parents trust. In that game, every green-colored button triggers a real money spend. Every red button declines a spend. Of course a small child, even before they know how to read, is taught that green is good and red is bad so they know which buttons to push. The green ones are often made a bit larger, and flash/pulse/glow/throb/etc.[34]

Candy Crush was built from the ground up to make as much money as possible. There is obviously nothing wrong with this as a general goal, and we would be foolish to imagine any game company isn't thinking about the bottom line to some extent, but there is a difference in degree with *Candy Crush* that can't be overlooked. Everything is subservient to the goal of manipulating the consumer to spend money on the game—*everything*, including the concept of "fun." With this in mind, many of the design decisions of the game begin to make sense.

Sugar Theme

Candy Crush is targeted to a Western audience with Western tastes. A similar game aimed at the East would have a different texture and flavor; in many Asian cultures, candy/sweets are not as beloved and indulged as in the West. There is a good reason players are not looking at fish or abstract blobs or hardware store items: the glossy candies in the game look good enough to eat, and they remind one of childhood fantasies of excess—a chocolate river or a swimming pool full of gumdrops. It's a game about candy. How dangerous can that be? This is an overt play for upping the overall innocence of the game itself; not only is it not scary to look at, it seems absurd to imagine that such a game might be capable of doing something nefarious in the background.

Bright, Cartoonish Color Scheme

Not only is *Candy Crush* cartoonish, it features an infantile guide who ushers you into the game and squeals at every stage when you do well. Everything about the game is as cute as possible: the sounds it makes are cute, the cut scenes are cute, and the fonts and the pop-up windows are engineered to look like a computerized version of *Candyland*. Cute things are, by definition, both powerless and helpless[35]—it's not a coincidence that *Candy Crush* leverages cute to the max. Given the onslaught of cute, it's easy to feel deeply unsuspicious as to the game's motives—an extremely valuable position for a game from which to influence the consumer. Given its simplicity, the game looks and plays like a throwback—it's self-knowingly and childishly retro—and the last thing you would ever imagine is something so cute actively manipulating you.

Gameplay

The rules of the game are so simple a child could easily learn them. And while King denies targeting children, it's certainly the case that nothing about the game would be difficult for a four-year-old to master. *Candy Crush* is almost insultingly simple for adult: just swipe the screen, match similar candies, and progress to the next level. All you have to do is make the right moves—if you don't, well, sometimes you won't pass the level. It *appears* that the more you play *Candy Crush* the better you get at it. The game increases in difficulty as the levels fly by; pretty soon *Candy Crush* stops being the easy breeze the first ten or twenty levels were and progress is slowed and soon halted. The apparent goal is to keep playing, get better, improve your skills, and move to the next level. This would make sense as a strategy except for the fact that the game is dynamic; the difficulty scales; it does not want you to move ahead too fast. To proceed after a certain point it's often necessary to buy an extra life or purchase a boost to clear a stubborn level. What had been sold as a game of skill slowly begins to morph into a money game,[36] often without the player noticing. While it's possible to finish *Candy Crush* without spending a dime, it requires a huge amount of time, effort, and astonishing luck. Not only isn't *Candy Crush* an easy game, it's not fundamentally a game of skill. It's not clear that a randomly selected merely competent player does any worse on level 100 than the world's most sophisticated *Candy Crush* expert: at this point everyone is fighting the computer algorithm and depending on dumb luck to proceed.

More worryingly, *Candy Crush* is not interested in frustrating a player so much that the player stops playing. That's obviously bad business for a game that depends on players spending cash in-game to make any income. Instead, *Candy Crush* is calibrated to ensure that a player is neither moving too rapidly through the game and therefore has no incentive to purchase upgrades, nor getting so frustrated they stop playing. This requires a delicate adjustment, but given sufficient player data King is capable of making such judgments with astonishing accuracy for the average player, which is all that matters when you are talking about over two billion downloads.

Social Network Leveraging

Initially, *Candy Crush* relied heavily on Facebook friends to help spread the game's influence and consumer base. There are many in-game events that have out-of-game remedies. If you run out of *Candy Crush* lives, you can request more lives from your Facebook friends, who upon receiving your message and installing the game can give some to you—and you give *them* extra lives in return. *Candy Crush* tracks your advancement against the scores of these newly revealed social media friends, displaying the results for you and your circle of friends to see—allowing for good- or ill-natured competition. This is the most obviously self-serving of all of *Candy Crush*'s tricks; there is no valid "gameplay" reason for leveraging Facebook in this way. It has no mutual in-game function; *Candy Crush* does not allow direct player vs. player competition or cooperative play. The point of the Facebook feature is to outsource advertising from the company to its consumer base: if King can get players to convince their friends to install the game for a onetime benefit (more lives), it's clearly the company who benefits the most. It's a free form of the best sort of advertising: exhortations from a trusted friend.

OTHERS JUMP ON THE MANIPULATION BANDWAGON

The hugely successful and profitable *Candy Crush* example kicked video-game manipulation into high gear. In 2011, King was on the verge of bankruptcy; some of the founders and angel investors (affluent seed investors) sold their stake in the company due to its rather pedestrian growth potential. In February 2016, King was acquired by Activision Blizzard for $5.9 billion. This was made possible on the back of its *Candy Crush* and the *Candy Crush Saga* line of games. This was one of the fastest growth rates of any company in the history of the world if you throw out oil field strikes, diamond mine discoveries, and sunken ship recovery operations hitting it big. Essentially, King struck a vein of gold running through all of us and was able to leverage it on a global scale. Why would it not inspire legions of copycats?

Some of the most blatant examples of video-game manipulation are unbelievably crass in their presentation. As described by Ramin Shokrizade,

More than any game in the Zynga stable, [*FrontierVille*] seems the most child oriented. The gameplay is extremely simple, all characters are childlike and cartoonish, and the goal of the game is to build a homestead so that your sweetheart can relocate to you so that you can get married.

Within the first hour of play in *FrontierVille* the player will be shown a wounded, bloody, and crying baby deer. I described this as "Dying Bambi" in my 2011 paper. The player is told that the deer was attacked by coyotes and unless the player gives Zynga $5 quickly, Bambi will die. While such horrifying appeals might be easily resisted by an adult, it seems likely that a traumatized child might go to extraordinary lengths to save Bambi.[37]

Ramin is quite open and clear in his assessment of the current state-of-the-art in game design, and he finds ethical and moral lapses all over the place, driven by profit:

I think it is inevitable that some companies will iterate towards even more exploitation of children in games. The most aggressive companies will hire soft and hard scientists like myself, in addition to quantitative scientists, to optimize the exploitation of youth. The ultimate result will be national regulation, which is already happening in some parts of Asia. In the meantime, such agents will try to make as much money as possible in this Wild Wild West of gaming . . .

If you have your consumer enraptured by [an altered state of consciousness, complete with physiological changes, that might make them more vulnerable to certain suggestions]and then put them in distress, either by threatening them (by holding Bambi hostage), making them lose (*Candy Crush Saga* or *Puzzle and Dragons*), or putting them under time/economic/competitive pressure/threat (almost any competitive or midcore game today, including Kabam or Kixeye games, or *Clash of Clans*), then offer to sell them relief, you are engaging in Distressed Monetization. I consider Distressed Monetization unethical.[38]

Ramin Shokrizade has outlined far more subtle ways to influence players and get them spending, including the following techniques.

Threat Generation

It's incumbent upon many games to generate some sort of threat and to make the player feel under assault and willing to pay to reduce the current stress/threat. The major problem with this method is that too much stress causes players to stop playing the game as it is the game generating the stress. One way to reduce such stress is to delete the game, which isn't the desired outcome. Another way to get around this problem while still maintaining constant threats is to deflect the threat from the game to another in-game player. If you are busy fighting against another player in an online world and you have the possibility of spending money to ensure that you are not attacked for a day or two, or make the attack unlikely to succeed, the threat is actually coming (in the player's eyes) from the other player, not the game itself, even though the remedy (giving money to the game) implies that the game manufacturer has *something* to do with it.

Another example comes from online card games:

> The other popular genre of multiplayer mobile games using threat gener- ation is the "Trading Card Game" (TCG) genre. TCG's allow you to play a match against another player as a test of "skill." These games are a lot of fun as long as they remain a test of skill. Threat is generated by the knowl- edge that the other player could have purchased or otherwise acquired overpowered cards that will make skill of little importance in the match. Ideally the source of the threat will be deflected to the other players in the game so that they blame each other for the threat you have designed.
>
> The developer then sells the threatened player the same cards that are threatening them, as a source of durable protection. Since the best cards do make the player all but invulnerable to players that have not spent similarly, this can lead to essentially a threat-less situation. Because of this the prices are extraordinarily high in the TCG genre.

The only way to keep selling to a player that has bought all the cards you sell, is of course to make new cards that are so powerful that they again threaten players using the old cards.[39]

Regardless of how the mechanics work, the emotional link between threat and game has been broken; the threats come from in-game interactions with other players. The solution isn't to stop playing the game; the solution is to make sure your in-game character is well defended. If this requires an in-game purchase, so be it.

Coercive Monetization and Virtual Currencies

In the popular cooperative shoot-em-up game *Overwatch*, produced by Blizzard Entertainment, you can get a new "skin" for your character, changing its outward appearance, or a new "skin" for your weapon, changing its outward appearance, etc. You get the idea. These are purely cosmetic changes and have no gameplay effects at all, and are received by opening "loot boxes" that are awarded after a successful fight or two. Loot boxes are random, or at least they are presented as being random, and upon opening one you might end up with a coveted skin or not. You can also buy loot boxes directly from Blizzard in-game; this gives you more opportunities to get the skin you really desire.[40] Which makes you wonder: why don't they just have a "skin store" where you can buy these things directly without the interference of obviously artificial loot boxes? Isn't it annoying for a player who wants the Junkrat Jester skin to force them to wade through fifty loot boxes before getting what he or she desires?

Yes, but it's far more profitable to make them suffer in this way. Many people find opening loot boxes fun simply because they are an unknown quantity (the EU is on the verge of determining that loot boxes are a form of gambling and they might soon be regulated out of existence).[41] It's like a pull at the slot machine. It also obfuscates the true cost of the skin. Loot boxes and all types of in-game currencies, just like casino chips, transfer known and understood external fiat currency into unfamiliar and sometimes unknown values. If you buy twenty-five in-game jewels for $10, and want to buy a magic sword for four jewels, how much is that in dollars? It's not a hard calculation but it is a calculation that must be made to figure out the true cost in dollars and many times the cost is not equal to the value. Similarly, if you buy fifty loot boxes for $20 and after opening them all get two skins you *kinda* wanted but not the skin you *really* wanted, plus a mass of other stuff that might be occasionally fun to play with . . . what's the real cost of the skins? Who knows. The onus is on the player to rejigger and recalibrate what it means to make a good or a bad deal, getting around our trained lifelong skill at doing this using dollars and cents.

Skill Games and Money Games

A skill game is just that: a game based on skill, and the better your skills the better your results in the game. A money game depends on your spending money on the game in order to proceed or do well. If these choices are explicit in the game rules there is nothing wrong with either method, although I prefer to play games that don't require money to get ahead. The problem arises when a game of skill transforms into a money game, often without the player realizing that this is occurring. *Candy Crush* is, again, the canonical example: "King.com's *Candy Crush Saga* is designed masterfully in this regard. Early game play maps can be completed by almost anyone without spending money, and they slowly increase in difficulty. This presents a challenge to the skills of the player, making them feel good when they advance due to their abilities. Once the consumer has been marked as a spender . . . the game difficulty ramps up massively, shifting the game from a skill game to a money game as progression becomes more dependent on the use of premium boosts than on player skills."[42]

Many other such tricks and techniques are available for savvy game designers, and it's crucial to note that none of them involve inspired game design, creativity in presentation, or concerns about maximizing "fun." There is so much money to be made with modern free-to-play games that everything else has been thrown under the bus. Modern video games are becoming increasingly stressful and unpleasant gaming experiences for the simple fact that the monetary incentives are wildly out of alignment. You simply make more money chasing whales through manipulative and unfun gameplay than you do by creating a bright, complex, challenging, pay-once-up-front game of the old-school variety.

There is no way to argue that the most fun games are the most profitable, nor that the most inventive and creative games are the bestsellers. We are well beyond all that. The market has identified an apparently paradoxical fact about human beings: *we are willing to play, and spend money on, games that give us vanishingly little pleasure but that are distracting, engaging, and addictive.* This should not come as much of a shock given our historical understanding of gambling, gambling addiction, and the biological basis of such compulsive behavior. It's been found recently that a statistically significant portion of patients taking the antipsychotic drug aripiprazole undergo a sudden transformation into gambling addicts.[43] When the patient is taken off the drug, the urge to gamble dissipates as quickly as it had manifested.[44] That there are powerful biological triggers for gambling didn't require such an overt example as proof; humans the world over gamble and some do it obsessively. Slot machine addicts are known to wear adult diapers so they can relieve themselves without stopping play. More desperate slot players go where they sit and clean up later if they ever do clean up.[45]

Candy Crush is a virtual slot machine in the form of a feel-good game, leveraging the same biological triggers used by casinos the world over, and like slot machines the players are fairly up-front about their feelings about the game. Very few compulsive gamblers would admit to liking slot machines or enjoying their experience playing them; just the opposite. Most feel nothing but shame for what they are doing to their lives and the financial ruin they are causing. Almost all would gladly take a pill to remove the compulsion.[46] (The same can be said of many other types of addicts—for example, cigarette smokers loudly and honestly complain about their habit while lighting up.)

Modern Americans are doing exactly the opposite: we welcome the casinos into our homes, our lives, and our pockets—for the most part, unwittingly. The game designers certainly know. It's beyond time for the players to wake up to the fact.

Highly addictive games give rise to serious questions about choice, free will, the ethics of targeting vulnerable consumers, and unclear game rules that counter consumer expectations. These issues are not going away anytime soon as companies become ever more aware and sophisticated in their manipulations of consumers. Few gamers are aware of the problem or have any clue that they are, on occasion (and at least 3 percent of them in aggregate) the gaming industry's derided and desperately sought whales.[47]

CHAPTER SIX

PROFESSIONAL LEAGUES AND THE RISE OF ESPORTS —ARE THEY STILL GAMES?

In 1938 Johan Huizinga wrote *Homo Ludens*,[1] one of the fundamental texts anthropological game studies, and in it he claimed that a game stops being a game the moment it is monetized. What had been play is now a job. Professional players are just that: professionals, playing for pay and subject to market forces external to the experience of true games. One of the great myths of professional sports is that players play because they love the game. Professional football, in particular, is such a demanding sport, causing so many injuries of lasting consequence, that a vast majority of current players (though certainly not all of them) likely participate only for money or fame. Increasing numbers of NFL players are retiring from the game while still in relatively good health because the pain of the sport overshadows any hope of enjoyment while playing. Many players have a financial goal in mind after which they abruptly quit playing—this total might be $10 million or $100 million, depending upon ability and inclination. Once that goal is reached the game is left behind, often with relief.[2]

Early exiting of a NFL career is still a relatively rare event but has been spiking over last few years as concussion concerns have become more apparent.[3] An NFL career, for everyone except the top 1 percent of players, is a constant battle against the ever-present risk of a career-ending injury or slow degradation of ability from an accumulation of violent collisions. Remarkably and notably, NFL contracts are almost always fully unguaranteed—a signing bonus is often paid up front but after that every player, no matter how famous or lauded, is one injury away from being cut and the contract discarded. This leaves players in a constant state of unrest and insecurity; not only are contracts voidable, they might at any time be traded to another team without notice. Taken together, along with the NFL's notoriously arbitrary and unforgiving behavior policy, overseen by its much-hated commissioner who operates as both judge and jury,[4] it's very difficult to be an game idealist in an NFL locker room.

It's not unusual for NFL veterans, after seeing a rookie coming in who might someday take their place on the roster, to quietly sabotage the rookie's development—giving them poor or contradictory advice, or gently backstab them with an assistant coach.[5] At the same time, players love a good locker room; they love playing for teams who enjoy each other's company and work well together on the field. It's not uncommon for players to dislike their owners and coaches, to dislike their home city or even their fan base, yet make sacrifices to not let down their team-mates.[6] Coaches do all they can to accentuate and reinforce this feeling, as it leads to less locker room tension and better results on the field—yet this is a one-way bargain. Owners feel no loyalty to their fan base nor to players when they rip up a franchise and move to a new city, as recently happened with the now-LA Rams,[7] nor do such concerns play a part when a player is cut or traded. When a player holds out for more money or puts in insufficient work in the off-season he's a traitor to his team; when an owner does something similar—well, that's business.

These factors make watching an NFL game difficult for a fan. The ever-present possibility of serious injury hovering in the background—leading some to call viewing a game as an immoral act[8]—and the knowledge that most players are playing for no greater goal than money, removes much of the idealistic enjoyment of the sport understood as a game.

Yet something like the Super Bowl obviously retains the external trappings of a sports game: the logical rules, the delineated field, the time-limited extent of the competition, the athletic competition. But we also have, inevitably intruding, a tidal wave of influences outside the pure unadulter-ated sphere of play: it's impossible not to worry about player health when seeing world-class speed and strength applied to the task of crushing the ball carrier into the turf. It's impossible not to be aware of the widely publi-cized salaries (public because of salary cap concerns) of the many stars and lower-tier supporting players; it's common to hear a fan ask another fan if a given player is "worth it"—not only for what he brings to the field but the player's "hit" to the salary cap. Part of the game is managing the team's finances; one of biggest and still exponentially expanding new games for sport-loving Americans is "Fantasy X" (where X is football, baseball, bas-ketball, or another sport), a game in which players are given a set amount of pretend money to purchase rights to various professional players each week, with the best performing aggregate team winning that week's compe-tition—and often a real-money pot.

On one level it's absurd to call an NFL or NBA game *not* a game because the players are being paid. They are playing the same game as the pickup game at the local Y—just with better equipment and the benefit of paid referees. But in Huizinga's view it's crucially not enough to be going through the motions of a game to call something a game; a game "played" at gunpoint is obviously following the rules of the game but everyone par-ticipates under great duress—nobody can be said to be having any fun at all.

It's reasonable to think of games in more flexible terms than a binary category—either game or not-game—and imagine games existing along a spectrum with fun and play on one end and cold-hearted business interests on the other. Turn the knob from pure fun—children rushing around playing an involved game of tag—and slowly move up the gra-dient. At some point it's difficult to maintain that those participating in what seems to be a game—following all the rules of the game—are really "playing" the game. The extreme end, such as the NFL, gives us two groups of opposing participants who go through the motions of game play bereft of either joy or fun, minds torn between doing well in the game, keeping them employed, while never forgetting what the game is giving them: astonishing salaries (at least at the professional level). At this point, a sports game resembles any other highly structured system. We don't think about a lawyer in court, arguing a case in front of judge and jury, as participating in a game, although sometimes we metaphorically couch their actions in these terms ("The defense really won that round"). Yet it's easy to view the American trial process as a game, as it has all the required categories: a clear-cut delineation of physical space (the Hall of Justice), Team A and Team B (prosecutor and defense), referees (judge and jury), and a long and extremely intricate list of rules about what can and can't be done, based on law and precedent. The environment of the court is a distinct sphere of action; what occurs there is unique compared to our everyday social reality. There is a definitive start and end time to the process, which, while it can extend for weeks or months, nevertheless has a clear-cut conclusion: guilty or not guilty (or the jury is hung).

Many have termed such structures game-like in how they operate, but it's unclear to me what insight this grants. Does the trial system feel natural because it is game-like, drawing upon the power of games, which are fundamental to human growth and experience? Or are games just another type of highly structured organizational activity? Does Wall Street play the game of "making money" by following or not following a long list of rules and regulations, or is this just an unhelpful mapping of "game" onto activities that should not qualify?

Where are other modern professional teams located along this sliding scale? The NBA offers us a lot of evidence, because almost all NBA contracts are guaranteed, and much hand wringing follows the signing of any given player to a team because the question that inevitably arises—and it should, given NBA history—is whether the player is going to "live up to the contract" or alternatively take it easy. He's been paid, the money is guaranteed, so why expect them to work very hard? It's a real issue, and many players fail to live up to their promise given lack of monetary motivation after a big contract is signed, which leads to the inevitable conclusion that for many players the game isn't about fun or love of the game so

146

much as money, pure and simple, else they would work just as hard after a big payday out of love (or respect) for the game.[9]

While it's painful for a fan to squarely face the facts, it's hard to avoid the conclusion that professional sports are not truly games but rather monetized competitions outwardly resembling games that for the participants are often as tense and fun as Russian roulette. This does not have to diminish one's love of such events. It's quite possible to enjoy professional sports far more than amateur games, which are a purer example of undiluted play, while at the same time understanding that what is being seen on the television, the motions of the player and the ball, are simulations one step removed from the reality of a real game: well-paid actors "playing" the part with exquisite scenery and garish matching costumes and sometimes jaw-dropping athleticism. It's fundamentally *work*.

The English language has difficulty representing this distinction, which is amusing because *Homo Ludens*[10] spends a lot of time in historical linguistic investigation looking at how other cultures and languages define "play" and what it means for something to be a game. Is it better for English-speakers to distinguish between play/not play and claim that many high-end athletes are "participants" in a game? We might continue to distinguish: are NBA employees "participating in a game-like exhibition"?

The game/not game distinction doesn't bother me personally; I enjoy watching somebody else mow my lawn, but I'm also not under any illusion that he would bother to do so if I didn't pay him promptly after the last blade's cut. It doesn't lesson my enjoyment—otherwise I'd have to do it myself—but it does keep the true reason for his effort at the forefront: cash.

It's also possible that professional sports experience evolution (or devolution). Early NFL football players were notoriously poorly paid and often took jobs during the summer to make ends meet. NFL salaries were not only modest but insufficient, and benefits (if they existed at all) failed to match or make up for ongoing health problems. Yet the NFL prospered in a way it could not have had these early players not loved the game as a game and loved playing it. Otherwise—why would they have bothered? As television rolled into American households and the NFL proved itself to be remarkably amenable to broadcasting, as constant breaks in the action formed easy and natural advertising slots, total profits shot up, as did player contract values. At some point in the last thirty years it seems reasonable to conclude that a tipping point was reached: enough money was now available for players to convince them to continue playing however they felt about the game itself.

On the one hand we should applaud the fact that the early, extremely abusive pay structure was overturned for something far more fair to the players; on the other hand, the "purity of the game" was fatally punctured.[11] Given current salaries and openly discussed player commentary[12] about why players play (for the money), it's worth asking how much pleasure we are able to derive from a team of hardened mercenaries battling another team of hardened mercenaries. Or maybe this doesn't matter: just as it's possible for an animal to play a game without an implied understanding of what it is doing, humans are capable of enjoying a game despite the knowledge that nobody playing it is having any fun at all—and might suffer catastrophic injury for our viewing pleasure. There is satisfaction to be gained from observing the highest levels of athleticism regardless of its spur. The Romans certainly didn't suffer any qualms or diminution of interest when watching slaves fighting for their lives against an assortment of horrors, despite the slaves' desperate desire to be doing anything but participating in that particular game of arena combat.

The latest iteration of for-profit broadcast sports are esports (electronic sports, i.e. video games): games such as Blizzard Entertainment's *Overwatch* are regularly covered by ESPN's esports division and feature international teams competing in front of large and rambunctious crowds with impressive production values (check out the APEX *Overwatch* competition streams on YouTube for an eye-opening example of high-tech set design and live "caster" commentary). Humans apparently have an innate craving for these sorts of structured competitive tournaments, but we can't escape their fundamental paradox: money is necessarily involved in their organization, sponsorship, and participation, but money drains from the game many of the qualities we most admire in games.

As of 2017, esports are the fastest-growing segment of the sport industry—nothing is close to its snowballing growth:

> The coming year will see the Esports Economy grow to $696 million, a year-on-year growth of 41.3%. Brands are expected to spend $517 million, broken down into $155 million on advertising, $266 million on sponsorship, and a further $95 million on media rights. Brand investment will double by 2020, pushing the total market to $1.5 billion. Consumer spending this year on tickets and merchandise will amount to $64 million. Another $116 million is invested by game publishers into the esports industry through partnership deals with white-label organizers.[13]

While $1.5 billion by 2020 is far below Major League Baseball's 2017 $9 billion market size, these sports are moving in diametrically opposite directions. The audience for esports is one of the most coveted in the advertising world: both young and middle- or upper-middle class. The audience for baseball is famously elderly and averages out to fifty-three years old; for esports in America the average audience member is twenty-eight. While esports' 41 percent yearly growth from 2016 to 2017 obviously isn't sustainable, it's not a stretch to claim that esports are bound to match and exceed Major League Baseball in the near future: already by 2016, "22% of American male millennials watch esports, putting it virtually equal with baseball and hockey in terms of viewership among that demographic."[14] It's not only going to happen, for some segments of the population it's already happened, and given that the younger generation takes video games even more seriously than their older peers (both playing more and spending more on games) there isn't any reason to think that the esports boom is anywhere near played out.

The majority of Americans don't really have a clear understanding of this subterranean movement in the economy and culture, and for those who do please excuse this brief digression. The rest of us are trying to figure out what's going on and catch up.

THE RISE OF EnVyUs

Blizzard released *Overwatch* in May 2016, part of the genre loosely termed a "team-based multiplayer online first-person shooter video game." This definition doesn't explain much. A better description goes something like this: the action takes place in an online battle environment where your team of six fights against another team of six. The environment consists of futuristic, highly stylized, and often cartoonish landscapes; the precise goal of the competition changes depending on the challenge (map). The eventual winner might have to capture a crucial area and keep it under control longer than the competition. One of the teams might be tasked with escorting a car, tank, or battering ram from the start of the map to the end of the map under a strict time control, with the enemy attempting at every step to stop or delay progress. The challenge can also be hybrid—first control an area for a while, and then escort a released vehicle to the end of the map.

Each team of six players must select six characters from the character pool without duplicates: if you have a Junkrat on your team that's the only one allowed. Of course the enemy team might also have a Junkrat, but they too are limited to one (not that you would necessarily want more). In general, the overall winner is the team that manages the greatest distance in the least amount of time for the escort maps, or who is first able to capture and hold the control point for a specific amount of time. This is a game of communal victories; there are eagerly tracked individual stats but no way for a single individual to really win or lose a high-level game. It's a rigorously constructed team game, stressing cooperation and group tactics. The goals are basic and clear. The method of achieving them is always the same: efficient killing of the enemies using as few resources as possible.

Team EnVyUs formed in early 2016, and while its roster has varied considerably over the last two years the core players have remained stable: Taimou (Timo Kettunen), HarryHook (Jonathan Rua), cocco (Christian Jonsson), INTERNETHULK (Dennis Hawelka), and chipshajen (Sebastian Widlund). Mickie (Pongphop Rattanasangchod) joined at the end of 2016, EFFECT (Kim Hyeon) in April 2017, and Seagull (Brandon Larned) is the newcomer. (The last two were not yet part of the team fight that follows).

Initial Fight of the Match:
Numbani Hybrid Escort/Assault Map

To see how the game functions both as a game and as a broadcast event, let's look at the *Overwatch* Major League Gaming finals in 2016, pitting EnVyUs against FaZe Clan (FaZe).

Our Heroes (Team EnVyUs): Taimou, HarryHook, cocco, chip-shajen, Mickie, and INTERNETHULK.

The Villains (Team FaZe Clan): TwoEasy, ShaDowBurn, Forsak3n, zombs, FCTFCTN, and Rawkus.

The place: The Major League Gaming 2016 tournament, Las Vegas, Nevada.

The setup: The final match of the competition. The winning team gets $40,000 (and glory), the loser $20,000.

FaZe is on the attack for the first map, Numbani, and has to take the first control point. To do this they must travel through the streets near the spawn toward a maze of buildings and corridors surrounding a central square—the map's control point, which they must capture and hold for thirty seconds. The decide to ignore a straight-line approach, moving openly through the streets, and instead enter a building that connects to another building that contains a stair leading to a series of balconies and platforms overlooking the control point. They want to gain a height advantage if possible by rushing up the stairway to take it unopposed or knock EnVyUs back if they should be waiting for this tactic and resist. It looks good initially; as a team they fly up the initial set of stairs, move to a second staircase, and crowd into the connected platform. They are met by INTERNETHULK controlling Winston (a massive space gorilla), who fires his auto-aiming short-range Tesla cannon into their midst, hitting all of them, slowing their progress.

INTERNETHULK falls back after doing light damage as the responding attack is too intense and will soon drop his health to zero, forcing him to respawn, but behind him cocco is playing Reinhardt, a futuristic Germanic knight with one of the best defenses in the game—a single-direction shield that protects anyone behind it until the shield takes two thousand points of damage, is whittled down, and cracks. INTERNETHULK could have hopped behind Reinhardt's shield for cover but instead drops to the lower street and immediately works his way around the enemy's back, flanking the attackers still busy on the higher ground. There he teams up with Taimou, controlling Roadhog, which is a nasty-looking bipedal pig creature, large and fat, wielding a short-range shotgun and a ranged "chain-and-grabber" combination. This weapon allows Roadhog, should he hit with it, to immobilize enemies at a moderate distance and pull them close (using the chain) and when at point-blank range blast them in the face with his trusty shotgun. Roadhog is slow but hardy, capable of doing a lot of damage up close but useless in wide-open areas of the map where his size and sluggishness makes him an easy target. EnVyUs obviously knows Roadhog's limitations and has him skirt around the main part of the battle, moving down narrow streets and through tight corridors where his vulnerabilities are masked and close-range combat is the rule not the exception.

INTERNETHULK and Taimou discover the enemy's damaged Reinhardt sitting in a room, unsupported and vulnerable, having taking significant damage from the fight at the top of the stairs and retreated in order to heal. In a frenzied burst of action both lay into the enemy, who doesn't last long under the dual assault. While shotgun blasts and Tesla cannon electricity shred Reinhardt, Mickie's D.Va (a mechanized bipedal tank) smoothly takes INTERNETHULK's place on the upper platform, standing next to cocco's Reinhardt, still defending the position, busy using his private shield to ward off most of the incoming fire. The whole time, from across the square, HarryHook is laying down moderate but incredibly consistent supporting fire with Soldier 76 (a grizzled machine gun-firing veteran), shooting harmlessly through his team's shields into the onrushing enemy. The last member of EnVyUs, chipshajen, is controlling the character Ana, and stands beside Soldier 76 shooting her biotic rifle, which has the unusual property of damaging enemies but healing team members. Chipshajen is able to keep his team relatively healthy by accurately striking allies and, when nobody needs a boost, switches to attacking the enemies directly, inflicting long-range damage alongside Soldier 76. So far, she's been able to keep cocco's Reinhardt relatively healthy.

The enemy keeps pushing onto the upper platform despite the withering incoming fire: cocco's Reinhardt is eventually forced to pull back and Mickie's D.Va launches herself into the air, retreating to the lower street level as she drops but still firing. It's a fighting retreat, and it looks like the enemy will soon occupy the upper platform. FaZe's plan seems to be working.

Back comes INTERNETHULK's Winston from his brief sortie against the enemy flank, and he relaunches himself onto the upper platform, using one of his short-term abilities to create a shield bubble around himself—temporarily protecting him from the concentrated fire heading his way. Immediately both D.Va and Reinhardt turn on their heels and join him, moving from retreat to attack with smooth synchronization. Soldier 76 remains untouched behind them, continuing to fire unhindered, and Ana is busy healing everyone within sight. What looked to be a successful assault is anything but: the attackers, already weakened from ongoing support fire and now faced with three relatively healthy and robust defenders, are forced to retreat or be utterly destroyed. They flee down the stairs.

D.Va instantly pursues but stops halfway down the stairway at a small platform, angling herself diagonal to the lower stair, not allowing the enemy (bunched below) to attack her. If they want to do some damage they'll have to poke their heads out of the lower staircase. D.Va is content to wait them out. It's a moment of calm in the midst of relentless action. FaZe's job is to capture the control point, unlock the payload, and escort it through the rest of the map. FaZe can't just sit and wait. Their need to attack, knock back EnVyUs, and capture the control point (the square surrounded by buildings). The longer they sit and wait the better EnVyUs's odds of stopping them.

Finally FaZe makes another push. FaZe's Reinhardt, already killed once by INTERNETHULK and Taimou, has respawned (come back into the game) from their respawn point; in *Overwatch* death isn't permanent but it does slow a player down. There is always a respawn delay, and the respawn point itself might be quite a distance from the location of the current battle. If a team is getting killed with great frequency they are unable to generate much momentum as they wait for their respawns to rejoin the team; until they are at full strength, the numerical disadvantage means that they don't have much hope of pushing forward. It's quite common in high-level *Overwatch* play for teams to abruptly break off an attack and retreat after an early causality; it's better to wait for their respawn to rejoin then continue to push ahead, risking even more deaths and further respawn delays. *Overwatch* is, fundamentally, a game about time.

FaZe's Reinhardt has his shield up and steps out from the top of the lower stair, turning to face D.Va and block her attack. The rest of FaZe boils out behind him, blasting away. Mickie's done his work; he's delayed them with D.Va for a few seconds, and as they push forward he retreats, dropping from a side door to the lower street, allowing FaZe to rush the upper stairs, again attacking the upper platform. It seems like FaZe will have a numbers advantage since D.Va's fled, but D.Va is a relatively swift character; almost immediately she spins, shoots into the air from the street, and cannonballs into the upper platform where FaZe is busy pushing back cocco's Reinhardt. D.Va's sudden appearance and ability to scatter or knock members of the enemy formation into the lower street means they have to pay attention to her, right away. She's right there, glee-fully machine gunning them.

D.Va ensures that there isn't time to deal with the long-distance threats both Ana and Soldier 76 pose, who continue to attack and support rel-atively unmolested. Winston joins D.Va on the upper platform for the counterattack, and cocco's Reinhart stops giving ground and again pushes ahead. FaZe is in disarray; they hadn't expected D.Va to plow into them so quickly and disrupt their attack. They begin to suffer losses. Soldier 76 takes out the enemy Reinhardt but FaZe is doing damage as well. FaZe bursts through and manages to swarm across the square to chipshajen's Ana, killing her, and cocco's space gorilla falls with a grunt. A few FaZe attackers manage to squirm forward to the control point, temporarily capturing it, but the rest of EnVyUs is healthy and prepared; they swarm the square in unison and easily take out the disjointed stragglers. Pretty soon it's a full team wipe. EnVyUs has lost two characters, who will quickly rejoin the team, while FaZe is forced to respawn as a group. EnVyUs has enough time to return to their original positions, heal up, and prepare for the next attack.

At the start of the map FaZe is given four minutes to control the point; the clock currently stands at 2:38. They essentially wasted a minute-and-a-half and made no progress, but it's even worse than that. All *Overwatch* characters have special abilities called "ultimates," which they earn by doing lots of character-specific things; the healing character gains her ultimate by healing a lot of damage; a damage-dealing character gains his by doing a lot of damage, etc. Ultimates are rare but devastating abilities that are sometimes enough to change the course of a given battle; D.Va, for example, can remove herself from her robotic carapace and shoot it into the air as a self-detonating bomb. When it returns to earth it explodes, and all enemies in the blast radius are killed (or at least take a big pile of damage). After an ultimate is used it needs to regenerate from scratch; depending on the character, an ultimate might take one, two, or three minutes to rebuild. The faster an ultimate charges the more modest its overall power; the most significant ultimates are the ones that take the longest to earn. Ultimates are relatively rare and need to be used with care and conservatively utilized. It also helps if you chain ultimates together as a team; Ana's nanoboost ultimate, temporarily increasing both survivability and damage-dealing potential for a single ally, can be added to Winston's primal rage ultimate, which increases his speed, survivability, and damage-dealing, to create a monstrous short-term beast of unparalleled ferocity. Both ultimates, which are considered relatively low power compared to other characters', could be used separately to good effect, but when stacked can cause real devastation. Smooth cooperation between teammates regarding synergistic ultimate use can almost immediately end a battle.

The problem with FaZe's initial attack is that they didn't actually do much damage to EnVyUs, and the damage they did cause was healed, for the most part, by Ana, charging her ultimate. Everyone on EnVyUs hurt the enemy more than they were hurt in return, and as a consequence three EnVyUs characters already have their ultimates charged up, compared to one for FaZe, and the other EnVyUs members aren't far behind. Because of the ultimate discrepancy FaZe is actually worse off than they were at the start of the game and still have the same goal. They're moving backward.

EnVyUs has a bit of extra time to push forward of their initial positions, and as FaZe comes out of their respawn point Soldier 76 takes a few pot shots from long range before falling back to his standard defensive position on an upper platform across from the control point. Mickie's D.Va is again on the high ground, near the exit of the upper staircase. Taimou's Roadhog is roaming the streets below but keeping close to the rest of the team. Ana is primed and waiting for the action to start.

This time FaZe forgoes the upper stairs (it hadn't worked last time) and rushes in a mass straight down the main street, heading for the control point in a direct line. EnVyUs is relatively well prepared; Winston creates a bubble shield, temporary blocks FaZe, and starts zapping away with his electrical gun. Soldier 76, completely untouched on the upper balcony, has all the time in the world to look down and pick the best targets, and does enough damage to kill FaZe's Rawkus. Now it's six (EnVyUs) versus five (FaZe). Soldier 76 manages to earn his ultimate just in time, due to his unhindered damage-dealing, and instantly enables it: for around ten seconds he no longer has to aim his machine gun. Every enemy he points at is automatically blasted.

It can be a devastating ultimate, but his angle on the balcony isn't that good; FaZe moves beneath it, using it as cover. Soldier 76 only manages to damage two or three characters before the enemies' D.Va flies up from below, squats in front of him, enables her shield, and begins a very unfair one-on-one. Soldier 76 has excellent ranged strength but poor defenses and close-combat skills. He soon falls. Now it's five versus five.

The trouble for FaZe is that before Soldier 76 died he finished off his ultimate, scattering damage far and wide. EnVyUs, hiding behind Reinhardt's shield, and receiving constant healing from Ana across the square (who, like Soldier 76, is a ranged weapon specialist), is in far better health. EnVyUs bunches together and Winston starts pounding the enemy with his simian fists. Reinhardt swings his hammer. Roadhog, behind the Reinhardt shield, blasts away with his shotgun. Somewhere in the distance FaZe's D.Va is having a battle with EnVyUs's D.Va, which will likely result in a slow-moving draw; both have excellent defenses and poor offenses. In the meantime, Ana remains untouched and FaZe is forced to fall back. Mickie's D.Va suddenly dies; now it's four (EnVyUs) versus five (FaZe), and both teams have two or three ultimates each. EnVyUs has retaken the control point, and the time reads 1:56. HarryHook's Soldier 76 respawns and rushes to join his friends. The enemy D.Va attempts to destroy Taimou's Roadhog but it's a half-hearted attempt; Roadhog is safe behind Reinhardt's shield and surrounded by friends. FaZe's D.Va flees, leaving EnVyUs completely in charge of the control point. The time reads 1:48.

It's soon six versus six as everyone who died respawned and rejoined their teams. Both teams have three ultimates, and each team has another character close to an additional ultimate. It's extremely even, but FaZe has to push the attack. EnVyUs can afford to regroup and wait.

FaZe's Reinhardt moves onto the control point, swiveling his shield toward EnVyUs, protecting himself and his team. It looks like FaZe is on the verge of colonizing a portion of the control point, when, from above, hidden on an upper balcony, INTERNETHULK's Winston leaps into the air, flies behind the enemy Reinhardt's shield, and throws himself into a mass of bunched enemy, his Gauss gun a-blazing. There are some second-line support characters here, including a sound-based character design (Lúcio), who both heals allies and speeds their movement. Lúcio has a weak attack and his best defense is speed; when confronted by Winston he is forced to flee, removing his support from FaZe's team. Winston then turns to the enemy D.Va and shoots electricity through her shield, which doesn't defend against these types of attacks, again causing chaos and forcing D.Va to retreat. Finally, as Winston starts to take damage, INTERNETHULK triggers his ultimate: primal rage. The annoying chimp is now a terrifying gorilla: fully healed, faster than before, and hitting far harder. The enemy player Rawkus goes down. FaZe is scattered, their support characters are all over the place, but so is EnVyUs; the chaos created by Winston split them up as they attempted to pick off lone characters one-by-one. The great ape is finally killed but certainly made an impression. The rest of the fight is a donnybrook.

Mickie's D.Va goes down again. FaZe pops an ultimate, graviton surge, creating a black hole that temporarily sticks together any member of EnVyUs caught within it (this is devastating when combined with D.Va's exploding bomb ultimate, which can't be run away from). Lots of damage is being laid down by both sides. Another member of FaZe goes down. EnVyUs respawns have rushed back to the fight and they swarm the enemy. FaZe's last character on the point, D.Va, is surrounded and blown to bits. EnVyUs stands alone. The clock is down to 1:09. Both teams are without ultimates. FaZe respawns are activated after five seconds, and their team begins to regroup for another attack—if they can manage it. EnVyUs presses their advantage after realizing that a few FaZe characters have dropped back and are waiting for reinforcements to show up. EnVyUs rushes forward, attempting to pick off one or two more, which would cause them to respawn and burn valuable time. FaZe continues to retreat successfully, flying backward, and EnVyUs gives up the pursuit and rushes back to the control point, taking up positions for defense. It's been a very disciplined battle from their side.

EnVyUs again takes the high ground and waits for what's to come. The timer's down to 0:46; FaZe has to do it now if they are ever going to do it. FaZe tries the staircase again, a replay of their first attack, but EnVyUs is prepared, and after a little back-and-forth damage-dealing manage to generate three ultimates (FaZe still has none). Taimou's Roadhog, on the top level this time instead of the streets, pops his head around a corner, spots the enemy coming out of the upper stairs, and throws his chain grabber. The enemy D.Va is grabbed, pulled close, and blasted with the shotgun, grievously injuring her. FaZe's Lúcio appears, attempting to heal his wounded ally, and Roadhog drops back to the lower road, still blasting away but giving himself a little more distance and looking for cover. So far the attack has been stymied; FaZe needs to regroup and re-engage. The timer reads 0:33.

Soldier 76 and Ana, on balconies across the square from the upper stair, again have the freedom to fire at will. Nobody is pressuring them; nobody is attacking them. Soldier 76 blasts into the enemy mass and eliminates FCTFCTN, meaning it's now five versus six. He continues to fire unopposed, and a few seconds later he picks off TwoEasy. Now it's four versus six, and the timer reads 0:15. The situation is dire, and the end of the game is pretty brutal. Soldier 76 has again earned his ultimate (tactical visor) and is perched above the control point. He knows FaZe has to take it within the next ten seconds, and Ana, beside him, knows it too. She's got her nanoboost ultimate charged up as well, and applies it to Soldier 76. Soldier 76 then triggers his ultimate, automatically hitting whatever he's pointing at, and because of the nanoboost they hit really, really hard. As FaZe streams onto the control point they are met by Reinhardt and his shield, Roadhog and his fat, tough, pig body, D.Va with fully charged defenses, and sheer death being dealt from above. Soldier 76 kills three enemies within seconds, and the rest are mopped up by the grunts on the ground. Time ticks down. The counter reaches zero. FaZe fails to take the first control.

Now it's EnVyUs's turn. All they have to do is capture the control point to win the entire map, since FaZe hadn't been able to achieve that objective. They have four minutes and do the sensible strategic thing. Their first attack is pushed back by FaZe, but EnVyUs builds up some ultimate charge in the process. EnVyUs regroups, and their second attack builds up even more ultimates, which they conserve and don't use when their attack is dispersed and destroyed. By the two-minute mark EnVyUs has three ultimates with a few more pending while FaZe has none, having used a few to power their so-far successful defense. The next attack is the real one: again Soldier 76 and Ana end up getting high-ground position without much pushback, and EnVyUs uses all their ultimates as they rush the control point, evict FaZe, and take the square with a minute left on the counter. It wasn't really as close as it looked; EnVyUs had generated a large ultimate advantage for themselves, and barring exceptional skill and/or luck on the part of FaZe the final attack was sure to push through.

The two teams fought over three more maps, but the results were similar. Team EnVyUs won the grand finals by a score of four maps to zero. FaZe got skunked.

WHAT TO MAKE OF *OVERWATCH*
AS A SPECTATOR SPORT?

First of all, viewing an *Overwatch* match is a very chaotic and confusing way to watch a video game. Because the maps are large and varied, it's unusual for a full team to be together on the same screen very often, which means that most streamed video is from the perspective of a specific character. There are twelve characters involved in any given combat when everyone's healthy, which means that the viewer is sometimes seeing only one-twelfth of the action. Of course, for the big fights most of the characters are clumped together and it's possible to get a sense of the overall flow of combat, and *Overwatch* broadcasts do include a fair amount of third-person, "omniscient" floating camera shots, where it's possible to see the broader action. But for the most part a stream consists of leaping from character POV to character POV with some general action shots and sequences intermixed. It's not easy to figure out what's going on the first time you watch the game, nor the second or third. But slowly you get used to the frenetic pace; the broadcasters have a pretty good sense of what characters, at what times, will generate exciting drama (i.e. right before a big attack ultimate is used, so we can watch the carnage first hand). The matches are broadcast live, which means important skirmishes or tactics are sometimes missed. There isn't any way to really solve this problem in the abstract; *Overwatch* producers do a good job given the challenge, and will surely do even better in the future.

Most notable, I think, are the "casters," who contribute ongoing audio commentary over the streamed gameplay and sound effects. Because the action is so fast and frenetic they are forced to narrate what's going on with a speed and accuracy that makes football or baseball color commentary feel positively antediluvian. In general I was impressed with their abilities; their average age hovers around twenty-four years old, but as a group they were extremely professional and took their jobs very seriously. They are not simply narrating a video game, they are contributing to the overall popularity and success of a legitimate sports event, and they feel the same pride in their work as whispering, slow-speaking golfing commentators.

As for the match itself, it's clear that the better team won. That's the point of *Overwatch*: it's a team game, both structurally and tactically. Some players might be better or worse than others, and some are transcendent talents in this little field of human endeavor, but individual skill can't compensate for poor or adequate team play. All team members are mic'd up and in constant communication. Successful teams must work together for enemy targeting, tactical positioning, ultimate use, healing, and other boosts, and be flexible enough to recognize sudden advantage and leverage these moments as a team, or alternatively know when to fall back in unison to regroup when something goes wrong. EnVyUs has excellent individual players but really excels at team-work, which accounts for the majority of their overall success.

While it seems difficult to imagine video games as large spectator sport events that's exactly what they have become, particularly in places such as South Korea, where the best players of the most respected games are able to make a comfortable living and garner enthusiastic media coverage. As of March 2018, there were forty-six esports millionaires in the world,[15] with many more surely to come; the top grossing player in the world at that point, KuroKy, had cleared almost $3.5 million. The monetary and social advantages are clear.

Video-game developers have more than enough money to support newly created professional video-game leagues, and salaries for players are still quite reasonable; these are the early days. Broadcasting costs, unlike traditional sports events, are modest but still significant: while you don't have to pay for television broadcast rights, since the stream will be distributed over the internet, you do need to create high-quality content, and this means a production team, commentators, sets, and quality equipment. But compared to traditional live sports these costs are trivial; the esports teams are small, crowd size moderate, and the price of even the fanciest computers and monitors are a drop in the bucket compared to security costs for your average Division I college football game.

It's easy to see why many experts view esports as the new big thing. Many of the most expensive costs of standard sports production are capped: there is no player's union, no cable TV negotiations to work through, no NCAA amateur association wielding reams of arcane rules, and there's already a large and enthusiastic audience. Competition between rival video-game leagues doesn't yet exist, as they actively work together to increase publicity and exposure under the theory that anyone watching esports for the first time (any esports, anywhere) will surely lead, down the line, to greater long-term success for everyone involved.

They might well be right. The rise of esports is reminiscent of what happened with mixed martial arts and the Ultimate Fighting Competition, which was founded in 1993 and was for years thought to be nothing more than the dirty and illegitimate red-headed stepbrother of traditional boxing—a place to go and slum around for a while but nothing to be taken seriously. In 2000 the entire UFC was bought for $2 million, which looking back on it was probably one of the best business decisions of the decade (barring early investment in Bitcoin in the late aughts). Growth exploded, stars were made, fights promoted, pay-per-view got onboard, and by 2017 the UFC was sold for $4 billion dollars—yes, $4 billion dollars, an increase in value I don't have the energy to figure out.

The UFC leverages humanity's innate enjoyment of watching people hammering away at each other. As a rule the fights are spectacularly raw and bloody, a clear counter to the increasingly skill-based and knockout-adverse professional boxing matches that still manage to garner global interest. This growth isn't possible in a void. It wasn't the case that the UFC generated their own growth due to canny advertising and the like (although they did an excellent job with this). The UFC slotted in perfectly with a modern desire for a different type of sport—one less mature, pristine, and fixed by history into its current form, and because of ongoing success slightly corrupt from associated money and interest. (In the case of boxing, *extremely* corrupt.) The UFC was a breath of fresh air, and its audience told the reigning elites, "Yes, we like this even though *you* think it's barbaric." And after a while the elites had to give in and go along, given the size of the audience and the money that was suddenly up for grabs. While still young and certainly raw, the UFC is busy becoming a legitimate industry, and I hope for its own sake that it doesn't turn on its audience and crack down on the things that made it popular in the first place.[16]

The main difference between esports and the UFC, the NFL, and all the other popular professional leagues is the fact that esports are not, fundamentally, an athletic competition. Playing a video game at the highest levels requires excellent hand-eye coordination and skill as well as a high degree of mental processing power, but we don't get absurd athletes doing insane things for our viewing enjoyment—feats of speed or strength that can be enjoyed in the abstract even if you dislike the specific game that's generating the action.

If you don't like *Overwatch* there isn't any way to enjoy an *Overwatch* broadcast. That's certainly a limitation. Almost everyone watching *Overwatch* broadcasts (author possibly uniquely excepted) has played the game and enjoyed the game and wants to learn more about the game. They want to see how the pros do it, and possibly pick up some tricks or strategy. This is a crucial difference; being able to relate to the game being played, or playing it yourself on the weekend, is a significant bond between audience and players, one increasingly distant from modern American childhood where sports of all kinds are being played less and less. From 2008 to 2015, youth basketball participation went down 3.9 percent, baseball participation went down 14 percent, football participation went down 28 percent, and softball participation went down 31 percent over the same time frame.[17] It's not just these sports; children are less physically active overall by 8.8 percent. There is less connection to sports across the board, making it difficult to truly appreciate the skill involved in high-level athletic competition because these skills are an unknown quantity. How hard it is to catch that type of ball in that situation, or shoot it from that distance? Who knows. On the other hand, it's easy to tell how good a pro player is at *Overwatch*. It's a trivial matter to put yourself in their place, fire up to the game, and realize, yeah, what they just did was really hard to pull off, and I certainly couldn't have managed it.

I don't want to overstate the importance of this type of sympathetic interaction between player and fan, but it's not negligible. As video games continue to become more mainstream, with younger players spending increasing time and energy focusing on them, it's unlikely that video games will suddenly be seen as anything other than a legitimate use of time and, more than that, intrinsically dramatic and interesting. If I was a betting man with a few million to spare, I'd be tempted to buy an investment share in one of the new professional video-game leagues. Sure, it seems exceedingly silly to imagine a stadium full of people watching a huge video screen, as players sitting at tables bang away at their controllers, but we don't have to imagine it. It's already here, happening, and profitable. Given the growth of games over the last two decades, and their increasing visibility and respectability across the culture, you might want to bet against professional video gaming as a long-term investment. But I wouldn't.

CHAPTER SEVEN
THE DANGERS OF THE VIRTUAL

MORE AND MORE GAMES

I t's a cliché to imagine life's a game: "You might not realise, but real life is a game of *strategy*. There are some fun mini-games—like dancing, driving, running, and sex—but the key to winning is managing your resources."[1] It's not clear how such an expansive view fits into our understanding of what constitutes a game; a lot of life is far removed from play, and the idea of growing old and feeble with burgeoning physical degradation and mental incapacitation doesn't seem fun—one might wonder if it would be possible at that point to quit playing? Yes, but the reset button is singular—you are only given one life, with no bonus men available—and involves the minor inconvenience of death. Is "life as a game" a useful metaphor for a happier and more productive existence?

As with anything, it depends upon implementation. "Life as a game" need not fare better or worse as a theory guiding one's life than, say, Catholicism or "money at all costs" or extreme Buddhist segregation from the concerns of the material world, inspiring a lifelong meditative retreat. At the very least, "life as a game" seems harmless and might be useful as a spur for action, but this isn't the focus of the chapter. I'm not looking at life played *as* a game, played in such a way as to ennoble existence by expanding possibilities and increasing complexity and possible rewards, but at life enveloped and defined by a game or games. A life where external games are inextricably woven into the fabric of everyday existence. For hardcore gamers, cautionary tales abound.

We might as well start with the first international gaming superstar hailing from America at a time when America was just beginning to flex its industrial might and was still thought, from a continental viewpoint, to be little more than a rough, unsophisticated former colony. Paul Morphy, born in New Orleans in 1837, was only twelve years old when he took on the European chess grandmaster Johann Jacob Loewenthal in 1850 and defeated him soundly over three games, winning two and drawing one.[2]

Morphy was the definition of a prodigy; he picked up the rules to chess almost instantly from watching his relatives play, and by the age of nine he was already one of the best players in New Orleans. After defeating Loewenthal, sending shock waves across the chess-playing world, Morphy participated in the first American Chess Championship in 1857 and easily captured the title. Knowing that his true competition lay in Europe, Morphy traveled to London in 1858 and at the age of twenty destroyed all challengers using a formidable mix of tactical wizardry and strategic genius, playing in a style thought by the experts to be at least fifty years ahead of its time. Prominent victories were scored over Adolf Anderssen, generally acknowledged as the best player in the world, and Loewenthal (again), as well as the formidable Parisian cafe player Daniel Harrwitz. After giving blindfold chess exhibitions in England (playing without seeing the boards and memorizing the pieces and moves against eight opponents simultaneously),[3] Morphy returned to America, triumphant and lauded, the undisputed chess champion of the world and an obvious source of pride for the entire nation.

At the height of his popularity and fame, Morphy suddenly and inexplicably announced his retirement from chess.

For Morphy, chess was an essentially amateur activity. Morphy came from a wealthy family and didn't need to play for money, and he loudly criticized money's influence on the game. He often refused to accept cash prizes and donated tournament winnings to less fortunate players. Before the world really had a chance to focus on what was happening with Morphy in New Orleans, the American Civil War arrived, embroiling the nation, making chess a complete afterthought. After the war ended, many made repeated attempts to get Morphy to return to Europe to defend his universally accepted if informal chess championship, or even play a few games by mail or in a casual setting, but Morphy was steadfast. Chess was a game played for fun, and if he was no longer having fun he was no longer interested in playing. Morphy turned his attention to "real life," studied law, and quickly managed to qualify after memorizing the entire Louisiana law code word-for-word (yes, Morphy was that type of anomaly). He soon set up practice but had trouble attracting clients. Nobody really knows why that was the case; it's possible that Morphy, while certainly an expert at the technicalities of law, lacked the social or rhetorical flair required to make a business out of it. I suspect he would have been an unbelievably good corporate lawyer—give him a case or legal problem and, in the obscurity of a back room, working alone, it's likely he would have come up with some wonderful strategies for others to argue and debate. That's not what happened, though. Morphy, for lack of a better term, languished in New Orleans and soon retired from law into comfortable obscurity. He died at the age of forty-nine, it is claimed, from a stroke induced by a cold bath taken after a long hot walk.[4]

While it sounds like a life misspent, or genius thrown away, Morphy is an unusual and *successful* example of a man escaping what was to become a tiresome and canonical feature of chess prodigies the world over: stunning childhood success, domination in early adulthood resulting in overwhelming fame and acclaim, leading to the fate that often waits for those truly blessed with both genius and obsessive work habits—paranoia, insanity, and a premature death. Chess grandmasters are not a stable lot, a fact documented by reams of historical evidence. The following grandmasters, some of them world champions, are only part of a long list of sad examples:

- Wilhelm Steinitz attempted to contact God using a wireless telephone to challenge him to a game of chess; he soon died miserable in an insane asylum.
- Aron Nimzowitsch was unable to slow the onset of creeping paranoia, and he refused to believe that people the world over were not attempting to starve him by serving him ever-smaller portions of food. He died of pneumonia, at age forty-eight, after being bedridden for three months.
- Carlos Torre found it increasingly difficult to keep his clothing on; he famously boarded a bus in Mexico City stark naked.
- Bobby Fischer, Morphy's closest American parallel, embraced the most extreme anti-Semitic conspiracy theories imaginable after his retirement.[5] He applauded 9/11 for giving America what it so richly deserved, and quietly drifted into increasingly paranoid seclusion in Iceland, an embarrassment to the chess community.[6]

It's not clear whether insanity follows those too closely involved with world-class chess play and its rigorous mental demands or if the only people who manage to become chess immortals are those suffering from forms of mental or emotional instability, enabling concentrated focus for years on end but coming at a very steep price. But it's important to tease out the link between games and life, starting with a fictional presentation of the typical scenario: the growth and decline of a Russian chess master, which delves into not only the overt dangers but the tenuous emotional bonds linking games to life.

NABOKOV'S *THE LUZHIN DEFENSE*

The canonical example illustrating the tendency for chess grandmasters to retreat into paranoia and insanity, and by far the best literary novel about chess ever written, is Nabokov's *The Luzhin Defense*, which I'll quickly summarize while highlighting crucial points along the way. In the novel we are introduced to the chess prodigy, Luzhin, who as a boy was awkward and socially inept. When his father (Luzhin Sr.) visits Luzhin in his new school, hoping the teachers would have recognized what he viewed as his son's exceptional abilities, their praise was torpid. Deciding instead to watch Luzhin's class during recess, hoping to see his son running around with the rest of the children playing with a "large grey rubber ball," Luzhin Sr. attempts to hide, but Luzhin catches sight of him. He slips back into the school's vestibule, and after his father leaves Luzhin returns to his traditional recess occupation: "Only then did he creep out again, and, carefully skirting the players, make his way left to where firewood was stacked under the archway. There, raising his collar, he sat down on a pile of logs. In this way he sat through approximately two hundred and fifty long intermissions, until the year that he was taken abroad."[7]

It wasn't a good or bad childhood, simply lonely. Luzhin had no real interests and no focus until the evening that a violinist, hired to play for his father's party, came across Luzhin hiding in a corner of what he had imagined to be an empty room. The violinist didn't really mind Luzhin sitting there quietly, and he soon became interested in a box sitting on a desk, a present given to Luzhin Sr. a few days before. It was chessboard. After fiddling with it, and pulling out a few pieces out to admire, the violinist deigned to talk to Luzhin: "'What a game, what a game,' said the violinist, tenderly closing the box. 'Combinations like melodies. You know, I can simply hear the moves. . . . The game of the gods. Infinite possibilities.'"[8]

The next morning Luzhin woke "with a feeling of incomprehensible excitement,"[9] and it was on this day that his "aunt" (actually his father's second cousin), who was having an affair with his father (unknown to Luzhin), taught him how the chess pieces were arranged on the board and their basic moves. Before Luzhin could actually play a game, however, his aunt was forced to leave the house following a tense argument; completely unaware of the adult drama being played out, but responsive to the emotional storm, Luzhin imagined everyone had gone mad. Luzhin took the board and pieces to his room and told nobody he had done so.

Chess had come to him surreptitiously, without his father being aware; it had been introduced in an environment of high emotional turmoil, and Luzhin viewed it as a somewhat disreputable secret. He still didn't know how to play, but he knew he wanted to play.

The following week at school Luzhin saw two other students playing the game, and from watching them Luzhin finally learned the rules. The next morning he went to school with his chess board, failed to enter, and instead walked to his aunt's house a few blocks away. When he knocked she was still sleeping; he eventually was given leave to see her and left her house two hours later, elated. He missed school for a few days, and during the following week he didn't attend at all. The school finally called home to see what the medical emergency was about. Luzhin was interrogated without effect. Chess was his secret, and he was going to keep it that way.

Luzhin was soon able to effortlessly beat his aunt, so his aunt had an older gentleman come at the same time as Luzhin every morning and play against him while she stepped out of the house. This was a real player, an expert, and he crushed Luzhin fifteen games in a row before Luzhin managed a draw—which was remarkable given that he had learned how to play only a few weeks before. The expert taught Luzhin to read chess notation and how to go through published games in magazines, transforming symbols into moves upon the sixty-four squares of the board. It was at this point that Luzhin's secret love transformed into an obsession; Luzhin found pleasure in nothing except going through old chess games, playing through them, and learning as much as he could.

Luzhin Sr. didn't know what his son was doing in his room all summer long. He was completely unaware of his son's burgeoning chess ability, and only after his aunt let it slip that Luzhin was a prodigy did Luzhin Sr. casually ask for a game, pretending it was nothing more than a way to pass time. It was over quickly. Luzhin Sr. was beaten four games in a row, but his son didn't like his worlds colliding. Luzhin took the family chessboard and buried it in the backyard, halting any more "casual" games of this sort. Chess was sacred and not to be shared with his father.

From this point on Luzhin is slowly thrust into the public spotlight; he moves from child prodigy to master to grandmaster to international star. Luzhin's life is focused on chess, and it's only after a nervous breakdown during the final game of a prestigious tournament that he's forced to stop playing, recover his sanity at a spa, and while there engage in one of the most awkward and slow-moving romances in all of fiction. He ends up getting married, but he is forced to renounce chess: it had caused his breakdown and is viewed by his friends and relatives as an active danger. His wife suggests he take up stamp collecting or follow politics; anything but that dreaded game.

Luzhin agrees to leave chess behind and makes a concerted attempt ... but the newspaper has a daily chess problem, which he surreptitiously scans and instantly solves. His fired chess manager makes a sudden appearance, bringing with him memories of past tournaments and events. Luzhin feels the world beginning to constrict. He wants to escape chess, but he can't escape chess. In any case, what is Luzhin without chess? Luzhin realizes that the game is taking over his life despite his best defensive efforts, and no longer is chess limited to the boundaries of the wooden board. Characters appear and disappear, moving like knights. Patterns of light and shade flicker on the hallway parquet, resembling the white and dark squares on the board. The world is the enemy, and Luzhin is the King, forever in motion, darting from side to side, searching for a defense against checkmate. Eventually the attacking patterns coalesce into hard unremitting pressure, and Luzhin realizes there's only one escape. During a horrific party (people filling his apartment, surrounding him, intent on talking to the famous former grandmaster), Luzhin retreats into the bathroom, opens a small frosted window, climbs up on the sill, and throws himself from the fifth story to the Berlin courtyard below. Surely this represents freedom and is the ultimate defense against the ever-present attack coming from all sides? But even as he's falling Luzhin realizes that the black-and-white pattern of the onrushing square courtyard is nothing less than an oversized chessboard—even in death Luzhin falls into the game he has come to hate and can't escape. His defense fails. The game consumes him.

TAKING GAMES FAR TOO SERIOUSLY

The historical record, Nabokov's fictional but realistic take on the problem, our evolved impulse to play games (ingrained, inescapable), and the increasing sophistication of game designers and manipulators make it increasingly difficult to extract oneself from games and focus on what people typically call "real life." The addictive dangers of games are broadly accepted as legitimate; both gambling addiction and video-game addiction are recognized and relatively commonplace problems in our society (the American Psychiatric Association now includes "Internet gaming disorder" [IGD] in the DSM-V, but only as a possible diagnosis for inclusion in future versions). Obsessive playing, hardly exclusive to chess, functions as a cautionary tale against a singular all-encompassing focus upon games. It's the flip side to Aristotle's "moderation in all things" and shows that any game, however deep and historical, and however intellectually engaging and beautiful in its movements and construction, poses a risk to the imaginative obsessive. To live one's life within the game of chess, to find fame and fortune and praise and glory within it—and possibly *only* in it, and nowhere else in what we call "reality"—places a terrible burden on a game that it ultimately can't support. It brings to mind Aristotle's corollary: "Any virtue taken to an extreme becomes a vice." Too much time spent doing any one thing, however rewarding or distracting or fun, is likely to spin a life out of balance. What's required are limits, the ability to step back and focus attention on the big picture, the imaginative ability to speculate about what's not being accomplished because of what's being done instead. Is it possible to critically review an intense ten-hour binge of *Grand Theft Auto* and wonder what you were not doing in the meantime?

We know that a game must be separate from reality, with specific rules and regulations and a well-defined physical demarcation distinguishing it from our everyday world. It's also crucial to remember that when we play a game, no matter how involved we become, we can still distinguish the game world from the real world. A soccer match can be engaging to such a degree that the rest of the world momentarily fades from existence; name, place, and personal history become blurred and hard to access, for what matters is the ball, the goal, and the flow of players across the field—yet when somebody twists an ankle and stumbles to the ground, play stops. We bend down and look; we lift the player up and guide them, hobbling, to a car. The game is a reality but not *the* reality, and when reality reasserts itself the game instantly evaporates. We are aware of the game reality and the fundamental unreality of the game at the same time, overlapping but distinct and of unequal importance.

The danger of obsessive game playing is a reversal of the formula, an acceptance not of the game as a game but the game as fundamental, with reality occasionally intruding but easy enough to push away—until it's no longer possible. I already mentioned the horrific case from South Korea where a married couple, Kim and his wife, Kim Yun-jeong, became so addicted to a video game that they allowed their three-month-old baby to starve to death in a back room.[10] The reversal in this instance was complete: the virtual game child and the real child swapped places. The maternal and paternal care the two Kims should have lavished on their daughter, who like all infants was demanding and sometimes messy and difficult to deal with, was instead morphed into virtual care for a virtual—and clean and well-behaving—child avatar. The culprit here is surely the intensely immersive world of online gaming, which has reached a point of technical sophistication unavailable to previous generations of players. It's difficult to break the spell of online gaming when you are well-balanced and living a happy life and playing for occasional fun. It's almost impossible when you are under stress, unhappy, eager for distraction, and just want to feel better for a moment (or hour) or two.

Games have always functioned as an escape from "reality," but in the past it was sometimes difficult or at least a struggle to enable this escape. If you wanted to play poker or bridge you needed other players. If you wanted to gamble you needed money, access to a casino or an illegitimate back room at the end of a dark alleyway, and time. Gaming rigs require a console, a television, controllers, and game cartridges (or an internet connection). The more engaging the game the more difficult it can be to realize the game: organized sports and high-level chess both demand significant resources before it's even possible to get a game underway. No longer. Most people carry the ultimate game console around with them 24/7 in their pocket.

As we have seen it's certainly possible to become unhealthily and obsessively addicted to chess and eventually view it as "reality" instead of what passes for reality by the rest of us, but this process generally requires a gifted individual, able to plumb the depths of the game, and happens only after many years of concentrated focus achieve a totality of self-delusion capable of causing real-world behavior at odds with both society and one's own wellbeing. With online games such as *Prius*, played by the deeply disturbed South Korean couple, the headlong dive into a completely immersive all-encompassing obsession took less than a year for two otherwise average adults, and resulted in a dead infant.

The ongoing distraction and fragmentation of our modern lives, accelerated by the intrusion of smart phones and communicative technologies, has been widely reported and written about, but these factors combined with the biologically immersive nature of games give rise to a powerful new threat: game addiction, either "hard" or "soft." It's an open question whether Americans can be said to be playing games as opposed to being played by games; the enjoyment (or distraction) potential games represent must be contrasted with our heightening awareness that game playing is gobbling up an ever-greater proportion of our already scarce free time and that, for many, games are no longer a hobby or a harmless pastime: they come with significant social and personal costs.

What happens when we play games too intensively, when we get so deep into the "virtual world" of a game that the real world fades and begins to lose meaning? High-level chess competition offers a dire historical warning, and deeply immersive modern video games are accelerating this schism with often tragic results.

A slightly overwrought but extraordinarily typical experience is supplied by the author Craig Mod, whose essay "How I Got My Attention Back" does an excellent job highlighting many of these issues.[11] Craig's basic claim is that modern technology is fragmenting our minds and attention, making it increasingly difficult to focus upon anything real and long-term. It's not just Facebook and Twitter that swallowed Craig's attention; he found himself, inexplicably, addicted to the online game *Clash of Clans*, and what he says about it is extremely interesting given our close inspection of *Candy Crush* and its manipulative tricks:

> As I got closer to my goal—that mythical league on the horizon—I felt the algorithms turn on me. I sensed they knew I had a goal, and they turned that goal into an unobtainable carrot. Was I being paranoid? Maybe. The last day I played, I played for ten hours straight. Play the game slowly, a few minutes a day over months, and the algorithms are insidious. Play the game in a manic burst, and suddenly the algorithms feel laid bare. I spent only $40 over those five months, but those last ten hours were grueling. The closer I got to the goal, the more the algorithm would knock me down, set me up with what appeared to be easy wins only to have me lose. Disheartened, I'd try again, this time beating someone against whom I should have lost. Over and over this continued. It was so perfectly tuned to my most primitive set of chemical desires that it was actually beautiful—a thing of beauty. I could feel it moving beneath the screen. Its tendrils and my neurons moving with an eerie synchronicity. But of course, the lock-step relationship was weighted heavily towards the house; just as victory was once again in sight, I was back to my position ten moves and an hour prior. Where did it end?
>
> It was ridiculous. I was ridiculous. And maybe I was just a bad player. But I couldn't help shake that I was caught in a con, a long and shitty con.[12]

Craig likely wasn't wrong about the game's algorithms. Online games with a global reach and a customer base of millions don't need to be particularly subtle; too much subtlety probably hurts the bottom line. If you are particularly sensitive to what a game is doing, and feel it's creepily in harmony with your basic biological impulses ("Its tendrils and my neurons moving with an eerie synchronicity"), you're probably right. The game is likely overplaying its hand because it can. Most players are not as self-conscious or self-aware as Craig Mod, nor do they necessarily feel bad about the game. While gaming, they might require a strong push occasionally, and this push will probably be recognized by those on the lookout for such manipulations. Craig found *Clash of Clans* too mechanically intrusive to play with much enjoyment: he understood, at some point, that the game was playing him, rather than the other way around.

Whose fault is playing a game too much, for too long, in a way that might end in addiction if taken to an extreme? It's easy to blame the players but they're not the only ones involved, and they have considerably less expertise resisting the forces arrayed against them from game designers and companies whose sole purpose is to encourage further gameplay. Bianca Bosker's article in the *Atlantic* shows that the decision to put down a smartphone or pick it up, or to stop playing a game or continue to play for just a moment or two more, is the central focus of much of the "attention economy"—the rather horrifying economic system, driven by advertising, whereby companies make more money the longer their product is interacted with by users. The longer a game is played, or a website browsed, the greater the eventual monetization. The decision to play a game, stop using an app, or leave a website isn't a simple independent decision; it's at the crux of the modern technological moment. Companies fail or succeed depending on how well they manage user attention. Millions of dollars are at stake:

> While some blame our collective tech addiction on personal failings, like weak willpower, [video-game-addiction activist Tristan] Harris

points a finger at the software itself. That itch to glance at our phone is a natural reaction to apps and websites engineered to get us scrolling as frequently as possible. The attention economy, which showers profits on companies that seize our focus, has kicked off what Harris calls a "race to the bottom of the brain stem." "You could say that it's my responsibility" to exert self-control when it comes to digital usage, he explains, "but that's not acknowledging that there's a thousand people on the other side of the screen whose job is to break down whatever responsibility I can maintain." In short, we've lost control of our relationship with technology because technology has become better at controlling us.[13]

It should be clear that game companies and smartphone app designers want users to engage with their applications as much as possible: either get them hooked and squeeze out in-game purchases or deliver ads alongside whatever else is being offered. There isn't anything wrong with this in theory. It's how we used to think about successful art. "The book was so good I couldn't put it down"—that's unqualified praise, not a warning against possible addiction. What's different now? What's so wrong with getting wrapped up in a book, or a game?

WHAT'S "REAL LIFE" AND WHAT'S "VIRTUAL"?

A wanderer stumbles across a rabbit hole, enters, and is never seen again . . . that's where this discussion can easily lead. The demarcation between real and virtual isn't always clear, and in the hands of a relatively unsophisticated theorist it can be obscured to the point of opacity. For theorists who really know what they are doing, the world can be made to seem like a mirage. Even an apparently simple examination of what it means for something to be a "tree" can result in philosophical monographs and linguistic confusion. Is a "tree" that thing outside with branches, a main trunk, branches, leaves, and some roots? Looks like it. Okay, let's take this common-sense definition as fundamental. Question: do "trees" really exist in the world? Of course: my house is made from the nailed and glued corpses of hundreds. That's proof enough, right? Yes and no. Philosophers are happy to point out that other cultures might have a very different understanding of what that thing outside with leaves is. Some cultures might view a "tree" as not just consisting of its trunk, branches, and leaves, but the circle of ground around its drip line, or alternatively exclude roots from their definition. Another culture might view a tree without leaves as a different thing, a "not tree," as it's only a tree when it has leaves. We are sometimes so caught up in our linguistic construction of the world, blindly assuming that the construction actually represents a perfect overlap with "reality," that the fundamental unreality of our lives takes a backseat. We live in a world of words, symbols, signs: does it even make sense to speak of a game world as "virtual" when our economy, and our lives, are hopelessly wrapped in a shroud of social, fiscal, and linguistic constructions?

Yes it does.

That thing you call a "tree" might have a definition with blurry edges but it's clearly a distinct thing, with a unique DNA and a specific type of bark and fruit and a definitive life cycle. The fact that the limits of what is a "tree" and what is a "not tree" are sometimes difficult to determine does not undermine the fundamental fact that it's solid legitimate thing in the world, capable of reaching sixty feet in height and a girth of ten feet (or whatever it happens to be for that species). A redwood isn't a pine and neither is a dandelion. Many linguistic objections arise from confusion arising from limit, or edge, cases; the fact that it's sometimes difficult to determine the precise boundary conditions of a concept does not invalidate the possibility that there is a communal, shared base for the concept. Of course there are trees in the world, and every culture has a different take on what constitutes a tree, but this does not mean that the core concept is corrupt; rather, it means that it's sometimes not possible to fully define all aspects of what makes up a "tree" using everyday language. If you were to use scientific language, probing the object for specifics, and carefully noting every detail, it would be a trivial matter to distinguish between yew and oak and the extent of its physical form, regardless of the language used.

We are born and grow and eventually perish. Complain as you might about fundamental certainties and living in a world of symbols, you can't really get around that fact. Death is a fundamental truth, not a cultural or linguistic construction. While denied and fought against, death will nevertheless win in the end. The idea that *everything* is virtual because humans are deeply virtual, and linguistic, and addicted to symbols of all kinds does not really hold up once you escape the academy. The truth of gravity, or of voltage and current in an electrical circuit, is immune to dialogue and discussion. Simply because many of the things humans care about are in one sense or another virtual does not mean that we wholly live in a shadowy world of reflections and symbolic representations. Any child can distinguish between play and "reality" a high percentage of the time—it's therefore reasonable to ask what happens when you spend too much time playing with the virtual instead of engaging with the real.

On a more down-to-earth level, surveys indicate that the vast majority of humans are happiest when they have a full and diverse life, not one obsessively focused upon games. Again, there are edge cases—people who are willing and happy to spend ten hours a day playing *Call of Duty* and don't care about anything else they are missing out on, or professional poker players who eat, sleep, and think about nothing but poker. These are the extremes. For the rest of us, too much game playing isn't healthy. Consider the case of twelve-year-old Brett, a seemingly normal American boy from Marin, California, who developed an unhealthy obsession with *Counter-Strike*. His love of the game, leading to what everyone agreed was an addiction, eventually led Brett, like Luzhin in *The Luzhin Defense*, to consider suicide by defenestration when unable to play his game of choice:

The withdrawal made Brett want to die. The 12-year-old had only been cut off for a few hours, and his mind was already wandering to a dark and dangerous place. Looking out the window of his family's three-story home in Wassenaar, a suburb of the Hague, in the Netherlands, the American transplant imagined swan-diving out of his room and falling to the ground below, with his skull cracking open against the pavement. A grim death, sure, but at the time he felt anything had to be better than not being allowed to play *Counter-Strike*.[14]

Can video-game addiction really get this serious? Yes. To delve again into the most depressing and extreme cases: "Rebecca Colleen Christie sat at her computer for hours at a time playing the fantasy role playing game 'World of Warcraft' as her three year old daughter Brandi slowly starved to death."[15] Video games are more than capable of surmounting some of the most powerful biological impulses humans have—maternal love and care.

These are extreme examples, and they don't say much about game-playing in the larger society; the same sorts of arguments could be waged against eating. Some people are addicted to food and essentially eat themselves to death; this doesn't say anything about the value or worth of eating. Mental illness is generally the cause of these types of edge cases, and games are the way the illness manifests—at least that's the counterargument, and the sensible, moderate way to view these types of dramatic episodes. A better way to approach the subject would be to look at larger studies and eschew the individual example, which has been done. Dr. Douglas Gentile, an experts on youth/adolescent video-game addiction, surveyed three thousand children:

> Gentile learned that there's a complex chicken-or-egg structure to pathological gaming and depression. People with mental health problems or attention disorders are more inclined toward escapism and, therefore, habitual gaming. But on top of that, people . . . [who] game consistently from a young age will develop attention disorders and social

anxiety, which cripple them in school, leading to more intense mental health problems and a stronger drive to game.[16]

Dr. Gentile isn't a moral purist, or looking to generate a trumped-up hysterical panic. When he first started to research the topic, "'I was absolutely sure that video game addiction couldn't be a real thing,' he said. Instead, he was converted and is now passionate about attracting attention to pathological gaming."[17]

It's not quite true to call this a chicken-and-egg problem because the chicken and the egg in this case did not suddenly appear out of nowhere, asking for an explanation about their existence. Game companies are actively targeting younger and younger players, and marketing via gaming has spread into the broader business community:

> *Create a Comic*, as it is called, was created by General Mills to help it sell Honey Nut Cheerios to children. Like many marketers, General Mills and other food companies are rewriting the rules for reaching children in the Internet age. These companies, often selling sugar cereals and junk food, are using multimedia games, online quizzes and cellphone apps to build deep ties with young consumers. And children . . . are sharing their messages through e-mail and social networks, effectively acting as marketers.[18]

This is a completely natural and expected expansion of gaming, incorporating *Candy Crush*'s leveraging of social media to get players and/or consumers to not just advertise a product but to generate the best sort of advertising, typically unavailable through other means: a peer-to-peer recommendation. It's one thing to read a Facebook advertisement while scrolling through the latest news article; it's another to receive a message from a personal friend asking you to look at the results of a product-sponsored game you played and inviting you to play as well.

In the marketing world this sort of thing is absolute gold. The cost of developing and delivering a simple game suitable for children (basic graphics, basic gameplay) is miniscule compared to what is required for a top-end wholly immersive 3-D game. It also has an incredibly long shelf life; normal advertising comes and goes in a flash. The advertisement is seen, or not, and the money is spent. *Create a Comic* might exist for months or years, blurring the boundaries of advertising/not advertising and further obscuring what it means for something to be a game. Is it possible to create a game whose only real goal is to generate brand loyalty ... yet it's still a game? Because outside forces are necessarily involved in such creations (financial, corporate), doesn't this puncture the pure sphere of the game as a world outside that of everyday life and contribute to the blending of the real and the not-real, the virtual and the everyday?

More to the point, the increasing focus upon capturing and exploiting children's love of games makes it clear that the "chicken and egg" analogy falls flat on its face. With billion-dollar global companies busy targeting children as potential game players, hooking them at ever-decreasing ages,[19] the slow and steady push to forever expand gaming's influence makes it far more likely that if you are somewhat vulnerable to such manipulations you will be caught up and exploited.

Let's remember what Dr. Gentile has to say about things: "People with mental health problems or attention disorders are more inclined toward escapism and, therefore, habitual gaming." If the gaming market, being pushed at Americans from all sides, is eager and willing to sweep up anyone with any type of innate weakness for their product, and capture them from an early age, and this capturing has poor long-term effects (creating the sort of gaming addictions that generate problems in later life), games are more *cause* than chicken/egg with respect to poor outcomes.

As a culture we now recognize and legally regulate this type of leveraging of consumer weakness in *some situations*, but it took a lot of effort to get to this point, involving drawn-out fights against entrenched power structures. We no longer allow children or young teens to smoke addictive cigarettes, yet to this day, despite it being illegal, tobacco companies continue to target children while denying they are doing any such thing. The Camel cigarette brand, for example, was roundly criticized in the 1990s for their "Joe Camel" advertising push, after it was revealed that it was children, rather than adults, who responded far more positively to the advertisements.[20] People were up in arms, and the truth eventually oozed out: "one of the nation's major tobacco companies, the Liggett Group, acknowledged that the industry focused on minors with its promotional efforts because virtually all smokers begin the habit as teenagers."[21] It got ugly, with charges filed by the Federal Trade Commission that the R. J. Reynolds Tobacco Company illegally aimed its Joe Camel advertising campaign specifically at minors. The issue was eventually settled out of court, with R. J. Reynolds Tobacco agreeing to pay a fine and redesign their "Joe Camel" campaign to make it less appealing to children. It was a repulsive if understandable risk; for tobacco companies, young customers are crucial for creating life-long brand loyalty, even if the length of that life is going to be negatively impacted.

It's hard to imagine that game companies are going to be more ethical than big tobacco with a product that's less obviously addictive and physically damaging than cigarettes. With games, it's far more difficult to see and prove cause and effect. You can't shrug your shoulders and look away if you catch sight of a five-year-old smoking a Camel, but you can when watching one immersed in the latest and greatest multiplayer game. The level of addiction for the two (games/cigarettes) doesn't feel the same; the dangers are not in alignment. One eats up your lungs and the other . . . well, it's easy to argue to yourself that it *probably* won't do anything.

The addiction potentials of the two are clearly different. But we don't find stories of nicotine addiction causing parents to starve their children. The baseline addictive power of nicotine has a faster and more obvious onset than gaming, and while gaming is less addictive to the population at large it's capable of far more damage to one's life (or other lives) when it reaches the limit cases. Cigarettes often kill the smoker and sometimes, through second-hand smoke, impact others. At its worst, game addiction can destroy families, kill children, get parents thrown in prison, etc.

The slow-moving effects of game addiction difficult to regulate; at the extremes it looks and feels like nothing more than insanity—you can always point to these unfortunates and claim, "The only people who get addicted to games *that seriously* are seriously screwed in the head." But I don't think it's that easy to determine, and I don't think there are any easy solutions. We have a lot of trouble regulating long-term and hard-to-spot dangers. It took us over fifty years to get the tobacco industry to admit that their product did cause health problems. It might take a hundred for the gaming industry to admit the same, if they ever do.

LET'S "GAMIFY" THE WORLD! EVERYONE WINS!

The blurring of lines between game/advertisement, or game/not game, parallels that taking place in a broader context: the desire to inject games into "reality" by means of "gamification." This is an ugly word roughly meaning: *The application of game-design elements and game principles in non-game contexts*. Broadly speaking, gamification is a way to live your life, or work at a task, by thinking of it as a game. The doyenne of this sort of theory is Jane McGonigal, a professional game designer and the director of Game Research and Development at Institute for the Future.[22] She also works for SuperBetter (a game design and consulting firm), where she is the Chief Creative Officer. It should come as no surprise, given her background, that her first book was titled *Reality Is Broken: Why Games Make Us Better and How They Can Change the World*.

While it's not fair to judge a book by its title, McGonigal or her publisher seems to have a knack for irritatingly cutesy offerings—in what way, and in what context, is "reality broken"? The answer appears to be: "In almost every way." Many still struggle with poverty. Inequality is skyrocketing. Healthcare is an ongoing societal challenge. What does McGonigal suggest we do to fix things? A *New York Times* book review summed up her solution nicely:

> The premise is that since games motivate us more effectively than real life, making them altruistic and bringing them into the physical world will promote altruistic behavior. But is this motivating power transferable? . . . Reality doesn't work this way. Floors need scrubbing. Garbage needs hauling. Invalids need their bedpans washed. This work isn't designed for your pleasure or stimulation. It just needs to be done.[23]

The following quote perfectly distills the fundamental problem with McGonigal's wildly enthusiastic and irrepressible gamephilia:

> If reality is inherently less attractive than games, then the virtual world won't save the physical world. It will empty it. Millions of gamers, in McGonigal's words, are "opting out" of the bummer of real life. . . . Halo 3, for example, has become a complete virtual world. . . . McGonigal calls this war game a model for inspiring mass cooperation. Two years ago, its 15 million players reached a long-sought objective: They killed their 10 billionth alien. "Fresh off one collective achievement, Halo players were ready to tackle an even more monumental goal," McGonigal writes. And what goal did they choose? Feeding the hungry? Clothing the poor? No. The new goal was to kill 100 billion aliens.[24]

As McGonigal infamously claimed in her TED talk in 2010, the planet spends three billion hours a week gaming, but "If we want to solve problems like hunger, poverty, climate change, global conflict and obesity that number should balloon to 21 billion."[25] This is a deeply perverse claim about how to solve intractable problems, and I couldn't come up with better satire if I tried.

In 2011 when journalist Andrew Moseman asked McGonigal directly about what current problems require gamification and how games *might solve the problem*, she had this to say:

The two biggest problems that will be solved together, potentially, are obesity and world peace. . . . So there's new, interesting thinking that the best way to create world peace would be to reduce the diabetes trend, which is tied to the obesity trend, which is our number one health concern in the U.S. There is this huge space of games that are being created for physical activity, and games have also historically had quite a lot of content around war—World of Warcraft, Starcraft, Call of Duty. But this idea that we could use games to reduce obesity, stop diabetes, and that that would lead to world peace, I think is really fascinating.[26]

This is absolutely typical for McGonigal: extremely light on details, and extremely heavy on claims. Regarding world peace and obesity: so far nothing we have tried has worked that well, but maybe sprinkling a little game theory over the problem will magically transform it into yesterday's problem. There is no indication that McGonigal has given any thought about how to create games to reduce obesity (or if this really a valid solution)—although it might be pointed out, gently, that we already have a large and vigorous class of games that reduce obesity. They are called sports. They are heavily subsidized, culturally applauded, for many a source of satisfaction, and for a lucky few a source of great monetary rewards. Yet the obesity epidemic rolls onward. Does the evidence really suggest that we are not playing enough games?

Another classic example of "gamification" comes from McGonigal's own life. While at work one day she apparently had an accident resulting in a concussion that was more serious than initially imagined. The concussion caused long-term effects, lasting a few weeks, and McGonigal was left feeling depressed and suicidal for the first time in her life. What was the solution she came up with to fix her real-world problem? "Gamification." While in recovery she created a video game titled *Jane the Concussion-Slayer* to help her deal with the trauma, a game she later enhanced into a commercial release called *SuperBetter*. McGonigal raised $1 million dollars to fund the commercial release, and I have to say she certainly did gamify her life successfully: from concussion to million-dollar game over the course of a year. There is a lesson to be learned here about active design versus passive play.[27]

SuperBetter, the game, attempts to generate real-world change under the rubric of game playing: "Users identify a problem they're focusing on, like getting over a breakup, sleeping better or reducing stress, and are given a 'power pack' of activities to do. *SuperBetter* includes detailed scientific explanations for its tasks . . . but it eschews traditional approaches. 'Ninja weight loss,' for instance, forbids you from dieting and encourages you to sneak up on weight loss by writing down which foods make you feel energized or to exercise a little more."[28]

SuperBetter isn't a game, it's a run-of-the-mill self-help book/ notification device in the form of a game, which leverages none of a game's truly powerful motivating elements. It might feel like a game in the terminology used ("power pack," etc.) but as a method to change human behavior it's incredibly ham-fisted. If somebody really wants to lose weight, forbidding them from dieting and suggesting they exercise is a dead end for everyone except those who are exceptionally motivated to lose weight and probably don't need *SuperBetter* in the first place. They're gonna do it anyway.

SuperBetter the game led to *SuperBetter: A Revolutionary Approach to Getting Stronger, Happier, Braver, and More Resilient* the nonfiction book, which is anything but revolutionary. It's more of the same, written with overwhelmingly gushing prose, which neither I nor the *New York Times* enjoyed:

> Like all self-help books, "SuperBetter" takes familiar techniques of personal care—drink plenty of water, cultivate a robust support network, keep mentally stimulated—and repackages them. The prose, true to genre, swings between lullaby and war cry, seeking either to woo us with promises or to rev us up with declarative sentences about inner strength and power. Each paragraph is a needle bed of exclamation points, and the book's wilder claims appear flimsy, the arguments irksomely oversold.[29]

The overarching problem with McGonigal is that she's as deeply embedded in the gaming community as anyone in the country. She writes glowingly about games, makes a lovely income from games, helps run a gaming company, and as anyone with one-size-fits-all solution every nail she sees is a problem to be fixed by a good solid swing of the gaming hammer. She's not a critical thinker, nor apparently interested in recognizing the problematic claim that games can and will change the world, ergo: game more. As a gaming insider she's absolutely invaluable: she's the perfect antidote for an industry nervous about the increasing number, and increasing press coverage, of time spent gaming by youth and adults. There is a general sense that blowback might occur; people might clamp down on the time they allow their children to game or experience unsupervised time on electronic devices. The solution isn't to claim that more people aren't playing games—that's a losing battle. The real answer is to confidently assert the following: *Yes, more people are playing more games than ever before, and that's a good thing. It's going to save the world!*[30]

Does McGonigal have much scientific research to back up her wildly optimistic claims that "gamification" will solve all the world's ills, or at least a small portion of them? Yes and no. Yes, in that there exist studies, which she cites, that show that "gamification" can positively impact the ability of groups to accomplish some specific tasks—which perfectly aligns with our common sense. For example, McGonigal discusses a study that claims to show that playing *Tetris* reduces PSTD effects for returning soldiers. However, the researcher authoring the study admits the lab findings "can't easily be applied to real-world situations."[31] In general scientific studies, when they exist, are far too tentative and unclear to support McGonigal's extravagant claims.

It's not even a new idea. We do gamification all the time in real life if we can manage it: throw a hundred hay bales onto the truck and take a break ("get a reward"). See if you can throw more bales than your work partner in a shorter time. Make a contest out of it. See if you can lose yourself in the game aspect and only when it's over look at the great big pile of moved hay and think: *Wow, I don't remember even doing that.*

This is an everyday example of "gamification" and both incredibly uninteresting and entirely dependent upon situation and circumstance. Who is their right mind wouldn't try to make a game out of an unpleasant task if it was possible? Who wouldn't want to structure their charity as a game, with points awarded for successful volunteering and neighborhood beautification projects? If you can pull it off it's magical. The problem is that setting up these games is incredibly specific to the task and extremely delicate. It's not hard to turn a proto-game into something else entirely. It's easy to decide, as a player, that game-theory components applied to the difficult task of weight loss or running a charity are not only unappealing but actively distasteful, as overtly creating a game to generate positive results often makes the game aspects feel artificial, manipulative, annoying, and easy to reject. McGonigal only offers the most basic and superficial suggestions for how games should be structured and implemented in ways that maximize success.

The hard part isn't the realization that games can be useful tools to effect social change. The hard part is specifying the details and setting up a few examples and testing the game structures in the real world to see how they turn out. McGonigal has tried at least: the Groundcrew application allows people to work together to achieve a list of stated goals in a game setting (you "play" by doing worthy real-world deeds). The results aren't surprising: "Where's the reliable evidence that this data translates to people's doing more real work? Projects like Groundcrew, McGonigal concedes, have produced 'modest if any results so far.'"[32]

McGonigal, a self-professed gaming expert, doesn't appear to understand the way games function or how they relate to the "real world" (if they do). The right way to accomplish "gamification" is to understand that it can only be applied to a small number of the problems facing the world. You can't slap a point system on "quantity of books read" and call it a game, hoping that the players (readers) will want to maximize their point total—this is just ham-fisted manipulation in the guise of a game. Her theory also has other severe problems.

"Gamification" is an extremely artificial method for inspiring what the game designer views as correct or positive behavior. It's possible to make a game so compelling and seamless that the lines between play and work blur, but it's very, very difficult, and I don't know anyone who has successfully deployed such a game for creating additional low-cost housing, for example. A successful attempt would have to be extremely sophisticated and subtle, and would probably be forced to actively hide parts of the "game playing" aspects to pull a runaround regarding the irritating artificiality of the game itself. This isn't something McGonigal has interest in exploring nor, from what I have read, the sophistication to pull off.

"Gamification" also harkens back to Jonathan Haidt's idea of moral dependency; it assumes that one of the best ways to solve a problem isn't to inspire people to solve the problem, or argue that for ethical or economic reasons a problem such as low-income housing should be tackled in order to ameliorate a social ill—rather, what's required is no thinking about the fundamental ideas at all, just participation in a game. The power to define what problems are to be focused upon, as well as the methods the game uses to potentially fix the problem, are in the hands of the game designer, not the participants, who are left in a state of passive play. That McGonigal finds this unproblematic isn't surprising, since in theory she or her peers will be the ones creating the games and deploying the games, while the game-players do all the messy real-world work. She's the active creator; everyone else is a passive slave.

"Gamification" requires a rigid hierarchy with game designers sitting on their thrones pulling the strings of their players, but it's a strange sort of hierarchy that hides its structure from both the game makers and game players. Because it's voluntary (you can play or not play, it's up to you) the idea is, I suppose, that it's neither coercive nor corporate in the traditional sense of the term. Of course it's both: overtly coercive (that's the whole point, getting people to do things that they otherwise wouldn't do) and exceedingly controlling (that's the way games are structured: limited sphere of action, limited number of possible choices, clear-cut goals, and rewards for meeting those goals). It's also possible that the energy and time people spend "playing" socially useful games (rather, games that are claimed to have socially useful effects) drains them of the energy or time they might otherwise have used to go out and do real work. If you can sit in your living room and "play" a game that claims to be solving world hunger, well, you have done your good deed for the day. Keep working at it a few hours a month and that's probably enough—you've contributed to the global good in some nebulous way. I can't imagine a more comforting thought for hardcore gamers.

McGonigal is yet another in a seemingly endless series of B-list celebrities or authors who achieved fame by sturdy application of the "but actually" trope. You know the one: hey, do you think exercise makes you live longer? I bet you do . . . *but it actually doesn't* (at this point in the article or speech one rat study is cited, all contradictory evidence is ignored, and the speaker breezily continues with the apparently contrarian point that everyone is exceedingly happy to embrace). McGonigal's doing that same sort of thing but pushes it to absurdly grand extremes. You think playing games is bad? I bet you do . . . *but it actually isn't, in fact more people should play games since games will change the world.* I wonder when this particular trope will be seen for what it is and firmly rejected, as it's not only deeply unhelpful but actively diverts energy and effort from other solutions that have a chance of actually working instead of functioning to make everyone feel better about their (generally) privileged and exceedingly comfortable lives.

Successful examples of "gamification" are hard to come by and generally tackle one small, extremely detailed problem. The best game in this genre, by far, is *Foldit*, an online puzzle-solving video game created by the University of Washington Center of Game Science to solve long-standing protein-folding problems that are mathematically intractable for modern computers.[33] Players are given a set of protein-folding tools, an image of the protein to be folded, and asked to compactly fold the specified protein. Particularly successful folding sequences are highlighted, sent to the scientists in charge of the project, and looked at with human eyes to determine if the sequence of folding makes biological sense, could be replicated, and might have some useful function. *Foldit* players have achieved real and notable successes, deciphering the crystal structure of the Mason-Pfizer monkey virus (M-PMV) retroviral protease, as well as an enzyme that catalyzed the Diels–Alder reaction. *Foldit* work continues, and by any standard this is a hugely successful example of "gamification" for a number of reasons, which should be obvious and taken into account when looking to "gamify" other problems.

1. The problem to be solved, protein folding, is by definition a puzzle to be solved using typical puzzle-solving actions. The fundamental gameplay activity is inherent in the question, not layered on top of an unrelated issue.

2. Puzzle solving based on 3-D manipulation of abstract forms is something humans are inherently good at and have doing for years before the idea of Foldit entered any researcher's mind. Even a simple video game such as *Tetris* uses these sorts of abstract rotation and puzzle-solving skills.

3. The problem is one that can't be solved using standard methods; computers are not very good at solving these types of problems efficiently and without inordinate power- and time-consumption.

4. The ultimate goal of the game is both clear and obviously useful. Learning more about how proteins fold will necessarily improve research and likely generate long-term benefits.

5. Gameplay can be distributed in small chunks over the internet and does not require inordinate effort on the part of the players. You can play in a burst for five minutes or settle down for five hours and still get a little/a lot accomplished.

6. The game is professionally designed and has the support of a well-respected university. It's also free to play.

It's not that "gamification" is by definition a bad way to approach a given problem, but it's not the right way to approach all (or even most) problems. Problems that are themselves game-like (such as protein-folding) are obviously amendable to "gamification" but even here there are serious limitations. The method for solving the puzzle must be able to be cheaply distributed to the players, and if this involves anything physical (such as a small bundle of chemicals) the game comes to a screeching halt. The problem to be solved also can't be too difficult—it helps a lot if you can make incremental progress or work with others in a team to tackle a larger challenge. It must be relatively fun in order to attract and keep players, and it can't be something distributed by a large petrochemical company, for example, leveraging crowdsourcing to get a bit of research done on the cheap. That won't fly. These are only some of the limitations and restrictions required for the successful creation of such a game, and they shrink the possible applications to a level that makes McGonigal's wildly optimistic claims for "gamification" seem either hollow or aggressively naive. I believe, deep in my heart, that McGonigal truly believes what she's saying, but that doesn't make it less silly or more practical.

GAMES TO IMPROVE THE WORLD

There's another way to approach the problem of merging "reality" with games, and it's not to force "gamification" upon innocent problems across the land. It's about changing the games that we play to accomplish something more useful than shooting electronic blips representing a hoard on onrushing aliens.

Erik Lehmann, based in Ithaca, New York, has a simple solution: get rid of violent games and replace them with more useful games or activities. He's founded the Game Changer Movement, whose goal is to redirect *Call of Duty* (and other shoot-em-up) players toward games that are more socially beneficial and personally rewarding—or get them away from a single-minded focus on gaming altogether.[34] Gloria DeGaetano, founder of the Parent Coaching Institute, is enthusiastic about the concept:

> The Game Changer Movement is a brilliant tactic to shift our youth's attention away from psychopathic play and engage them in healthy video games of their own design. When our kids artfully amplify life and what brings us all the best in life, they learn what it means to be and stay human in our screen world. While creating video games of significance, they are reminded that their contributions matter and that, in fact, we need their authentic voice and leadership so desperately. Our current crisis cannot be changed by the same old thinking. . . . We would be smart to listen to [Erik Lehmann] and wiser if we participated in his movement [Game Changer]. I'm all in. How about you?[35]

While some of the fundamental impulse to make radical change is based in the assumption that violent video games generate violent children and/or adults (a claim reviewed in the next chapter),[36] something more interesting is lurking just beneath the surface. Erik Lehmann takes it as a given that humans are addicted not so much to multiplayer games but, "addicted to or driven by the desire to feel significant, accomplished and part of a larger community."[37] This claim aligns with what we know about the most popular video games in the world, which are either extremely manipulative single-person puzzle games (such as *Candy Crush*), or multiplayer 3-D immersive games (such as *Call of Duty, Skyrim*, etc.). We already know what makes *Candy Crush* popular, so what about multiplayer games? Here I think Erik is onto something important. Just as *Candy Crush* relentlessly abuses various biological and mental processes to addict us and squeeze money out of us, there must be a biological basis for what's going on with multiplayer games. What makes them so incredibly popular and hard to put down?

Most of the reasons aren't difficult to discern and are broadly accepted by the academic gaming community. Multiplayer games have features that most of us would recognize as tapping into fundamental human needs or desires:

- **Communal**

  Play occurs within a group of friends/companions.

- **Smart, complex gameplay**

  The enemy tactics and strategies arise not from AI but from the best thinkers in the world: other humans.

- **Competition**

  Players compete against enemies as well as allies (to see who gets the most kills, had the best strategy, etc.).

- **Instant feedback and recognition**

  Players can show off during the game, display their skill, receive social cred, dispense praise and blame, and are able to gain something humans desperately desire: respect.

Candy Crush can't manage any of these things, yet it remains incredibly popular and additive. Is it any wonder that a game that taps into some (or all) of these socially mediated biological drives has a good chance of getting and keeping a player's attention?

There's obviously a significant different between multiplayer games and pure manipulative cash grabs such as *Candy Crush*. With *Candy Crush* our biology has been hijacked, our focus distracted and captured, our neural defenses avoided or eluded. That's not necessarily the case with multiplayer games.

When you are busy doing a mission in *Call of Duty* and your friend makes a joke and you laugh and somebody else piles on about something nearly but not quite unrelated and it turns into a real conversation, that's just as legitimate a discussion as one taking place over the telephone. It's not as good as face-to-face, of course, and much is lost by the technological remove, but there isn't any way *Call of Duty* can be said to be abusively manipulating your desire to talk to your friends. They have built it into the game, sure, and it makes the games much better and more profit-able, but the basic interaction isn't corrupt: it's presented in a relatively pure way. You can make and break friendships through *Call of Duty*. You are not limited to a certain amount of "radio time" every mission and forced to purchase more time should you desire a longer conversation.[38] These conversations can be, for want of a better term, both legitimate and real—people have met online playing *Call of Duty*, transitioned into real-world communication, and sometimes have ended up getting married.[39] That's about as real as it gets.

Moreover, an important interpersonal currency, *respect*, is granted by a human to another human as a result of actions taken and either reported or viewed first hand. It's possible to gain the respect of your *Call of Duty* squad by clever play, well-aimed shooting, consistent tactical acumen, or a million other ways. This type of respect is just as real as that earned on the street or in the corporate boardroom—it might not be as valu-able from a monetary standpoint, but for many it's incredibly important. Respect, working together, functioning as a well-oiled team, winning together and losing together: these are real outcomes, even if they take place in the virtual world. It's not clear that the ability to lead a squad in *Call of Duty* has any real-life applicability, but I could see it happening; a nervous teen ends up running a squad of twenty-year-olds and gains self-respect as he gains the respect of others. I could also see the game being incredibly depressing for those without adequate gameplay skills—who wants to play with *them*? Nobody.

It's now more clear what Erik Lehmann was talking about when he said that games are a way for people to "feel significant, accomplished and part of a larger community." It's not that *Call of Duty* or other first-person team-based games are incredibly addictive because they are manipulating the heck out of the players (although they do this as well). Crucially for their success is the opportunity they offer for the type of team coopera-tion that many young Americans can't get any other way. We don't need to use our imaginations very hard to see the attraction of these games. Consider an average ten-year-old boy bundled off to school, going through supervised classes, having a thirty-minute supervised recess (if lucky), and returning home at around 3:30 p.m. after a day of uninspired learning with little or no possibility to engage in free play or complex self-guided group interactions. It's often not possible or feasible to jump on a bike and ride over to a friend's house or gather in the dusty field next to the old oak tree; these things have been made essentially illegal by the incredibly watchful and fearful society that regards a child out in a street, running around alone, as a magnetic source of soon-to-arrive tragedy.

It's not that such a boy doesn't want to play or talk to his friends or have adventures and fall down and skin his knee while running in fear from a presumed monster shaking a bush in the back corner of the park. He does. So when a game appears that allows this sort of activity in what most consider to be a safe "virtual" environment, it's naturally going to be embraced. *Call of Duty* and games like it are wildly successful because, in a real sense, many people don't have anything better to do, or can't achieve the same type of interactions without the support of these types of virtual worlds.

Let's remember twelve-year-old Brett who was so addicted to *Counter-Strike* that its removal made him want to kill himself.[40] That's obviously a really bad outcome, and I sympathize with Brett and not just because of his game addiction. He's a child and unable to handle some of the incredibly appealing stuff being thrown at him by the game, which was designed to have this effect even on mature adult minds . . . but I'm also upset by the fact that Brett didn't have other outlets for his perfectly reasonable, rational, and human desire for companionship, to be part of a group working toward a larger goal, and to make a positive contribution and (if possible) gain the respect of somebody that he, in turn, respected. That Brett's culture was so barren as to offer no opportunities except those available in a commercial video game is a damning statement not so much of the game, which at least allowed him some outlet for these desires, but of our modern world. In cases such as this I think the problem is at least as much real as virtual; had Brett lived fifty years ago with the same technology there's a chance he would still become addicted to *Counter-Strike*, but there's an even larger chance (I suspect) that he would be too busy with his newfound freedom and ability to play with real friends, in the real world, to feel the need to obsessively master *Counter-Strike*. It's the chicken-and-egg story again; those most susceptible to video-game addiction are those whose lives are the most empty and meaningless, which in turn drives more video-game playing and a continual emptying-out of real-world interactions.

It's not so much that people love to virtually blast artificial 3-D representations of other humans to bits; it's that, "violent video games give all those who play, a sense of autonomy, competence, and relatedness."[41] We know this to be true from other types of immersive 3-D games; *Minecraft*, for example, can be played in such a way that it's essentially nonviolent, with a focus on building a communal world, creating and solving puzzles, and working with other players to achieve various goals. It's incredibly popular, far more so than *Call of Duty*. Violence isn't the root cause for the popularity of these types of games, it's simply the easiest/most widely accepted way to structure and design them. It's incredibly lazy game design, granted, but not the most important feature of a game's success.

What the Game Changers Movement wants to do is wean people away from "empty" games that offer social advantages but absolutely no productive game content (*Call of Duty* and its copycats) toward games that allow for plenty of personal interaction and team-building and also contain valuable content or generate a valuable result. The biggest problem with this goal is that such games are difficult to create and don't represent a known genre in the market. The amount of developer time that went into *Candy Crush* was significant, but just a drop in the bucket compared to 3-D immersive games. The free market does not reward socially useful and healthy game design unless it's extremely profitable.

Call of Duty: Modern Warfare 2 had production and advertising costs in excess of $280 million dollars, which is mindboggling. The fact that the average immersive 3-D game can cost as much or more than your average Hollywood movie means that, like Hollywood, the goal for producers is to not take any risks with the extremely expensive product. If you create a standard Hollywood movie, or a standard 3-D shoot-em-up, it's likely you will at least break even. The worst that can be said about you is that you are extremely uncreative and cowardly, but that is not a net negative from the accountant's perspective. On the other hand, if you take risks, think outside the proverbial box, and aim for something different, better, and unique, it might catastrophically fail, in which case all the blame is coming your way. Fingers will be pointing from every nook in the studio. You were given a high-flying supersonic jet and drove it straight into the ground. While the rewards of creating a middling Hollywood movie or middling shoot-em-up are modest and certainly far less than an unexpected hit, the downside is almost nonexistent. Producers don't lose their jobs for creating genre flicks, even if they fail. Most genre movies fail. That's the way it works. Producers lose their jobs after taking risks and reaching for something better and coming up empty.

Humans are risk-adverse. I understand why the *Call of Duty* franchise produced "more of the same" with their $280 million dollars, but I don't respect it. At the very least they might have dropped their advertising budget by $20 million (from $200 million) and used that money to fund an extremely sophisticated and professional game in a vastly different and interesting genre. What's required is professional buy-in from the current market leaders and major players.

Help might be on the way. The Social Venture Network (SVN) recently hosted a conference that sought to bring together Silicon Valley activists, game designers, and industry executives to generate just this sort of industry buy-in from those with enough money to make better games possible.[42] The Games for Change Festival hopes to inspire similar outcomes and has been in the public eye recently for their link to the prestigious Tribeca Film Festival.[43] Harvard University's Making Caring Common project recently developed the game *Quandary*, which focuses on, "perspective-taking, critical thinking, and ethical decision-making skills."[44] Lots of work is being done in this part of the gaming world and has been for over a decade. I wish them the best. It might be the case that the gaming community is on the edge of adopting, in a big way, a very different sort of game than the typical type of cookie-cutter bestsellers. It could happen. After all, a hip-hop musical about Alexander Hamilton recently made it big on Broadway, which proves that, in theory, anything is possible. From my perspective a truly meaningful, game-changing game can't arrive fast enough.

CHAPTER EIGHT

KEEP US SAFE BY GIVING THEM GAMES

THE COMIC-BOOK CODE COMES TO VIDEO GAMES

The mass media has long made the "common sense" argument that violent video games, violent movies, violent books, and depictions of violence in any genre, particularly when it's glorified and gory in its full bloody depiction of some gruesome event, has ill effects upon those experiencing the simulated violence. The argument *seems* to make sense. To progress through a level of a modern video game, a gamer might have to kill four virtual enemies and do it in four particularly expressive ways: one gets it with a shotgun blast in the gut, the other with a crossbow, the next via hit-and-run, and the last by a spiked baseball bat to the head. Despite the clear absurdity of the simulated scenario this surely can't be good for the psychological health of the player—can it?

Grand Theft Auto generated the loudest and most virulent press of this sort. The game unapologetically embraced gruesome, over-the-top video-game violence to a degree often assumed to be obvious satire. It famously allowed players to visit prostitutes and pay them to engage in typical prostitute/john behavior, "healing" some previously accrued in-game damage—presumably because, hey, sexual healing's a thing. It was permissible in-game, and certainly common, for *Grand Theft Auto* players to afterward murder the prostitute and retrieve their money.

Typical press reactions were along the lines of the following self-explanatory title:

THE KIDS AREN'T ALRIGHT: These "Grand Theft Auto" Rampage Videos Are Disturbing: "Simulating depravity and the most unspeakable of moral acts"[1]

The author of this screed, Paul Bois, makes it clear from the start that he does not think video-game violence creates real-world violence, and he also wants the reader to know he isn't promoting censorship. His argument is more personal and nuanced than most in these types of articles, and he asks the following question—why are people doing horrible things in these types of video games? He looks back on his own teenage years playing *Grand Theft Auto* and no longer recognizes the person he was then: "though I eventually grew [out of] this packaged insanity, many have not."[2] It's not clear why virtual violence is fun, but it certainly is for many teenage boys (and adults). This violence feels like something we should be very worried about; it certainly doesn't strike anyone as the most healthy thing in the world. But without evidence of significant real-world effects (violent or emotional) it's hard to know what to do about violent video games (or if something should be done).

The violence found in video games, while certainly hyperactive and over-the-top, can be compared to that found in modern horror movies such as the *Saw* franchise, where the action isn't virtual but simulated; human actors are busy pretending they are being decapitated, having their jaws ripped open, or getting a drill to the spine. This is far closer to "reality" than the virtual cartoonish world of *Grand Theft Auto* and should therefore be more disturbing—which is odd because violence is the fundamental draw and inescapable plot device for these types of movies. People pay money to see simulated violence—there isn't any doubt about it. There is little panicked media concern about horror movies, action movies, television shows with multiple gruesome deaths every twenty minutes or so . . . Why are video games targeted as being particularly problematic?

The major issue has to do with passive vs. active involvement. The fact that *Grand Theft Auto* players are the ones aiming the guns and directing the assassinations instead of passively watching them happen on the screen during a scripted narrative is taken to be both damning and consequential. It's not a bad theory, but it points directly back to the game design. The fact that such things are happening in *Grand Theft Auto* instead of *Minecraft* is because *Grand Theft Auto* was constructed to support these activates. They are the focus of the game, just as hor- rific mutilation and over-the-top misogyny seems to be the point of many horror movies. Part of the attraction of *Grand Theft Auto* is the fact that the game allows the player to do so many completely repulsive things— players are often shocked at how graphic and gross the game can get. In some ways the point of *Grand Theft Auto* is to plumb the depths of deg- radation and see how far you can go: what's the worst possible thing that can be attempted?

It's important to recognize that when playing *Grand Theft Auto* the most common response to these types of horrors isn't embarrassed silence . . . it's laughter. You could make the argument that instead of fos- tering or normalizing brutal violence, *Grand Theft Auto* instead allows it to come to the screen, flower fully, and be laughed at or experienced in a cathartic way. This claim was put to the test after children with higher-than- average mental health concerns were asked to play *Grand Theft Auto* as part of a study. The net result was deemed "therapeutic" by the clinician.[3] One study is just a single point of data and might be valueless depending on the quality of the research, but it at least makes sense given the indisputable numerical evidence that almost everyone agrees with: teen crime, and teen violence, is near its all-time low:

By 2014, the rate of violent victimization (which includes rape, robbery, aggravated and simple assaults) for adolescents ages 12 to 20 had fallen to a sixth of what it was from the mid 1990s, from a high of 181 victimizations per 1,000 population, to 27 victimizations per 1,000.[4]

It might be true that other factors are driving down the teen violence rate and that the rate would be even lower if violent video games were not so prevalent—in other words, we are doing a wonderful job at stopping this sort of crime, but could do even better by removing *Grand Theft Auto* and its like from the world. It's a hard argument to make, given that a concerted effort to find a link between violent games and violent behavior has so far resulted in no universal scientific consensus. Occam's razor suggests that whatever's going on regarding cause-and-effect probably isn't an unusual, extreme event. If something appears to have little effect on teen violence, and teen violence has been steadily dropping . . . that something is probably not a major cause of violence, if it's even a cause at all. For all we really know, that something might be helping matters instead of hurting them.

In 1954 a similar public panic took place in the world of comic books. In retrospect the entire fuss appears ridiculous, but the public outcry led to the creation of the infamous comics code, forcing comic book publishers to "voluntarily" censor themselves to ward off direct governmental regulation. People were outraged by what they saw as gory, violent, and scandalous behavior in comic books, and, because comic books were read almost exclusively by the young (men-children had yet to make an appearance), do-gooders everywhere argued that such depictions surely had harmful effects upon the otherwise pristine youth of the land. According to the new comic book code rules, "good must always triumph over evil," "lurid, unsavory, gruesome illustrations" were not allowed, and absolutely banned, without doubt, were all instances of "sexual abnormalities"—a long list of which was helpfully included, such as seduction, rape, sadism, and masochism.[5] The goal was to remove stimulation of the "lower and baser emotions," and as a result hemlines were lowered and cleavage became a thing of the past, which seems barely credible given the state-of-the-art in the current comic-book world, which wholeheartedly embraces the scantiest possible outfits for the most buxom women.

Much scholarly work has investigated a possible link between comic book (fictional) violence and real-life parallels, and it's important to note that a stringent correlation is something many have eagerly sought, as it would scientifically confirm many people's view of likely cause and effect and would without doubt make the researcher's career. He or she would be a star. But direct correlations have been difficult to find. Simplistic cause-and-effect studies, such as a massive increase in violent behavior by those reading about fictional violence in comic books or novels for hours on end, proved elusive. Current scientific debate in this area is ongoing and heated, but all for the most part agree that the effect of media violence, if it exists at all, is most damaging to young children, but even for the young it's at most a minor effect, dwarfed by other tradeoffs accepted without qualm (such as allowing states to raise automobile speed limits, killing thousands of children a year[6]). Since our society is perfectly fine with accepting outsized risks to children's health and wellbeing through extremely obvious harm or death arising from high-speed automobile accidents, is worrying about possibly nonexistent but (if it exists) certainly minor emotional damage from media violence either sensible or logical? Isn't this a bit like focusing on the dangers of tooth cavities when faced with cancer?

The most convincing theory accounting for dropping teen crime rates does not depend upon psychological effects on the mind by simulated violence, enabling a cathartic draining of otherwise violent emotions, but the fact that when teenage boys are busy playing video games they are not wandering the streets, bored, and getting into a little or a lot of very serious trouble.[7] It's eminently reasonable to suggest that even if violent video games do trigger aggression in a small minority already primed for aggressive behavior, this effect is far overshadowed by the benefits of keeping teens off the streets and plugged into consoles. The overall gains seems to be positive if you just focus on generated violence.

Typical worries about the dangers of virtual violence in comic books or video games seem wildly overblown and ignore what is emerging as the real hazard. Significant harm comes from a genre of games that are relatively new and bereft of guns, bombs, and laser beams: games larded with manipulative machinations targeting the psychologically vulnerable, created by sophisticated experts capable of constructing games of maximum addictive power. These games are still a minority and relatively new to the scene. Many modern and retro games are not so manipulative, and they can serve as the basis for thriving subcultures with enthusiastic fans, capable of both inspiring and creating meaning. Video games are not necessarily bad, despite most of what I've written about them so far. There are plenty of positive examples.

GAMES INSPIRING THE GOOD LIFE

Like any other hobby indulged in moderation[8] video games can function as a source for real community in a way that's generative and intensely rewarding. Games can even be said to define a lifestyle that appears, from a distance, to have nothing but positive benefits. A good example is John Jacobsen, aka the host and producer of the *John's Arcade* YouTube channel—an insanely busy individual for whom pinball and arcade games have become part of his life's work and a huge source of fulfillment.

John's main venture is his YouTube channel, featuring videos that often exceed two hours in length and cover a variety of game topics: pinball reviews and playfield fixit tutorials; video game monitor capacitor replacement and general electrical troubleshooting; arcade cabinet bondo work and sanding and "rattle-canning" (spray painting); best methods for generating backlit replacement art for marquees; and his most watched video, with over a hundred thousand views—how to play the extremely rare and strange-looking half-length *Super Mario Brothers Mushroom World* pinball machine. That might be enough for a normal mortal, but

John's got another YouTube channel, *John Sucks at Video Games*, which features him playing various beloved video games extremely badly. John's also the host of the *Arcade Outsiders* podcast (focused on "Retro Arcade and Pinball Collectors"), which has one hundred episodes,[9] he's the former cohost of the *Warcraft Outsiders* podcast (focused on the game *Warcraft*),[10] and he's part of a joint business effort with Ian Kellogg selling *John's Arcade* branded cap (capacitor) kits,[11] and he even had the energy to organize an annual event ("BroFest") at Funspot (the "Largest Arcade in the World"),[12] as well as play in an indie rock band, *The Kill Screens*[13] (referencing the famous "kill screen" bug that ends the video game *Donkey Kong* after level 117). In addition John is married, has a full time job, and at least one child. This can't be a case of depressing and commonplace video-game addiction—John's functioning at *much* too high a level.

What John represents is the positive, beneficial, and even ennobling power of video games, which are able to expand the mind's attention toward the real world, rather than limit it through an obsessive inward and virtual focus. John's love of games has expanded his community of friends and contacts throughout the country and extended his understanding in fields as eclectic as music, electronic board repair, and graphic design—in short enriched his life in ways powerfully fulfilling. The key to John's positive relationship to games is that he is, in a word, *active*. Games are not a method of passively passing the time or escaping into distraction; games are a gateway to active involvement with other people, other hobbies, and other interests. If all gamers the world over were as active as John I would be writing a very different book.

Similar real-world complexity and a desire to tackle significant issues are found in games such as *That Dragon, Cancer*, which has pushed games closer to containing meaningful and complex emotional depth, as well as helping families struggling with cancer overcome the challenges they face.[14] The game centers around the autobiographical story of its primary creators, Ryan and Amy Green, whose son was diagnosed with rapid-onset cancer when he turned one, and who only lived another four years.

The game was created in response to this trauma; according to most game reviewers it's a noble and groundbreaking video game, unafraid to delve into territory infinitely distant emotionally and psychologically from guiding a yellow Pac-Man blob around a fixed screen as it eats dots of varying colors. It's more than possible for video games to expand the mind and broaden one's life. The question is how often this actually happens.

THE BENEFITS OF SPORTS

The ability of athletic games to "develop character" is spoken of with a reverence that makes one suspect such claims are being oversold, but a look at the basic research broadly supports the fundamental assertions, which argue that sports allow athletes to learn about cooperation, hone their bodies, and enable a suite of strategic and tactical centers in the brain to activate and expand. Athletics also comes with a broad array of cultural and social benefits. For example, collegiate scholarships are available for the gifted in a wide variety of sports, and more spectacular monetary rewards are offered for those capable of reaching the professional level, however tenuous the length of their stay. While the chance of becoming an NBA player is far better than the likelihood of winning the lottery (roughly .03 percent of high school basketball players turn pro but only one in 175 million win a state lottery), it's still a terrible percentage and an unrealistic goal for any but the best athletes. Yet this route to astonishing wealth functions as an oversized symbolic commentary on American individualism as filtered through a genetic mesh. If you work hard and are extremely tall and are extremely good at basketball and don't get injured and actually like training for the game and playing the game, it's possible to become a multimillionaire, or even a billionaire if you happen to be Michael Jordan, achieving fame and wealth beyond the average person's wildest (realistic) dreams. Such success is rare, and it's not clear if the downsides of pursuing this dream should be considered too severe, considering the heavy burden it places upon those who unrealistically view professional sports as not only a possibility but a probability—ignoring other paths far more likely to lead to prosperity.

Before any American has a chance to get to the professional ranks, they must first run the gauntlet through the assiduously regulated NCAA sports monopoly.[15] Most NCAA collegiate sports are modest both in participation and money needed (water polo, for example, can't be said to consume many university resources), but others are in an entirely different category. The leader of the pack is without doubt college football, which is astonishingly huge: "just the 123 teams in the Football Bowl Subdivision (the uppermost echelon of college sports) reported $3.2 billion in revenue in the last fiscal year."[16] And college football not only brings in the most money, it also spends the most.

College football is the third biggest sport in America by revenue, lagging the NFL by a few billion and professional baseball by far less—possibly no more than five million. Revenue does not equate to profit, however; the vast majority of college football programs are net losers, requiring subsidies from university budgets to keep operating given high voluntary costs (new stadiums, new training facilities, exploding coach and assistant coach salaries) and required expenses (NCAA-mandated administrative bureaucracy, athletic directors, PR departments).[17] Only 10 percent of football programs are profitable year to year, and these are the cream of the crop: all are in the top three college football conferences, and include names such as Texas, LSU, and Notre Dame. They are likely to remain profitable in the short- and long-term given their history of success, high name recognition, fan and alumni base, and huge television contracts, which lesser conferences and schools can't hope to match. It's a clearly delineated system of winners and losers, with very little movement between the two groups.

Europeans look with puzzled bewilderment at the fact that globally recognized schools such as Yale and Stanford spend an inordinate amount of money and time fielding football and other athletic teams, greatly impacting student-body composition. Students with impeccable academic records who otherwise might have been admitted are instead sidelined for the latest five-star linebacker of dubious academic value. Almost no European schools offer scholarships based on athletics; organized sports there are a casual and informal affair without a governing body like the NCAA controlling the process and handing down draconian and arbitrary decisions. There seems to be no good reason for American schools to focus so intensively on athletics given the public university mission to educate. What was the purpose and role of college sports in the first place? How did these games become so important that they overrode sensible objections about the best way to spend public funds, the best way to educate the public, the best way to operate a university?[18]

The ultimate source linking sports and school comes from part of the Roman poet Juvenal's *Satire X*, often translated as the following:

> You should pray for a healthy mind in a healthy body.
> Ask for a stout heart that has no fear of death,
> and deems length of days the least of Nature's gifts
> that can endure any kind of toil.[19]

The fundamental assertion of the poem, taken up by Locke and greatly expanded in his *Some Thoughts Concerning Education* (1693), is that the mind, viewed as a *tabula rasa* (a blank slate), requires three things to grow and achieve its maximal potential: 1) the development of a healthy body, 2) the formation of a virtuous character, and 3) the choice of an appropriate academic curriculum. As Locke puts is, games and play are crucial to the development of a child's education: "This gamesome humor, which is widely adopted by Nature to their Age and Temper, should rather be encouraged to keep up their Spirits, and improve their Strength and Health, than curbed, or restrained, and the chief Art too is to make all they have to do sport and play too."[20] This prescription isn't just for children; there is constant interplay in Locke between the mind and body, as a healthy body enables the mind to better learn, and a strong mind allows care of development of the body. "Sport and play" are part of the overall package.

Locke's work was hugely influential, and educators took the first sentence of *Some Thoughts Concerning Education* to heart: "A sound mind and a sound body, is a short, but full description of a Happy state in this world"[21]—clearly evoking Juvenal's *Mens sana in corpore sano* ("a healthy mind in a healthy body"). The point of athletics is to link the development of the mind with that of the body and vice versa; a feeble body can't, in Locke's view, help the mind flourish, but a strong and active body surely can.

Endless scientific studies have shown that a combination of intense exercise and intense academic work produce excellent results, as exercise hones the mind and prepares it for learning. European universities are not against sports; multiuse gymnasiums and swimming pools and tennis courts are widely available, and informal leagues pit teams against each other in spirited if relatively low-level amateur competition. In Europe sports are encouraged up to a point; the question isn't whether sports and education are in alignment—they can be. It's a matter of degree. At what point does a focus on sport overtake and damage the possibility of education?

Modern American college football has diverged radically from its initial goal of living harmoniously with education. Football has become an end unto itself. College players are faced with a daunting task when arriving to campus; the average time spent on football exceeds forty hours a week. That's over five hours a day, with games being played on Saturday, and Sunday consisting of recovery and postgame workouts and tape analysis and other preparatory tasks. It's not possible to "catch up" during the summer; off season proves no less intensive, with no time off for the weary.[22] Universities have players over a barrel in this regard. Rule changes have only recently allowed scholarships to be granted for a full four years regardless of subsequent athletic performance—yet almost no schools offer them, instead opting for one-year deals, forcing players to conform to expectations and make their coaches happy or risk having their scholarships removed. If a player is injured, the NCAA has no rule against immediately "cutting" the player from the team, taking away the scholarship and forcing them to leave school or pay their own way.

Scandals plague college football; the massive amounts of money flowing in from television contracts and ticket receipts almost ensure that NCAA rules will be flouted, ignored, or carefully stepped around. There has been widespread public outrage about the disparity between money going to those running the programs and the unpaid labor (student athletes), who are explicitly barred from monetary compensation[23]—yet people still love college football. What's the reason?

Considering how long the United States has been around, college football is ancient. The first game was played in 1869, and by 1950 it had been solidly entrenched in the culture, far bigger and more popular at the time than the newly born NFL. Because of their deep historical roots and immovable links to educational institutions—college football programs can't pick up and move to another city, as professional teams often do—college football is able to effortless evoke one of the most powerful and irrational human emotions: nostalgia. Even for students who never attended a game while they were in school, watching their alma mater's team moving down the field in color-coordinated school jerseys often brings to mind a four-year chunk of time that most people look back upon as if not the best period of one's life at least one far more engaging, immersive, and exciting than what they are currently experiencing. Former students aren't the only ones who get on board; a single fan can infect a whole family with football fever, and entire communities have grown up with a specific school as a mascot. "Half the people in that stadium can't spell LSU," famously stated James Carville, a Louisiana State University alumnus and former adviser to Bill Clinton, "It doesn't matter. They identify with it. It's culturally such a big deal."[24]

College football represents the ultimate power of games in our society. What might have once been a classically inspired sporting event meant to help students hone their body for the goal of education has been transformed into something far bigger, metastasized into a mutually reinforcing mix of symbols—football is military precision and conformity write large; football is nostalgia for one's previous self; football is regulation of chaos, with a massive rulebook overseeing the action and giving the illusion of perfect control; football is athletic prowess and occasional flashes of beauty; football lauds the goal of hiding one's individuality while at the same time promoting individual "stars"; football is unpredictable, violent, and unexpected, as is life. College football offers its fans immediate excitement and deep satisfaction and allows many—almost all—to overlook the hypocrisy of the NCAA, the poor treatment of the majority of players, and the undisputed perversion of public university's educational mandate.

The power of football is a warning, if one is needed at this point, to take games seriously. Sports are both big business and capable of driving otherwise rational human fans to acts of casual violence[25] more easily than almost any other human invention, excepting religion. It is nationalism written small: community building with all the good and ill that comes from it. Colleges and universities aren't the only institutions that promote sports, though; the government has a large and continuing investment in promoting sports on all levels for a variety of reasons, some of them exceedingly dubious. For example, the New York Yankees built a new stadium in 2009 that cost an estimated $2.5 billion dollars and used $1.2 billion of New York City municipal bonds to help finance it. Since the federal government can't tax interest on these types of bonds the money, which would otherwise have been taxed, wasn't. The results aren't pretty:

> The loss in federal tax revenues was even higher than the subsidy to the stadium. High-income taxpayers holding the bonds receive a windfall tax break, resulting in an even greater loss of revenue to the federal government. In the case of Yankee Stadium, the additional loss was $61

million. That is, the federal government subsidized the construction of Yankee Stadium to the tune of $431 million federal taxpayer dollars, and high-income bond holders received an additional $61 million.[26]

You might make the argument that such subsidies are a good thing because sport stadiums generate positive economic value over the long run, and that a stronger economy produces more tax revenue and that, eventually, the initial investment will be paid off and a net profit realized. You would be even more inclined to make such an argument if you were the millionaire/billionaire owner of one of these bond-financed stadiums, but real-world studies don't support the claim:

> There is little evidence that stadiums provide even local economic benefits. Decades of academic studies consistently find no discernible positive relationship between sports facilities and local economic development, income growth, or job creation. And local benefits aside, there is clearly no economic justification for federal subsidies for sports stadiums. Residents of, say, Wyoming, Maine, or Alaska have nothing to gain from the Washington-area football team's decision to locate in Virginia, Maryland, or the District of Columbia.[27]

Fixing this problem on a federal level would be a relatively trivial matter. The straightforward solution would involve changing the current law to ban federal tax-exempt financing for all private stadiums: problem solved. This change would remove the current incentives to seek city or state support for private stadiums and, like the rest of us when confronted by a large construction project, those building the stadium would seek financing from banks, Wall Street, or other sources of funding and pay interest on the loans with some of their millions.

The reason sport stadiums have these types of tax breaks (and other incentives) is predicated on the assumption that the value of sports is a net positive from a social or economic point of view and an activity that should be supported by the government. This is true not just in America; European countries are busy spending tax dollars on any number of sport-related projects. Is this rosy view of the worth of sports justified by the facts?

Fred Coalter, writing about English government spending on sports in *A Wider Social Role for Sport: Who's Keeping the Score?* concludes that there isn't much justification for it:

> In recent years sport has achieved an increasingly high profile as part of New Labour's social inclusion agenda, based on assumptions about its potential contribution to areas such as social and economic regeneration, crime reduction, health improvement and education achievement. However these new opportunities (welcome by many in sport) have been accompanied by a potential threat—evidence-based policy-making.[28]

Mr. Coalter had been commissioned to review historical and current research and identify evidence for the "presumed social and economic impacts of sport."[29] It had been imagined to be a slam-dunk: of course sports are good for the public health, of course they lower crime and improve morale. Mr. Coalter, to his surprise, and certainly to those he worked for, came to a conclusion warranted by the evidence but sourly viewed by many in the government:

> To the disappointment of the commissioning clients, all reviews have produced rather ambiguous and inconclusive conclusions—equivalent to the Scottish legal verdict of "not proven." There are no "killer facts" and few "best buys."[30]

The evidence on the ground is at best inconclusive, which means those campaigning on behalf of government-funded sport spending don't have a particularly strong position from which to justify continued expenditures for activities that can't be shown to generate benefits. It's throwing money into a pit. Why do governments continue to do it?

The question doesn't just concern money spent on programs that have poor evidence-based outcomes. Time spent playing sports, practicing sports, and recovering from sports injuries is time not used in other ways. It's the old problem of opportunity cost again—what's not being done because everyone is so busy getting ready for the next football season? Is there any way to tell for certain?

THE TOWN THAT KILLED FOOTBALL

Getting rid of a publicly funded sport has been done before. This is what happened: the Premont Independent School District, in Texas, in dire financial straits and suffering from poor academic performance across the board, decided to do something absurdly rational and suspend all organized sports. Expenditures were in dire misalignment: football cost $1,300 per player while math spending was only $618 per student. As soon as the news broke the Texas media was agog—this was unthinkable. No more football in Premont? The typical concerns floated to the surface: "How many football players would drop out? How many cheerleaders would transfer to the next town's school? How would kids learn about grit, teamwork, and fair play?"[31]

This experiment only happened because the school district didn't have any other choice. In a small high school (roughly 280 students) in a Texas town hit hard by low tax revenues following the diminishment of once-profitable oil fields, there wasn't much financial wiggle room. In addition to a low tax base, the school finances had been so mismanaged for the previous decade that the state was ready to swoop in and take over if the district didn't make serious changes fast. Ernest Singleton was the new school superintendent, with the unenviable task of righting the ship any way he saw fit. He probably didn't have any choice in the matter.

Because the school district was on the edge of dissolution, most people took the news better than they might have otherwise. The new year rolled around, and Singleton looked to see what effect, if any, the sports ban had had on the educational outcomes:

> "The first 12 weeks of school were the most peaceful beginning weeks I've ever witnessed at a high school," Singleton says. "It was calm. There was a level of energy devoted to planning and lessons, to after-school tutoring. I saw such a difference."[32]

We are not going to take Singleton at his word. He has a vested interest in putting a rosy spin on the outcome, whatever the outcome was. The best way to tell what effect banning sports had is to look at the hard evidence. In the first semester of the year, the number of students failing one or more classes in Premont dropped from 50 percent to 20 percent. During the first parent-teacher night, attendance shot up from 6 the previous year to 160. The number of fights in school dropped from roughly one every few weeks to almost nil. Every educational metric ticked up as school discipline and attendance problems tanked. What was the reason for the drastic improvement?

> [The former captain of the football team] missed the adrenaline rush of running out onto the field and the sense of purpose he got from the sport. But he began playing flag football for a club team on the weekends, and he admitted to one advantage during the week: "It did make you focus. There was just all this extra time. You never got behind on your work."[33]

The reasons aren't difficult to figure out. In 1927, Roy Henderson, the athletic director of the University Interscholastic League in Texas, was particularly clear-headed in his understanding of the role of sport in an educational system: "Football cannot be defended in the high school unless it is subordinated, controlled, and made to contribute something definite in the cause of education."[34]

The situation in Premont was clearly off-kilter from a perspective of resource management. The school district was spending too much money on the minority who actually participated in organized sports, taking away from the majority and hurting the school as a whole. The focus on sports also drained too much time and energy from the players swept up in the intense competition and weekly games, who viewed high school not as a place to learn but as a convenient location for the hosting of athletic events. To speak of the "culture of a school" is to delve into nebulous concepts that are easy to ridicule and hard to justify, but something did happen at Premont. There were fewer fights. Grades improved. There was less tension, more support, and greater parental involvement. The simple fact that the high school no longer had any reason to exist except to teach was a symbolic move that seems to have carried some weight. In addition to having more time to eat, sleep, and read, students were faced with the fact, every day, that the cultural and structural powers in charge had decided that sports were not what was important about high school—learning was. It mattered.

Sports did eventually return to Premont but in a far more limited form. Volleyball, cross-country, basketball, track, and tennis all made an appearance, with strict limitations on the number of games played and how often (and how far) they were allowed to travel during the season. These are low-cost sports with stable and preexisting infrastructure, requiring little or no upkeep, but the same can't be said of football, which has high yearly and ongoing costs. Unfortunately, after a 5 years hiatus, Premont reinstituted the football program in 2017. This looks like a case of refusing to see the truth despite it being thrust in front of one's eyes.

The story of Premont is easy to argue against by claiming it's just another anecdote and as such not particularly representative. It's not difficult to find student-athletes who are both athletes and students in deed, not just in word. They work hard, play hard, and manage to get a scholarship to a college that they otherwise would not have been able to attend. The "system" works for them and rewards their effort, and everyone is able to see the result and praise it. These are the bright points of light showing how sports and education can meaningfully interact. These student-athletes are easy to spot, often charismatic, and make for good stories. The downside of sports is generally hidden. It's very difficult to determine just how much a given school district spends on sports (including security and travel expenses). It's nearly impossible to notice somebody's grades slowly slipping because they are too worn out from football to do their homework or sleep well. The truly hidden activities are the ones that never take place: the teachers not hired because that money was dedicated to the sports team, the students who were never inspired by an art or music or math class because they lacked a dynamic teacher or facilities. These are hidden costs that all the students bear but don't make for a clear and easy argument. You can't really make an emotional appeal by pointing to lower class failure rates following the banning of football at Premont. Even though it's obviously true, these are dry statistics. What is indisputable is Jonny Throwgood's full scholarship to Dartmouth, which makes for an unfair fight.

Blindly giving in to rah-rah sports boosterism isn't acceptable. The simple story is the emotional story: everyone feels bad for the football players when their game is taken away. In the meantime, the United States is being outpaced in the global educational race: "American high-school students will once again display their limited skills in math and reading. They will once again be outscored not just by students in Poland but also by students in places like South Korea, Belgium, the Netherlands, Finland, Singapore, New Zealand, Canada, Switzerland, and Japan. (In the last round of PISA [Programme for International Student Assessment] tests, administered in 2009, US students ranked thirty-first in math and seventeenth in reading, among seventy-four countries.)"[35]

Most if not all of these countries spend far less per capita on education than the United States, and most also have limited organized sports at their high schools (and those that exist are vastly less important than sports at American schools). The problem isn't money, nor culture, nor early-age interventions or lack thereof. The biggest educational problem seems to be America's extreme focus on high school sports, athletics, and organized competition. Such things are perfectly fine in moderation, but that's no longer what we have, and it's no coincidence that the states with the worst high school educational rates are also those where sports, particularly high school football, are taken as seriously as religion. Texas is in the bottom ten states in the nation for the amount of money spent per student for educational instruction,[36] while at the same time the Katy (Texas) Independent School District recently opened a new $70 million dollar football stadium, the largest and most expensive in the country, which also comes with huge yearly maintenance expenses.[37] It's hard to see this type of thing as indicative of anything other than priorities wildly out of alignment. How can this be justified?

Yes, games and sports are sometimes fun, but before spending $70 million on a football stadium it must be definitively and convincingly argued that the stadium helps students learn. Needless to say, this argument wasn't made by the Katy School District, which had other very real concerns they should have been addressing:

> On the same day that *Covering Katy* [the local paper] discovered an additional $9 million was spent on the football stadium project with little fanfare, the school board was also attempting to figure out how to pay for school overcrowding.... Chief Operations Officer Thomas Gunnell was asked for an estimation of how many schools will be needed in the short-term to address growth. "Maybe four elementary schools. Maybe two junior highs and a high school," Gunnell responded.[38]

This is far worse than initially imagined. It's not just that the football stadium is taking away money that could be spent on student education. The school district was busy spending money on the football stadium instead of taking care of the most basic needs of their students: as many as seven new schools must be built to relieve current and soon-to-arrive overcrowding. This isn't a corner case where high school football can be said to potentially impact student educational outcomes. This is a clear case of high school football actively harming student educational outcomes in the most obvious way. Thankfully, the Katy School Board was recently shaken up in the 2016 elections when Joe Adams, a twenty-seven-year incumbent, was beaten by "education activist and blogger George Scott."[39] Joe Adams is asking for a recount and professes deep confusion as to why he lost: "[I] expected to win. I've been on the board 27 years, and I've done a great job. We really don't have an explanation."[40] Is it possible Joe Adams hasn't a clue? Sadly, the answer is probably yes. Who, after all, wouldn't want a $70 million dollar high school football stadium deep in the heart of Texas?

CHAPTER NINE
FLOODING THE COLOSSEUM

The facts speak for themselves: Americans are spending more money on games than ever before and *far* more time watching, playing, and talking about them. The game economy, broadly speaking, is growing four times as fast as the rest of the economy and shows no sign of slowing down—its growth rate is rapidly increasing, not levelling off.[1] At some point a limit will be reached: our economy and our time will achieve maximum gaming saturation. Where is that point, when will that time arrive, and what are the costs of getting to the end of that particular road?

I don't think it's as far away as we think. Games have achieved unprecedented economic and coercive power. The origin of their power lies deep in our biological roots—we did not all grow up making music or writing poetry, but we did all grow up creating and playing games. Despite the size and growth of games in our economic and cultural life, little attention has been paid to the dangers they pose for our short- and long-term health as a nation. Taken along with the entertainment sector (writ large) and the four trillion dollar healthcare sector, at least half of our national economy is consumed with entertaining us or keeping us healthy—both worthy goals but requiring a vast quantity of resources. Where is this taking us? Are we destined to become a nation of gamers, and is this a productive and worthy result?

HAVING TOO MUCH FUN TO WORK

The growth of gaming is an underreported topic with very few critics paying attention to what's going on, but there are a couple of important exceptions. Recently, people have woken up to the fact that many able-bodied men of working age are not choosing to work and are instead finding sufficient pleasure and challenge from video games to opt out of the everyday economy: "22 percent of men between the ages of 21 and 30 with less than a bachelor's degree reported not working in the previous year—up from only 9.5 percent in 2000."[2]

The problem isn't so much a lack of desire to work or some newfangled type of modern laziness. The issue is that work is nowhere near as rewarding as many of the games: "'When I play a game, I know if I have a few hours I will be rewarded,' [one of these young men] said. 'With a job, it's always been up in the air with the amount of work I put in and the reward.'"[3] The "reward" in this case is more than financial: it's emotional and clearly linked to competence and skill.

More disturbing from a social perspective but not for the individual gamers in question is that this group of unemployed but game-playing young men are actually happier than their peers:

> "Happiness has gone up for this group, despite employment percentages having fallen, and the percentage living with parents going up. And that's different than for any other group," says the University of Chicago's Erik Hurst, an economist at the Booth School of Business who helped lead the research.[4]

The source of this newfound happiness is video games: 75 percent of the time this group used to spend working is now dedicated to the computer, and the majority of that computer time is spent playing games. It's not only that more young men are playing video games, the real problem seems to be innovation in what researchers call "gaming/

recreational computing."[5] While it's typical for leisure time to expand and contract with increasing or decreasing opportunities for leisure activities (and how fun they are), what is happening now is different from in the past. What researchers claim in the 2017 paper "Leisure Luxuries and the Labor Supply of Young Men" is that innovations in gaming and recreational computing are the cause of about half the increase in video-game playing since 2004. This is a strong causal claim: it's not that young men are playing more games because they have more time, it's that they are playing more games in large part because the games themselves are more rewarding. Increasing sophistication in the video-game market, better targeting of potential customers, more manipulative and addictive gameplay—these are just as important as choices individual gamers are making about whether to play or not to play.

This sounds a bit fishy. Is it really possible to create demand and create more gamers who play longer just by enhancing the games being designed and released? This seems like an unlikely claim, but nobody has a problem when comparing it to a corollary from the world of television. The so-called Golden Age of American television, typified by shows such as *The Sopranos*, *The Wire*, and *Breaking Bad*, generated huge numbers of new viewers because of their higher-than-average quality and entertainment value. When thinking of television or movies we have no trouble assuming that better quality products drive increased audience numbers. People are still choosing to watch or not watch the television shows, but it's possible to distinguish between viewers who watch television regularly (and would have seen the shows anyway) and those who are drawn to television based upon their interest in specific high-quality shows (and who would otherwise not be watching television). The same sort of dynamic takes place in the video-game industry. More entertaining video games don't just reward current players but bring in new players and increase the time everyone spends playing them.

This sort of thing can be tracked, and that's exactly what was done. Cheaper gaming options, along with higher-quality video games across the board, contributed to the majority of the increase in time spent playing them. Salaries for young men don't lag those of their older peers for equivalent work. Demand for labor in the United States remains relatively high and robust. It's not that these men are having more problems finding work than they ever had before. Yet something is happening: "There is a large and growing segment of this population that appears detached from the labor market: 15 percent of younger men, excluding full-time students, worked zero weeks over the prior year as of 2016. The comparable number in 2000 was only 8 percent."[6]

The short-term pleasures of gaming are difficult to compare to the negative long-term effects of dropping out of the job market, not pushing for a better job, or failing to search for work as hard as one might. Gaming is an immediately enjoyable but empty pleasure; figuring out how to get a better job is difficult but might have significant and meaningful long-term value. I find it hard to imagine that any mature man will look back on a five-year slice of his twenties during which he was living with his parents and spending the majority of his time playing video games and consider it a positive experience. Yes, it might have been fun at the time, but it also represents a complete dereliction of responsibility. It's putting off the inevitable. You can't live with your parents your whole life. You can't get a less-depressing and higher-paying (or intellectually rewarding) job by not engaging with the real world. You can't meet real friends, go on trips, or find the love of your life by sitting at home playing video games. Doing so winnows away the possibilities for a dynamic life, stripping them down to the most basic level: the game.

This data shows the power of sophisticated and addictive games taken to the extreme: millions of young men opting out of the economy because the lure of games has become too strong—a force far more powerful than the more nebulous reward of economic benefits, societal expectations, or education beyond a high school or college degree. In one sense these are true rebels, unafraid of the charge that they are living in their parent's basement wasting their lives . . . their retort would be, simply, that they are doing what makes them happy. This emotional claim is hard to argue against, however damaging it might be to them or our country in the long run, since removing a growing portion of a generation of men from the workforce has huge consequences for our economy's long-term health. These men are not just missing out on prime earning and learning years, they are turning their back on further education, entrepreneurial opportunities, and the most fundamental unit of any society: family.

Will this slice of the generation ever decide to marry and have children, and if they do how long will it take? Can we conceive of a culture with so much easy-to-access gaming pleasure that the choice to reproduce seems, if not irrational, at least a very open question given that it necessarily cuts into one's gaming time. One possible result is augmenting the ongoing decline in global birth rates, which are already below replacement value in much of the world (the global leader for sub-replacement birth rate is Singapore, coming in at a shocking 0.85, meaning that every couple produces, on average, 0.85 of a child).

GAMES ARE DIFFERENT

The power of books comes from what they contain: the ideas and themes, the interplay of plot and character, the making and breaking of arguments. Books linger in the mind long after being read. Games draw their power from immediacy and ongoing interaction. We forget the sensation of reading a book but not the book itself; what is remembered about a video game is the experience of controlling one aspect of a virtual world, of being lost in that world, not the information contained within it.[7]

The immersive power of games, in particular modern video games, powerfully distinguishes them from other artistic genres. It is in part a natural byproduct of time spent interacting with them. Watching a movie can transport the viewer to another universe, but this universe is limited in time and bounded in space: two hours in a darkened movie theater.

Video games, particularly interactive online games, are essentially unlimited time sinks; even when a player runs out of content it's possible, and from a dedicated gamer's point of view necessary, to start over and play the game in a fresh way, with new virtual companions, in a different order, with different goals.

The games themselves are huge; *Grand Theft Auto 5* has over 250 hours of content for the typical player, assuming a single playthrough without restarts and maximizing efficiency in a way not to be found in the behavior of real-world players. The actual time spent playing a game such as *Grand Theft Auto 5* can consume months of real-world time; when players self-report their total time spent playing, automatically logged by the game, many totals are well in excess of fifty full days. That's 50 * 24 = 1,200 hours, or thirty full weeks of work, or twenty-five weekends where the player did nothing except play video games straight from morning until evening and back till morning. One former record holder for time spent playing *GTA 5* clocked in at over 218 full days, more than a year of daylight hours consumed by a single game.[8] It's rare for players to finish an open-game world to their satisfaction—there was still more fun to be had in one obscure corner or other.

This is something new to our human brains. A sufficiently complicated and flexible video game can engage serious players for week, months . . . even years. As such, they are hugely successful entertainment products, and they piggyback on American's longstanding love of games in various forms, digital or not: professional sports, gambling, college football, and the amateur pickup basketball games being played everywhere across the country.

Games can be engaging to the point of addiction, a fact blindingly obvious to anyone with rudimentary knowledge of "problem gamblers" the world over. Like the repetitive stories of drug addicts, all gamblers tell the same tale, deeply rooted in a universal biological drive. Games belong, unlike farming or quilting or organic chemistry, in a special class of behavior that includes opiate ingestion, binge-drinking alcohol, and frequent, random, and often dangerous sex. These activates have a repetitive pull sufficiently strong to create overwhelming addiction and objectively and subjectively ruin lives. Legal regulations and cultural norms typically constrain addictive substances and behaviors; everyone would think it not only obscene but unethical to give a child chewing tobacco before school, allowing them to "dip" on the bus and face first-grade mathematics with a keener mind. Yet parents routinely purchase games for their children with little thought of possible long-term consequences—there is no other addictive behavior whose dangers have been so blandly overlooked.

America overreacted to marijuana, giving us the "War on Drugs," yet we allow adults to vote and serve in the army before legally drinking a beer. There are few regulations concerning non-gambling games, which make up the vast majority of the overall gaming economy. Fussy legal definitions regarding what does and does not constitute gambling elide the fact that a slot machine dispensing virtual tokens for virtual games still returns a reward. The draw of the game, and the lure of gambling, does not depend upon cash changing hands. We recognize this with other addictive behaviors—trading a chunk of steak for a bottle of wine does not constrain the addictive allure of alcohol, nor is it considered a legal exchange for underage drinkers. It's not the money changing hands that's the problem, it's the effect of the exchange.

Modern video games have slipped through our legal and cultural filters.

A WARNING

We ought to be wary of the power of games, yet games and gaming are fundamental to our civilization and our human psyche; everyone played games growing up, either structured or on the fly, and, as we have seen, we share this drive with other mammals, who both play and include humans in their play, easily communicating the boundaries and "rules" of the game. A young child playing with a mature dog is a typical and unremarkable case; the child is allowed to push the dog much further than normal, trying his patience and possibly causing a small amount of discomfort, yet the dog comes back for more until he decides he's had enough. Playtime is over: the dog growls, turns, and walks away. The virtual world created by the dog/child interaction crumbles.

It's not surprising that Western democracies, flush with cash, advanced technology, and guarantees of personal safety vastly greater than any civilization in the history of the world, embrace fundamental drives such as gaming. The Romans found themselves in a comparable situation, and at the height of their power hosted Colosseum games of ludicrous extravagance both in expense and lives lost—Emperor Trajan once forced 10,000 gladiators to fight each other over the course of one hundred days to celebrate a military victory.[9] Trajan's absurdly expensive sacrifice ensured that the demanding public, temporarily sated with each arena-gaming advancement and visual titillation, required even more for future satisfaction.

Gladiator contests in ancient Rome were initially a modest spiritual ritual, spilling blood to reward and honor the dead. They soon metamorphosed into vast spectacles full of propaganda, money-grubbing on the part of the promoters, and naked manipulation. Money that could have been spent on infrastructure, the expensive Roman army and its pension load, and many other necessary projects was funneled with increasing speed into games of growing size and extravagance. The more the public grumbled and complained of food prices and taxation, the more eager the rulers were to produce games, mollifying critics through vast distraction. It was a vicious circle: more expensive games led to greater expectations and fewer benefits from every game, which increased the need and demand for such games, causing more taxation—and more disgruntlement. There was no point of equilibrium; attempts to limit the number of Colosseum games failed due to public pressure and outrage, and what had been a relief valve ultimately helped weaken and destroy Rome from within. This is a clear example of a gaming culture out of control in a way unhealthy for the body politic, yet unable or unwilling to change even if it hastened the destruction of Rome.

At what point can we say that our culture, and our economy, is spending too much money and time on games?

Games are often a pleasure and serve as a sometimes necessary retreat from reality by creating a virtual reality just as "real" during the game as anything you might point to in the "real world." The problem this poses for modern societies is multiform; the gaming economy is busy gobbling up a larger and larger share of our national attention and technological focus—dedicated gaming computers sport features that would have only existed on supercomputers fifteen years ago, for example—yet we suffer from a decaying infrastructure, an electrical grid teetering on obsolescence, and ever-growing education and income inequality. At the same time games have become intensely engaging; teams of PhD's work in unison to create the most immersive and addictive gaming experiences possible, leveraging our collective mental and biological weaknesses to keep us engaged and forever playing. Children are playing games at younger ages for longer periods of time; the complete conquering of our lives by smart phones allows for gaming at any time of the day, regardless of location.

There has been some pushback against this onrush of gaming; children are now barred from "in game" purchases after an initial and horrifying period that saw millions of dollars spent by button-clicking children behaving without any real understanding of what they were doing and very little parental oversight. But for the most part the fixes have been gentle and around the edges. And it's not just children who are having problems. Here is a shocking statement from the mouth of a game designer specializing in creating addictive products, as outlined in a rather horrifying how-to manual called *Hooked: How to Build Habit Forming Products*:

Seventy-nine percent of smartphone owners check their device within fifteen minutes of waking up every morning . . . one-third of Americans say they would rather give up sex than lose their cell phones. . . . Face it: We're hooked. The technologies we use have turned into compulsions, if not full-fledged addictions.[10]

It's well past time to reconsider what games mean to us personally and as a nation, and to focus on how they can be used and, more significantly, abused.

ADDICTION AND DISTRACTION: IT'S NOT JUST GAMES

Games aren't the only things that are creeping deeper into our minds and habits. What everyone expected to be true from their casual use of Facebook has been shown to be the case after a recent and thorough study of Facebook use by five thousand users over three years. On average Facebook makes everyone unhappier in the long run, and some people become extremely unhappy extremely quickly. Despite the facts found by the study ("Association of Facebook Use With Compromised Well-Being: A Longitudinal Study"),[11] actual Facebook use by the participants didn't significantly decline even though many people complained about its effect upon their mood and life. Why would anyone continue to use something that's so unpleasant?

Facebook cofounder and ex-president, the billionaire Sean Parker, was pretty clear about why this might be the case:

He explained that when Facebook was being developed the objective was: "How do we consume as much of your time and conscious attention as possible?" It was this mindset that led to the creation of features such as the "like" button that would give users "a little dopamine hit" to encourage them to upload more content.

"It's a social-validation feedback loop . . . exactly the kind of thing that a hacker like myself would come up with, because you're exploiting a vulnerability in human psychology."[12]

Sound familiar? Facebook used the same tricks as the *Candy Crush* game designers, and everyone in the "attention economy" is being pressured to do the same thing.

When the only way for a company to make money is to attract eyeballs to their site or app and maximize how long those eyeballs are viewing ads and using the interface, the long-term solution demands exactly what we find: an ongoing free-market frenzy to create the most addictive, hard-to-put-down, and time-consuming user experience possible. Disposable in this calculation is end-user fun or enjoyment, or the desire to give end users quality content in return for time consumed. Why is this the case? Because end users have shown themselves to be incapable of extracting themselves from their phones and apps even if what they are getting is obviously manipulative and has low informational content and is making them actively unhappy.

A very basic example of this type of interface arose early in the development of the public internet. It used to be the case that if you wanted to read a news article or blog post you would click on a link and read the article. That was in the naive early days, which now feel incredibly ancient. What quickly transpired was a "development" irritating to the end user and obviously put in place only for the bottom line of the hosting company: a single article was broken up and spread over many pages. The user reads the first bit and is forced to click on a link titled "next section" or some such to load a new page and read the next section, and then click on another link titled "next section" or some such to load a new page and read the next section, and so on.

What had been a smooth, easy-to-digest reading experience became an annoying clickfest for purely business reasons: more clicks on more links results in higher reported usage rates, higher ad revenue, and more user "engagement" (even if the user is irritated by being forced to hop through these sorts of hoops).

You might think people would revolt against such an overt and clunky manipulation of their behavior, but the pushback wasn't strong enough to stop anything.[13] For every person who grew annoyed and failed to click on the next link in order to read the next section there were hundreds if not thousands who did exactly that. In the long run, clicks and page-load numbers skyrocketed.

The current goal for many internet companies desirous of clicks and attention is to be as manipulative and annoying as possible up to the very limit of the end user's patience, which they are often able to calculate mathematically given the easy and powerful feedback mechanisms available to web-based businesses. They'll keep pushing their user base for more and more until people start to drop away, and then they'll scale back a bit and achieve equilibrium, whereby the unpleasantness of the current user experience is just below the drop-off point. The goal isn't to give users the best possible experience, it's to extract as much attention from them as possible, limited only by user annoyance, which *does* have a limit. Finding that limit is key. Making the end user happy isn't part of the equation.

Google doesn't get off any easier, nor does anyone else in Silicon Valley. Tristan Harris, formerly Google's "in-house design ethicist and product philosopher,"[14] had grown dissatisfied by what he viewed as an ongoing attempt by Google, Snapchat, LinkedIn, Facebook, YouTube, and other companies to actively control and guide people's behavior with very little attention paid to what they are doing from an ethical viewpoint. His essential take on the matter is this: "All of us are jacked into this system. . . . All of our minds can be hijacked. Our choices are not as free as we think they are."[15] As an example, he discusses the "variable rewards" mechanism whereby an action such as swiping across a phone after a notification gives different results depending on what is being fed to the user. The result of the action is the same jolt of excitement that drives gamblers: "Each time you're swiping down, it's like a slot machine. . . . You don't know what's coming next. Sometimes it's a beautiful photo. Sometimes it's just an ad."

James Williams, another ex-Google employee, who built the metrics system for Google's global search advertising business (this is one of Google's primary sources of revenue), makes a similar argument: "The attention economy incentivizes the design of technologies that grab our attention. . . . In so doing, it privileges our impulses over our intentions."[16] He views what's happening in Silicon Valley as part of the "largest, most standardized and most centralized form of attentional control in human history. . . . The dynamics of the attention economy are structurally set up to undermine the human will."

WHAT CAN BE DONE?
WE KNOW BUT DON'T WANT TO KNOW

I think it's incredibly important to realize that the people most vocal and clear in their claims about the ethical failings of the attention economy, the ongoing destruction of our ability to focus and concentrate, the additive potential of games and social networking sites, and all the other rather obvious but hard-to-face facts of our always-connected modern life are the same people who either helped create these systems or were intimately connected with them. If anyone knows what's going on they certainly do. If anyone is aware of how powerful and disturbing these control mechanisms are it's them. The solutions they offer are the same we already suspect to be true and have (sometimes) already attempted to implement on a personal level:

Block, Ban, and Take Back Control

Justin Rosenstein, who created Gchat at Google, installed programs on his phone and computer to block Reddit and ban Snapchat, and he uses parental-control applications to limit his internet time. Loren Brichter, creator of the addictive and now-ubiquitous "pull-to-refresh" app design feature, blocks various sites, disallowed all push notifications, and refuses to pick up his phone after 7:00 p.m. Leah Pearlman, a former Facebook employee who was part of the team that came up with the Facebook "like" feature, installed a plug-in to delete her Facebook news feed and hired a consultant to run her Facebook page so she never has to deal with it personally. The solution they offer isn't to force yourself to stop using these sites by sheer effort, or refrain from playing a game using willpower, but to install utilities and put procedures in place that make it difficult if not impossible for you to give in to momentary impulses and short-term desires that are, by and large, harmful.[17]

Be Aware of Your Addictive Behavior and Be Offended by Those Who Helped Create It

One of the most important things anyone can do is to regulate how they are spending their time, but it's not enough to consider and review time already spent on this or that activity. Take the next crucial step and consider what is *not being done* because of what is *being done*. Humans are not very good at this sort of thing because it involves speculating about an unknown variable. It's not clear what benefits might have accrued that are greater in the long run than the short-term distraction offered by another hour of playing *Candy Crush*. But if this is never considered, the long-term effects of short-term distraction from games, Facebook, or other addictive apps allow these products, as a group, to evade their collective responsibility for real-world effects. The ultimate goal of the attention economy is to capture your attention and keep it for as long as possible, and if this involves addiction in some form (minor or major) . . . that's a feature, not a bug. It's cowardly to let companies who embrace this as their business model off the hook for their attempt to capture and retain your attention, pulling you away from your family, the external world, and harming your wellbeing. Taking offense is the correct response; anger's even better if you can manage it. It's a game that's being played in your brain for control of your brain, and very few people are aware of the psychological warfare that occurs every time they turn on a smart phone. It's my hope that people will begin to realize that Facebook, Google, and modern video-game designers are not friends making tools or games that either simplify or enhance one's life, but cold-hearted businessmen leveraging biological weaknesses with one goal in mind: making money. If they make you miserable while pulling in record profits . . . they will. And they are.

Nir Eyal, the author of *Hooked: How to Build Habit-Forming Products* (mentioned above) and a recognized world expert at how to create manipulative and compulsive products, confessed his personal solution to the problem posed by the attention economy, which he put in place to protect his own family: His home's WiFi router is hooked up to a timed power-cutoff switch and stops transmitting the internet to everyone in the house at the same time every day. The man who helps companies design addictive products knows that the ultimate solution isn't personal willpower or "choosing" to stop visiting Facebook or playing *Call of Duty*. The true solution involves pulling the plug.

WHAT'S TO COME?

What's terrifying about the current state of affairs with gaming and the "attention economy" is both the ongoing damage being done to people's happiness and wellbeing and the incredibly strong effects that are being produced using relatively basic technology. A good iPhone with a fast connection can get you distracted into unhappiness, a primitive phone with a slow connection doesn't work quite as well—but it still works. If we take a step back and consider the ongoing and expected move from standard screen-based games to immersive virtual-reality (VR) games, the stakes rise considerably. VR games include sensory input mechanisms (visual, audio, tactile) but also sensory recording devices (for measuring heart rate, body temperature, and breathing speed). This puts both input and output data streams on an entirely new level compared to a middle-of-the-road smartphone, which begins to look a bit old fashioned from this not-too-distant future perspective.

It also places game developers in an entirely new and powerful position from which to control and guide players. *Candy Crush* has shown that humans can be manipulated by a sophisticated implementation of relatively primitive technology to realize hundreds of millions of dollars in profits; now that game companies know how to generate the effects they want, imagine how much more powerfully the next generation of VR games will be able to manipulate their players. Game designers will be able to carefully calibrate their game mechanics and in-game offerings to match a player's heart rate, put them in realistic 360-degree peril before asking for an extra life or upgrade, use all the tricks learned and implemented on a small screen and multiply their effect a thousandfold, surrounding players with a dazzling immersive experience that very few people would be able to resist.

The future might not turn out to be a tragic apocalyptic fancy of the sort cooked up by a moviemaker—a wasteland of ongoing danger and ever-present horror—but something far more staid. I'm not the first to suggest that technology is just as capable of enslaving as freeing, and there isn't much evidence to suggest that human beings in 2018 are very good, or have much interest in, limiting the power given to those offering pleasurable technological distractions. In my opinion, a far more likely future scenario, given the current state of affairs, would simply continue the status quo in greatly enhanced fashion: people willingly giving up their lives to virtual puppeteers in exchange for distraction, pleasure, and the immersive power of games—happily ignoring those controlling the action and gently tugging at this or that string.

ACKNOWLEDGMENTS

This book would not have been possible without the patience and literary acumen of my wife, Jennifer Wilder, during a "year to remember." She's absolutely irreplaceable and I love her dearly. I would also like to thank Sheree Bykofsky, my agent, and everyone who helped me understand how games are produced and distributed—particularly Ramin Shokrizade, who gave me an insider's view of what's going on. Many more helped in direct or indirect ways: Amy Reading and Jay Farmer for emotional support and helpful research material; the Constance Saltonstall Foundation, who got me into gear during a writing retreat; my parents for a game-filled and trauma-free childhood; Nancy and Tim Wilder for stepping up to the plate during various minor disasters and cheerfully lending a hand; the Prometheus team (Steven and Hanna and Mark and all the rest); and my long-suffering editor, Sheila Stewart, who was placed in a wringer as the handle was vigorously turned.

Last but certainly not least I'd like to thank my two daughters, Poppy and Effie, whose high spirits and ongoing support (variously indicated) made every day a bit easier and propelled me toward the finish line a bit faster.

NOTES

INTRODUCTION

    1. Nina Strochlic, "'Love Child' Game Over: Internet Addicts Let Their Baby Starve to Death," *Daily Beast*, July 21, 2014, http://www.thedailybeast.com/articles/2014/07/21/love-child-game-over-internet-addicts-let-their-baby-starve-to-death.html (accessed February 5, 2018).

    2. One twenty-two-year-old mother, Alexandra V. Tobias, shook her infant to death for interrupting her game of *FarmVille*. (Catharine Smith, "Mother Alexandra V. Tobias Shakes Baby for Interrupting FarmVille, Pleads Guilty to Murder," *Huffington Post*, October 28, 2010, https://www.huffingtonpost.com/2010/10/28/alexandra-v-tobias-farmville_n_775264.html [accessed April 16, 2018].)

    Tony Lamont Bragg Sr., twenty-four, grew angry with his infant for bothering him during a heated game of *EverQuest* and squeezed the interrupting infant so hard that his heart was punctured by a rib. The baby bled to death in a utility closet where he had been stuffed. ("Obsessed EverQuest Fan Found Guilty of Manslaughter," *IGN*, January 3, 2001, http://www.ign.com/articles/2001/01/04/obsessed-everquest-fan-found-guilty-of-manslaughter [accessed April 16, 2018].)

    Twenty-seven-year-old Tyrone Spellman beat his seventeen-month-old child to death for pulling down his Xbox console. (Susan Arendt, "Man Convicted of Killing Daughter over Xbox Accident," *Wired*, January 30, 2008, https://www.wired.com/2008/01/man-convicted-o/ [accessed April 16, 2018].)

    Christina Cordell left her child in a hot car while she played *EverQuest* (it turns out this game is notoriously addictive), and after a few hours the child died from overheating. (Thomas Layton, "Games Cited in Recent Deaths," Gamespot, August 28, 2003, https://www.gamespot.com/articles/games-cited-in-recent-deaths/1100-6074253/ [accessed April 16, 2018].)

    I could go on, as examples abound, but I haven't the heart.

CHAPTER ONE: BIRDS DO IT, BEES DON'T DO IT, BUT SOME PIG-FACED TURTLES DO IT

1. The pre-cocoon caterpillar ate quite a lot, so this is perhaps unjustified.

2. Gordon M. Burghardt, *The Genesis of Animal Play: Testing the Limits* (Cambridge, MA: MIT Press, 2005), p. 108.

3. For a good overview of the frustrations of animal researchers, see Lynda Sharpe, "So You Think You Know Why Animals Play . ." *Scientific American*, May 17, 2011, https://blogs.scientificamerican.com/guest-blog/so-you-think-you-know-why-animals-play/ (accessed February 5, 2018).

4. Robert Mitchell, in Burghardt, *Genesis of Animal Play*, p. 108.

5. The world consists of games, play, linguistic give-and-take based on power relationships . . . there is no objective reality; etc.

6. Of course, sophisticated evolutionary theory is incredibly complex and accepts outcomes such as spandrels as legitimate. Spandrels represent nonfunctional behavior or biological results arising as a byproduct of other functions. Play might be an adjunct to other evolutionary processes, and might not be independently functional.

7. A phrase never used by Darwin but taken up by his bulldog supporter Herbert Spencer during the "evolution wars" following the publication of *On the Origin of Species*.

8. Those shrimp (*Synalpheus regalis*), like bees, have a complicated social hierarchy. They have one "queen shrimp" and live in an underwater "hive" consisting of the well-defended interior of a host sponge.

9. Karl Groos, *The Play of Animals* (Boston: D. Appleton, 1898), p. 12.

10. Ibid.

11. For details, see Marc Bekoff and John A. Byers, *Animal Play: Evolutionary, Comparative, and Ecological Perspectives* (Cambridge, UK: Cambridge University Press, 1998), pp. 11–13.

12. Ibid.

13. Martha A. Mann and Roger L. Mellgren, "Sea Turtle Interactions with Inanimate Objects: Autogrooming or Play Behavior?" in *Proceedings of the Sixteenth Annual Symposium on Sea Turtle Biology and Conservation*, comp. Richard Byles and Yvonne Fernandez (NOAA Technical Memorandum NMFS-SEFSC-412, 1998), pp. 93–94, http://www.nmfs.noaa.gov/pr/pdfs/species/turtlesymposium1996.pdf (accessed April 5, 2018).

14. Burghardt, *Genesis of Animal Play*, p. 12.

15. Rachel Feltman, "Video Catches Space Geckos Playing," *Washington Post*, April 22, 2015, https://www.washingtonpost.com/news/speaking-of-science/wp/2015/04/22/video-catches-space-geckos-playing (accessed April 5, 2018).

16. Aaron M. Bauer, *Geckos: The Animal Answer Guide* (Baltimore: Johns Hopkins University Press, 2013), p. 54.

17. Valerij Barabanov, Victoria Gulimova, Rustam Berdiev, and Sergey Saveliev, "Object Play in Thick-Toed Geckos during a Space Experiment," *Journal of Ethology* 33, no. 2 (May 2015): 109–15.

18. Jaak Panksepp and Jeffrey Burgdorf, "Laughing Rats? Playful Tickling Arouses High-Frequency Ultrasonic Chirping in Young Rodents," in *Toward a Science of Consciousness III: The Third Tucson Discussions and Debates*, ed. Stuart R. Hameroff, Alfred W. Kaszniak, and David John Chalmers (Cambridge, MA: MIT Press, 1999), p. 231.

19. You could claim, from a rational/scientific perspective, that play is so important to the rats (for various reasons, many yet unknown) that evolution has generated a mechanism for allowing play to continue even when one rat is dominant, allowing other rats to hone their skills against the master. This elides the question: why do rats not wish to wrestle against another rat who never loses? You can still gain skills and knowledge from a loss. Why would a rat "throw" a competition? What does he have to gain, since further wrestling does not improve his skills (which can't be beat)?

20. Pankseep and Burgdorf, "Laughing Rats?" p. 231.

21. Ibid.

CHAPTER TWO: ALL WORK AND NO UNSTRUCTURED PLAY MAKES JANE WHINY

1. Lynda Sharpe, "So You Think You Know Why Animals Play . . ." *Scientific American*, May 17, 2011, https://blogs.scientificamerican.com/guest-blog/so-you-think-you-know-why -animals-play/ (accessed February 5, 2018).

2. Sergio M. Pellis, Lauren A. Williams, and Vivien C. Pellis, "Adult-Juvenile Play Fighting in Rats: Insight into the Experiences That Facilitate the Development of Socio-Cognitive Skills," *UCLA International Journal of Comparative Psychology* 30 (2017), https:// escholarship.org/uc/item/30b7d05g (accessed February 5, 2018).

3. Sergio M. Pellis, Vivien C. Pellis, and Heather C. Bell, "The Function of Play in the Development of the Social Brain," *American Journal of Play* 2, no. 3 (Winter 2010): 278–96.

4. Ben Adler, "When Did Letting Your Kids Walk Home Alone Become a Crime?" *Grist*, January 21, 2015, https://grist.org/cities/when-did-letting-your-kids-walk-home-alone-become-a-crime/ (accessed February 5, 2018). It should be noted that this was a case of police overreach, but it nevertheless indicates the depth of the "supervision" mindset.

5. George Lowery, "A Campus Takeover That Symbolized an Era of Change," *Cornell Chronicle*, April 16, 2009, http://news.cornell.edu/stories/2009/04/campus-takeover-symbolized-era-change (accessed February 5, 2018).

6. Ben Cosman, "Universities Are Cutting Tenured Faculty While They Load Up on 'Non-Academic' Administrators," *Atlantic*, February 7, 2014.

NOTES

7. Ibid.

8. Lee Hall, "I Am an Adjunct Professor Who Teaches Five Classes. I Earn Less than a Pet-Sitter," *Guardian*, June 22, 2015, https://www.theguardian.com/commentisfree/2015/jun/22/adjunct-professor-earn-less-than-pet-sitter (accessed March 15, 2018).

9. Mary Ellen Flannery, "The Homeless Professor Who Lives in Her Car," *neaToday*, November 1, 2017, http://neatoday.org/2017/11/01/homeless-professor/ (accessed February 5, 2018).

10. The rate of increase is staggering: "There are now two nonacademic employees at public and two and a half at private universities and colleges for every one full-time, tenure-track member of the faculty. 'In no other industry would overhead costs be allowed to grow at this rate—executives would lose their jobs'" (Jon Marcus, "New Analysis Shows Problematic Boom In Higher Ed Administrators," *Huffington Post*, February 6, 2014, https://www.huffingtonpost.com/2014/02/06/higher-ed-administrators-growth_n_4738584.html [accessed March 15, 2018].)

11. According to the US Department of Education's CSS statistics, criminal offenses on campus have been halved since 2005 and are at an all-time low, reported arrests are at an all-time low, etc. The only significant statistic showing an increase is "Reported Hate Crimes," moving from 44 in 2005 to 1,029 in 2015. Note that this is simply "reported" crime; there isn't any way to tell how many of these reports were determined to actually constitute a "hate crime." In any case, the total number of these types of events across all schools (11,306 campuses) isn't a serious social issue. "Hate crimes" are obviously bad things but extraordinarily rare, and indicate that the perpetrators of most criminal activity are not committing racial/gender/sexual orientation "hate-based violence."

12. Elizabeth Nolan Brown, "Moral Outrage Is Self-Serving, Say Psychologists," *Hit and Run* (blog), *Reason*, March 1, 2017, http://reason.com/blog/2017/03/01/moral-outrage-is-self-serving (accessed March 15, 2018).

13. Haidt is quite open about the effect upon his teaching and his own practice of self-censorship, causing him to actively change his syllabus to bow to student "offense-taking" pressure. Haidt states, "Under the 2013 Department of Education revised guidelines that we describe in the article [Lukianoff and Haidt, 'Coddling of the American Mind'], any student who deems what a professor says to be 'unwelcome' can file harassment charges. These charges must be adjudicated by some body created by the university. This adjudication forces the professor to spend dozens of hours to write defenses, sit through testimony, and respond to official emails. It is a nightmare and a time drain dropped into a busy semester. . . . [After] this happened to me too, in a more abbreviated form. I am now gun-shy; I am afraid of offending the most sensitive student that I can imagine, and so I am now a more cautious, less spontaneous, and less interesting teacher" (quoted in Chris Bodenner, "Are Professors Being the Oversensitive Ones?" *Atlantic*, August 31, 2015, https://www.theatlantic.com/notes/2015/08/are-professors-being-the-oversensitive-ones/402904/ (accessed March 15, 2018).

For student self-censorship, see the following: Emily Zanotti, "Study: Most College

Students Self-Censor, Support On-Campus Censorship," *Daily Wire*, October 12, 2017, https://www.dailywire.com/news/22217/study-most-college-students-self-censor-support -emily-zanotti (accessed March 15, 2018).

14. Ruth Sherlock, "How Political Correctness Rules in America's Student 'Safe Spaces,'" *Telegraph*, November 28, 2015, https://www.telegraph.co.uk/news/worldnews/northamerica/ usa/12022041/How-political-correctness-rules-in-Americas-student-safe-spaces.html (accessed March 15, 2018).

15. Consider the tale of Bret Weinstein at Evergreen State College (accused of racism for coming to campus on a day when white people were suggested to "absent themselves"), or Erika Christakis at Yale (accused of racism for a mild letter to students about Halloween costumes), or Lindsay Shepherd (accused of transphobia and racism after showing a short video from an extremely bland by-the-book Canadian televised debate about personal pronouns, of all things), etc.

For details, see:

Bret Weinstein—Bari Weiss, "When the Left Turns on Its Own," *New York Times*, June 1, 2017, https://www.nytimes.com/2017/06/01/opinion/when-the-left-turns-on-its-own.html (accessed March 15, 2018).

Erika Christakis—Conor Friedersdorf, "The Perils of Writing a Provocative Email at Yale," *Atlantic*, May 26, 2016, https://www.theatlantic.com/politics/archive/2016/05/the-peril-of -writing-a-provocative-email-at-yale/484418/ (accessed March 15, 2018).

Lindsay Shepherd—Aaron Hutchins, "What Really Happened at Wilfrid Laurier University," *Maclean's*, December 11, 2017, http://www.macleans.ca/lindsay-shepherd-wilfrid -laurier/ (accessed March 15, 2018).

16. "New Survey: Majority of College Students Self-Censor, Support Disinvitations, Don't Know Hate Speech Is Protected by First Amendment," FIRE, October 11, 2017, https:// www.thefire.org/new-survey-majority-of-college-students-self-censor-support-disinvitations -dont-know-hate-speech-is-protected-by-first-amendment/ (accessed February 5, 2018).

17. Susan Svrluga, "Someone Wrote 'Trump 2016' on Emory's Campus in Chalk. Some Students Said They No Longer Feel Safe," *New York Times*, March 24, 2016, https://www.washingtonpost.com/ news/grade-point/wp/2016/03/24/someone-wrote-trump-2016-on-emorys-campus-in-chalk-some -students-said-they-no-longer-feel-safe/?utm_term=.c3d490162141 (accessed February 5, 2018).

18. This strange document can be found here: SVP and Dean for Campus Life, *Policy 8.14: Respect for Open Expression Policy* (Atlanta, GA: Emory University Campus Life, last revised April 12, 2017), http://policies.emory.edu/8.14 (accessed February 5, 2018).

19. The quasi-legal details can be found here: *In Re Donald Trump Chalkings and Related Matters: Opinion of the Emory University Senate Standing Committee for Open Expression* (Atlanta, GA: Emory University, April 26, 2016), http://senate.emory.edu/documents/past _documents/Open%20Expression%20Trump.pdf (accessed February 5, 2018).

20. The one notable exception is, perhaps, Evergreen College, where a significant proportion of the student body was involved in relatively extreme protests, but even here it was not the *majority* of students, most of whom just wanted to go to class and graduate on time.

21. The more problems that are perceived to exist on campus, the greater the need for administrative oversight, increased number of employees, higher salaries, etc.

22. For an interesting first-person take on how Wall Street functions, see: Chris Arnade, "What I Saw as a Wall Street Trader: A Culture of Bad Behavior," *Guardian*, October 1, 2013, https://www.theguardian.com/global/2013/oct/01/wall-street-banks-shared-responsibility -risks-investing (accessed March 15, 2018).

In general, short-term profit incentives far outweigh long-term interests; even during the run-up to a bubble, traders will attempt to grab as much profit as possible, helping to inflate the bubble, rather than pulling back after recognizing that the future risks far outweigh slightly higher short-term individual gains.

23. "What Is Unconscious Bias?" UCSF Office of Diversity and Outreach, https:// diversity.ucsf.edu/resources/unconscious-bias (accessed March 15, 2018).

24. To get a better understanding of what the IAT was attempting to ferret out, see: Anthony G. Greenwald and Mahzarin R. Banaji, "Implicit Social Cognition: Attitudes, Self-Esteem, and Stereotypes," *Psychological Review* 102, no. 1 (January 1995): 4–27.

The IAT test design is explained in the following article: Anthony G. Greenwald, Debbie E. McGhee, and Jordan L. K. Schwartz, "Measuring Individual Differences in Implicit Cognition: The Implicit Association Test," *Journal of Personality and Social Psychology* 74, no. 6 (June 1998): 1464–80.

25. Jesse Singal, "Psychology's Favorite Tool for Measuring Racism Isn't Up to the Job: Almost Two Decades after Its Introduction, the Implicit Association Test Has Failed to Deliver on Its Lofty Promises," *The Cut*, January 11, 2017, https://www.thecut.com/2017/01/ psychologys-racism-measuring-tool-isnt-up-to-the-job.html (accessed February 5, 2018).

26. Patrick Forscher, Calvin Lai, Jordan Axt, Charles Ebersole, Michelle Herman, Patricia Devine, and Brian Nosek, "A Meta-Analysis of Change in Implicit Bias," PsyArXiv, October 5, 2017, https://psyarxiv.com/dv8tu/ (accessed February 5, 2018).

27. Singal, "Psychology's Favorite Tool for Measuring Racism Isn't Up to the Job." Singal notes research done by Jacquie Vorauer in Canada, who writes, "if completing the IAT enhances caution and inhibition, reduces self-efficacy, or primes categorical thinking, the test may instead have negative effects."

28. For an overview of the current situation (many scholars can't even agree on basic definitions, such as "subconscious," "subliminal," or "unconscious"), see: John A. Bargh and Ezequiel Morsella, "The Unconscious Mind," *Perspectives on Psychological Science* 3, no. 1 (January 2008): 73–79, https://www.ncbi.nlm.nih.gov/pmc/articles/PMC2440575/ (accessed March 15, 2018).

Freud, while definitely not a scientist, nevertheless had a huge effect on the topic and claimed "the unconscious" was extremely powerful, subtle, and in constant communication with "the conscious" mind and required years of hard work to modify. Far more rigorous researchers, such as psychologist Elizabeth Loftus, maintain that the "unconscious" is both dumb and primitive. You can find academic support for every assertion between these extremes; there is no accepted standard. The idea that it's easy to plumb the depths of the mind and tweak the unconscious/subconscious control centers is pure whimsy. If this were the case, drug addiction would be a thing of the past—simply tweak the unconscious impulses driving one to consume the drug.

29. Bonnie Klimes-Dougan and Chih-Yuan Steven Lee, "Suicide Prevention Public Service Announcements: Perceptions of Young Adults," *Crisis* 31, no. 5 (2010): 247–54.

30. Timothy Sawa and Lori Ward, "Sex Assault Reporting on Canadian Campuses Worryingly Low, Say Experts," CBC News, February 6, 2015, http://www.cbc.ca/news/canada/sex-assault-reporting-on-canadian-campuses-worryingly-low-say-experts-1.2948321 (accessed February 5, 2018).

31. Ibid. [Italics added.]

32. Ibid.

33. "Ryerson, Acadia University Statements on CBC's Campus Sexual Assaults report," CBC News, February 9, 2015, http://www.cbc.ca/news/canada/ryerson-acadia-university-statements-on-cbc-s-campus-sexual-assaults-report-1.2948917 (accessed March 15, 2018).

34. I'm not a libertarian by any stretch of the imagination, but sometimes things are taken to extremes, and it's worth wondering if these extremes are reasonable. White supremacists march through town bearing swastikas and burning crosses; sure, it's legal, and an instance of individuals using their individual rights to meet and march, but it's almost always going to end with violence (minor or major) and will exacerbate and inflame social tensions. Still, it's legal: we accept it as a part of a free society. The canonical instance here is gun rights: extreme positions taken regarding the second amendment, limiting laws controlling guns, inflict direct harm upon our society yet are accepted as a necessary outcome to individual liberties.

35. Amanda Hess, "How Drunk Is Too Drunk to Have Sex?" *Slate*, February 11, 2015, http://www.slate.com/articles/double_x/doublex/2015/02/drunk_sex_on_campus_universities_are_struggling_to_determine_when_intoxicated.html (accessed March 15, 2018).

36. Bradley Campbell and Jason Manning, "Microaggression and Moral Cultures," *Comparative Sociology* 13, no. 6 (January 2014): 692–726, https://www.researchgate.net/publication/272408166_Microaggression_and_Moral_Cultures (accessed February 5, 2018).

37. Ibid. [Italics added.]

CHAPTER THREE: MASSIVE SIZE IS MASSIVE

1. Bureau of Labor Statistics, "Consumer Expenditures (Annual) News Release," news release, August 29, 2017, https://www.bls.gov/news.release/cesan.htm (accessed February 5, 2018).

2. Entertainment Software Association, "US Video Game Industry Generates $30.4 Billion in Revenue for 2016," press release, January 19, 2017, http://www.theesa.com/article/u-s-video-game-industry-generates-30-4-billion-revenue-2016/ (accessed February 5, 2018).

3. "North America Sports Market Size from 2009 to 2021 (in Billion US Dollars)," Statista: The Statistics Portal, December 2017, https://www.statista.com/statistics/214960/revenue-of-the-north-american-sports-market/ (accessed March 19, 2018).

4. "The Outdoor Recreation Economy—Support an $887 Billion American Industry," Outdoor Industry Association, https://outdoorindustry.org/the-outdoor-recreation-economy-support-an-887-billion-american-industry/ (accessed March 19, 2018).

5. Robert Johnson, "US Grabs Biggest Global Gambling Industry Win Share in 2016," *Casino News Daily*, February 12, 2017, http://www.casinonewsdaily.com/2017/02/12/us-grabs-biggest-global-gambling-industry-win-share-2016/ (accessed March 19, 2018).

6. Felix Richter, "Gaming Is a $30 Billion Market in the US," Statista: The Statistics Portal, June 15, 2017, https://www.statista.com/chart/9838/consumer-spending-on-video-games/ (accessed March 19, 2018).

7. Milton Griepp, "Hobby Games Market Over $1.4 Billion," *ICv2*, July 20, 2017, https://icv2.com/articles/news/view/38012/hobby-games-market-over-1-4-billion (accessed March 19, 2018).

8. Owen Duffy, "Board Games' Golden Age: Sociable, Brilliant, and Driven by the Internet," *Guardian*, November 25, 2014, https://www.theguardian.com/technology/2014/nov/25/board-games-internet-playstation-xbox (accessed February 5, 2018).

9. Michael Kismet, "The Top Ten Board Games of All Time," *HobbyLark*, January 14, 2018, https://hobbylark.com/board-games/The-Top-Ten-Board-Games-Of-All-Time (accessed March 15, 2018).

10. Matthew Byrd, "When Did Dungeons & Dragons Become Cool?" *Screen Rant*, September 14, 2016, https://screenrant.com/dungeons-dragons-popularity-critical-role/ (accessed February 5, 2018).

11. In their paper "Getting the Ball Rolling: Basis for Assessing the Sports Economy," Stuart Russell, Douglas Barrios, and Matt Andrews attempt to tease out the difference between direct and indirect economic effects of sports on the economy. A popular model (the "Vilnius definition of sport") results in a revenue total that's roughly six times as big as the direct sport outlay. The authors term this excessive, stating, "We believe that definition of the sports economy is too broad." They suggest a much smaller multiplier (2x – 4x) and better data acquisition and reporting to get a more accurate estimate of the total economic impact. With this in mind, I'm using an extremely conservative multiplier: 1.5x. In other words, direct "sports/gaming" spending comes in at roughly $1 trillion for American in 2017, so it's reasonable (if not an underestimate) to assume the total contribution is at least $1.5 trillion. (Stuart Russell, Douglas Barrios, and Matt Andrews, "Getting the Ball Rolling: Basis for Assessing the Sports Economy," CID Working Paper No. 321, July 2016, https://growthlab.cid.harvard.edu/files/growthlab/files/cidwp_321_assessing_sports_economy.pdf (accessed March 15, 2018).

12. "CMS: US health care spending to reach nearly 20% of GDP by 2025," Advisory Board, February 16, 2017, https://www.advisory.com/daily-briefing/2017/02/16/spending-growth (accessed March 15, 2018).

13. "Table A-1. Time Spent in Detailed Primary Activities and Percent of the Civilian

Population Engaging in Each Activity, Averages per Day by Sex, 2016 Annual Averages," *American Time Use Survey*, Bureau of Labor Statistics, 2016, https://www.bls.gov/tus/a1_2016.pdf (accessed February 5, 2018).

14. Christopher Ingraham, "It's Not Just Young Men—Everyone's Playing a Lot More Video Games," *Washington Post*, July 11, 2017, https://www.washingtonpost.com/news/wonk/wp/2017/07/11/its-not-just-young-men-everyones-playing-a-lot-more-video-games (accessed February 5, 2018).

15. Ibid.

16. Ana Swanson, "Why Amazing Video Games Could Be Causing a Big Problem for America," *Washington Post*, September 23, 2016, https://www.washingtonpost.com/news/wonk/wp/2016/09/23/why-amazing-video-games-could-be-causing-a-big-problem-for-america/ (accessed March 15, 2018).

17. Allegra Frank, "Take a Look at the Average American Gamer in New Survey Findings," *Polygon*, April 29, 2016, https://www.polygon.com/2016/4/29/11539102/gaming-stats-2016-esa-essential-facts (accessed February 5, 2018).

18. Simon Khalaf and Lali Kesiraju, "US Consumers Time-Spent on Mobile Crosses 5 Hours a Day," *Flurry Analytics Blog*, March 2, 2017, http://flurrymobile.tumblr.com/post/157921590345/us-consumers-time-spent-on-mobile-crosses-5 (accessed February 5, 2018).

19. Feliz Solomon, "YouTube Could Be about to Overtake TV as America's Most Watched Platform," *Fortune*, February 28, 2017, http://fortune.com/2017/02/28/youtube-1-billion-hours-television/ (accessed February 5, 2018).

20. A typical high-quality example is "bandersentv" (YouTube channel, joined August 31, 2009, https://www.youtube.com/channel/UCJ6nWQ7UO-Lve9ji2FUNYwg [accessed February 5, 2018]), who focuses on antique television and radios, or "AvE" (YouTube channel, joined February 24, 2012, https://www.youtube.com/channel/UChWv6Pn_zP0rI6lgGt3MyfA [accessed February 5, 2018]), who focuses on tool reviews, electronic teardowns, and injecting a new type of grumpy foul-mouthed Canadian jargon into the American linguistic gumbo.

21. "The Most Subscribed Youtube Users," Trackanalytics, https://www.trackalytics.com/the-most-subscribed-youtube-users/page/1/ (accessed March 19, 2018).

22. Andrew Webster, "Cuphead: Creating a Game That Looks like a 1930s Cartoon," *Verge*, September 28, 2017, https://www.theverge.com/2017/9/28/16378364/cuphead-art-design-1930s-animation (accessed February 5, 2018).

23. The official YouTube category name for the type of video in which you record yourself playing a video game as content for upload.

24. For a typical example, see, "Please Don't Feel Bad Watching This Gameplay," YouTube video, 19:10, posted by PewDiePie, October 7, 2017, https://www.youtube.com/watch?v=P5mnhYQC9qU (accessed March 19, 2018).

25. The numbers vary over time and content provider, but a typical estimate from a real-world experiment/example can be found here, and results in a claim of $2,000 per million views: Team Filmora, "How Much Does YouTube Pay for 1 Million Views?" *Growing Your*

Channel (blog), Filmora, November 8, 2017, https://www.filmora.io/community-blog/how
-much-does-youtube-pay-for-1-million-views-295.html (accessed March 15, 2018).

26. Julia Reiss, "Controversial YouTube Star PewDiePie No Longer the Richest YouTuber
in the World," *Complex*, December 8, 2017, http://www.complex.com/pop-culture/2017/12/
pewdiepie-no-longer-richest-youtuber (accessed February 5, 2018).

27. "YouTube's Demonetizing Algorithm Should be DESTROYED," YouTube video,
5:30, posted by The Guitologist, November 20, 2017, https://www.youtube.com/watch
?v=3e6sDc3IwX8 (accessed March 15, 2018).

28. Zontar, reply to "Youtube Demonetization," *Escapist* (forums), September 29, 2017,
http://www.escapistmagazine.com/forums/jump/18.1022773.24131828 (accessed March 15,
2018) [italics added].

29. "Advertiser-Friendly Content Guidelines," YouTube Help, 2018, https://support
.google.com/youtube/answer/6162278?hl=en (accessed February 5, 2018).

30. Robert Kraychick, "YouTube Demonetizes ANOTHER Dissident Channel," *Daily
Wire*, September 7, 2017, https://www.dailywire.com/news/20788/youtube-demonetizes
-another-dissident-channel-robert-kraychik (accessed February 5, 2018).

31. Sahil Patel, "The 'Demonetized': YouTube's Brand-Safety Crackdown Has Collateral
Damage," *Digiday*, September 6, 2017, https://digiday.com/media/advertisers-may-have
-returned-to-youtube-but-creators-are-still-losing-out-on-revenue/ (accessed February 5, 2018).

32. A site unrelated to YouTube that allows direct monetary support of YouTube and other
content creators, based upon the historical artistic "patron model."

33. Jonathan Ore, "Is Playing Video Games on YouTube a Copyright Infringement?
No One Wants to Find Out," CBS News, October 7, 2017, http://www.cbc.ca/news/
entertainment/youtube-gaming-pewdiepie-fair-use-1.4309312 (accessed March 19, 2018).

34. LDShadowLady, "Description," YouTube, joined January 9, 2010, https://www
.youtube.com/user/ldshadowlady/about (accessed February 5, 2018).

35. Dr. Brent Conrad, "Media Statistics: Children's Use of TV, Internet, and Video
Games," TechAddiction, last updated February 5, 2018, http://www.techaddiction.ca/media
-statistics.html (accessed February 5, 2018).

36. Shannon Younger, "Kids and Video Games: What Games Are Safe, and How Much
Should They Play?" *ChicagoNow* (blog), February 27, 2013, http://www.chicagonow.com/
between-us-parents/2013/02/kids-video-games-safe-benefits-length-time-play/ (accessed
February 5, 2018).

37. Jacqueline Howard, "Kids Under 9 Spend More Than 2 Hours a Day on Screen,
Report Shows," CNN, October 19, 2017, https://www.cnn.com/2017/10/19/health/children
-smartphone-tablet-use-report/index.html (accessed April 10, 2018).

CHAPTER FOUR: ANATOMY OF A BESTSELLER

1. Both John F. Kennedy and Henry Kissinger were big fans of *Diplomacy*; for a reason why, see Haoran Un, "Diplomacy: The Most Evil Board Game Ever Made," Lifehacker, November 10, 2017, https://www.lifehacker.com.au/2017/11/diplomacy-the-most-evil-board-game-ever-made/ (accessed February 6, 2018).

2. A typical formulation of this argument (sometimes called "radical relativism" but sometimes considered a not-very-interesting flavor of postmodernism) goes as follows:

> To privilege one reading as normative (the one correct interpretation) would be to priv-ilege one contingent situationality or tradition over another—a move that would be impossible to justify precisely because of the locatedness of any such justification. There is not *a* reading that is *the* reading of the world or a text.

(James K. A. Smith, *The Fall of Interpretation: Philosophical Foundations for a Creational Hermeneutic* (Downers Grove, IL: InterVarsity Press, 2000), page 164.)

3. It's obvious to every book reviewer that Johnson is an excellent writer and able to carry the reader along into unusual historical cul-de-sacs, but the overall thesis of *Wonderland: How Play Made the Modern World* (New York: Riverhead Books, 2016) is incredibly broad: "Johnson's idea of play is fuzzier: it includes fashion, shopping, food, taste, phantasmagoria, magic, sport, gambling, coffee houses, mountaineering and zoos. With a little finessing, his book might easily have been a history of serendipity or of aimless curiosity." Joe Moran, "Wonderland: How Play Made the Modern World by Steven Johnson Review—The Future Is Fun," *Guardian*, March 2, 2017, https://www.theguardian.com/books/2017/mar/02/how-play-made-the-modern-world-by-steven-johnson-review (accessed February 6, 2018).

4. Marc Prensky, "H. Sapiens Digital: From Digital Immigrants and Digital Natives to Digital Wisdom," *Innovate: Journal of Online Education* 5, no. 3, article 1 (February/March 2009).

5. Richard Van Eck, "Digital Game-Based Learning: It's Not Just the Digital Natives Who Are Restless," *EDUCAUSE Review* 41, no. 2 (March/April 2006): 16–30, available online at: https://er.educause.edu/articles/2006/1/digital-gamebased-learning-its-not-just-the-digital-natives-who-are-restless (accessed February 6, 2018).

6. Tom Chatfield, "Rage against the Machines," *Prospect Magazine* (June 2008), available online at: http://tomchatfield.net/portfolio/rage-against-the-machines/ (accessed February 6, 2008).

7. In my and many other people's view, Gladwell's not to be trusted with either history or science. In his *New York Times* book review of *What the Dog Saw*, Steven Pinker took him to task and in the process coined a new term: "In the spirit of Gladwell, who likes to give portentous names to his aperçus, I will call this the Igon Value Problem: when a writer's education on a topic consists in interviewing an expert, he is apt to offer generalizations that are

banal, obtuse or flat wrong" (Steven Pinker, "Malcolm Gladwell, Eclectic Detective," *New York Times*, November 7, 2009, https://www.nytimes.com/2009/11/15/books/review/Pinker-t.html [accessed April 16, 2018]).

Gladwell responds to such criticism in the following way: "I am a story-teller, and I look to academic research . . . for ways of augmenting story-telling. The reason I don't do things their way is because their way has a cost: it makes their writing inaccessible. If you are someone who has as their goal . . . to reach a lay audience . . . you can't do it their way. . . . [A]s I've written more books I've realized there are certain things that writers and critics prize, and readers don't. So we're obsessed with things like coherence, consistency, neatness of argument. Readers are indifferent to those things." This extremely illuminating quote can be found in Christopher Chabris, "Why Malcolm Gladwell Matters (And Why That's Unfortunate)," *Christopher Chabris* (blog), October 4, 2013, http://blog.chabris.com/2013/10/why-malcolm-gladwell-matters -and-why.html (accessed February 6, 2018). Gladwell openly states that he's not worried about "coherence."

8. Brad King, "Malcolm Gladwell Book Review on Games and Popular Culture," *MIT Technology Review*, May 23, 2005, https://www.technologyreview.com/s/404133/malcolm -gladwell-book-review-on-games-and-popular-culture (accessed February 6, 2018).

9. Nicolas Carr, "Grand Theft Attention: Video Games and the Brain," *Rough Type* (blog), April 1, 2011, http://www.roughtype.com/?p=1471 (accessed February 6, 2018). Carr, however, is extremely critical of both Gladwell and Johnson—he's citing Johnson's importance as an early writer on the subject, not as a trusted thinker.

10. General intelligence (GI) is extremely well-documented in the literature, and modern intelligence testing is sophisticated enough to pick out and predict long-term trends in people's lives to a statistically significant degree. In other words, higher scores on modern IQ tests indicate higher levels of GI, which map directly to longer life, greater happiness, better careers, and more emotional stability. The findings also map onto common sense: it's far better to be smart than dumb, and the smarter you are the better your general outcome. This is a statistical assertion, so individual instances vary; plenty of very smart people are extremely unhappy or living hand-to-mouth. There are just fewer of them by percentage than in the general population, and far fewer than found on the left side of the IQ bell curve. The old canard that IQ tests only test ability to take IQ tests, or that IQ tests are somehow culturally biased (an extremely easy problem to solve should it appear), simply mask their power. Our culture is uncomfortable with difference despite proclaiming our love of difference. It's easier to believe that tests can't in fact tease out an ingrained biological function such as GI, which has shown itself to be resistant to positive (not negative) environmental forces. You can negatively affect a child's GI with beatings and deprivation, or return them to their natural baseline state with good treatment instead of ill, but nobody has yet figured out a way to generate long-lasting GI increases. It's almost as if our culture resists engaging with things that are relatively immutable but hugely impactful.

11. Steven Johnson, *Everything Bad Is Good for You* (New York: Riverhead Books, 2005), p. 27.

12. Ibid.

13. Johnson is a stylistically excellent and convincing writer even if what he's writing about is probably, or certainly, false.

14. The point of talking about a border wall was never to build a border wall but to clearly point out that the speaker is somebody who cares about borders, both concrete (keeping others out of our country) and metaphorical (marriage means a man and a woman, neither more nor less; what is good for the world is not necessarily good for America; there do exist clear-cut distinctions between us/them; morality is not a broad swath of grey between the fuzzy endpoints of good and bad; etc.). A world with strict and distinct borders is a better place than one where people, and ideas, and money, are free to circulate around the world. It's one of the paradigmatic if often-unspoken tenants of conservatism that "fences make good neighbors." A key point is that rhetoric often flatters and convinces a listener without making crucial claims about the way the world actually functions—the truth value of a given speech act is secondary or insignificant. This is a good parallel to how faux contrarianism works, which flatters and panders as it attempts to convince and only engages shallowly with hard data and critical-minded objections. The ultimate point isn't to teach and explain how the complex world functions, it's to pacify and quell potential change while augmenting the status quo.

CHAPTER FIVE: *CANDY CRUSH*(ING) THE COMPETITION, AND HARPOONING WHALES

1. As the most profitable video game ever made, *Candy Crush* is going to have a long highly monetized afterlife. It's been so successful that some of its sequels have escaped the bounds of gaming, such as the *Candy Crush* live-action television show, which debuted on July 9, 2017, on CBS.

2. I'm using *Candy Crush* generically to describe both *Candy Crush* (as a Facebook or web game) and *Candy Crush Saga* (which was ported to mobile devices of all kinds, and has almost identical gameplay). When there are exceptions, I call them out directly.

3. Emilee Pham, "Why I Absolutely Hate Candy Crush" SF State Entertainment News: Uloop, March 30, 2013, http://sfsu.uloop.com/news/view.php/76601/why-i-absolutely-hate-candy-crush (accessed February 6, 2018).

Similar articles and complaints are legion, from across society. Here is an example from the bleeding edge: June Thomas, "Sugar Coma: Candy Crush Teaches Me Nothing and Steals My Time and Money. I Can't Stop Playing It," *Slate*, July 3, 2013, http://www.slate.com/articles/technology/technology/2013/07/candy_crush_saga_the_most_addictive_game_since_angry_birds.html (accessed February 6, 2018), and here is one from everyday people: Rheana Murray, "Cautionary Tales from People Obsessed with Candy Crush," ABC News, November

6, 2014, http://abcnews.go.com/Technology/cautionary-tales-people-obsessed-candy-crush/story?id=26712231 (accessed February 6, 2018).

4. Loulla-Mae Eleftheriou-Smith, "Tory MP Nigel Mills Admits to Playing Candy Crush on His iPad during Parliamentary Meeting," *Independent*, December 8, 2014, http://www.independent.co.uk/news/uk/politics/tory-mp-admits-to-playing-candy-crush-on-his-ipad-during-parliamentary-meeting-9909436.html (accessed February 6, 2018).

5. Murray, "Cautionary Tales."

6. Consumer complaints about *Candy Crush* fill the internet to a degree not seen with any previous game. Most take the form, "I used to love the game but now I can't stop playing."

7. Ramin was "tapped in 2013 to advise over 70 governments on this issue at the ICPEN summit in Panama as they were crafting regulations primarily for the EU governing how these products could be sold to children." (Ramin Shokrizade, private email correspondence, November 2016.)

8. Ibid.

9. You have to identify (match) three or more symbols in a randomized grid or table in order to make progress.

10. "Towards the End of Poverty," *Economist*, June 1, 2013, http://www.economist.com/news/leaders/21578665-nearly-1-billion-people-have-been-taken-out-extreme-poverty-20-years-world-should-aim (accessed February 6, 2018).

11. Max Roser and Esteban Ortiz-Ospina, "Global Extreme Poverty," Our World in Data, March 27, 2017, https://ourworldindata.org/extreme-poverty/ (accessed February 6, 2018).

12. Clive Crook, "Why Does Capitalism Get Such a Bum Rap?" *Atlantic*, May 2005, https://www.theatlantic.com/magazine/archive/2005/05/why-does-capitalism-get-such-a-bum-rap/304032/ (accessed March 18, 2018).

13. Elizabeth Day, "Candy Crush Saga: Sweet Success for Global Flavour of the Moment," *Guardian*, May 11, 2014, https://www.theguardian.com/technology/2014/may/11/candy-crush-saga-games (accessed March 18, 2018).

14. Shokrizade, private email correspondence.

15. Note: these rooms might otherwise be empty had the casino not filled them with "winners," essentially costing them nothing.

16. Bill Friedman, "Casino Design and Its Impact on Player Behavior," in *Stripping Las Vegas: A Contextual Review of Casino Resort Architecture*, ed. Karin Jaschke and Silke Ötsch (Weimar, Germany: Bauhaus-Universität, 2003), p. 70.

17. It's a chaotic environment, barn-like with a high ceiling, and everything is extremely bright, loud, dynamic, and ever-changing.

18. Anthony Curtis, "What's the Deal with Casino Carpeting?" Las Vegas Advisor, https://www.lasvegasadvisor.com/faq/general/casino-carpet/ (accessed February 6, 2018).

19. Excepting, perhaps, European cathedrals, which aim for the exact opposite goals: beauty and inspiration.

20. David G. Schwartz, "*Nevada Gaming Revenues, 1984–2016: Calendar Year Results*

for Selected Reporting Areas" (Las Vegas: Center for Gaming Research, University Libraries, University of Nevada Las Vegas, January 2017), http://gaming.unlv.edu/reports/NV_1984 _present.pdf (accessed February 8, 2018).

21. "Historical Las Vegas Visitor Statistics (1970–2015)," Las Vegas Convention and Visitors Authority, 2016, http://www.lvcva.com/includes/content/images/media/docs/ Historical-1970-to-2015.pdf (accessed February 6, 2018).

22. Jim Motavalli, "The Cantankerous Mr. Wynn: Why the Las Vegas Hotelier, 72, Thinks He's Got Another Hotel to Build," *Success*, August 12, 2014, http://www.success.com/article/ the-cantankerous-mr-wynn (accessed February 6, 2018).

23. Later versions of the game, *Candy Crush Saga* and the like, include levels where the goals are slightly different, but the process to achieve them is always the same: Match 3.

24. It's actually fewer since the width of the piece and the current board configuration likely inhibits possible moves, but the total number of moves remains far too huge to calculate.

25. After ten pieces fall there are 48^{10} possible board combinations, which is a number so large it would take a supercomputer years to calculate all the possible board configurations.

26. Stories of players of being "stuck" on a given *Candy Crush* level are legendary; people sometimes spend a week or more getting past a particularly difficult level, which should make it overwhelmingly clear that moving past the chokepoint is simply a matter of time—it depends on the right board configuration, which depends on luck. If there is skill involved it has such a minor effect that a week's worth of playing is still needed to get the job done.

27. Brendan Sinclair, "No One Is Actually Good at Candy Crush," GameIndustry.biz, November 11, 2015, https://www.gamesindustry.biz/articles/2015-11-11-no-one-is-actually -good-at-candy-crush-divnich (accessed March 15, 2018).

28. Stokes, "When Games Pretend to Be Games They Aren't," Overthinking It, September 5, 2013, https://www.overthinkingit.com/2013/09/05/candy-crush/ (accessed March 13, 2018).

29. Free at first. The original *Candy Crush* has a capped upper-level limit, and if you reach that using the free game the game is essentially over; for more levels you are forced to pay. As such, it is really an example of a free but gimped version of the full game, despite the upper limit of free play being very high.

30. Kevin Spence, "Candy Crush Represents Everything That's Wrong with Mobile Gaming," *GameSkinny*, April 4, 2013, https://www.gameskinny.com/1b054/candy-crush -represents-everything-thats-wrong-with-mobile-gaming (accessed March 13, 2018).

31. This is not *technically* true; it's possible to spend a fair amount of money on upgrades or other in-game benefits to a basic game, but even these totals are rather low. Even a big spender will only pay two to three times the cost of the initial game for upgrades and the like. In general, this type of "in-game content" is looked down upon by serious gamers as offending their sense of fairness; anteing up for a more-powerful, gun-in-an-arena combat setting simply rewards those willing to pay with a competitive advantage. Game companies have been careful not to cross this barrier; if "average" players feel that they need to spend money to achieve competitive balance, the game is in danger of tanking (i.e., losing all of its average customers, causing the online gaming

community to death-spiral). This is a long-term money losing strategy. More typical is what you can purchase in the video game *Overwatch*—cosmetic "skins" giving your character a unique look not available to the average gamer, but having absolutely no effect upon actual game play.

32. Dean Takahashi, "Candy Crush Saga: 2.73 Billion Downloads in Five Years and Still Counting," VentureBeat, November 17, 2017, https://venturebeat.com/2017/11/17/candy -crush-saga-2-73-billion-downloads-in-five-years-and-still-counting/ (accessed March 13, 2018).

33. Shokrizade, private email correspondence.

34. Ibid.

35. For a really interesting look at what makes things cute, see Sianne Ngai, *Our Aesthetic Categories: Zany, Cute, Interesting* (Cambridge, MA: Harvard University Press, 2012).

36. This is a well-known division in game development. Chess is a game of skill since there is no way to spend money within the game to achieve an advantage; however, there also exist games termed money games, where the player who spends the most money gains disproportional and overwhelming advantages over non-spending players. Many of these are extremely straightforward, and some even include auctions where players bid real money for the most powerful weapon or item, which essentially allows for an in-game insta-win by spending the most money. These sorts of games have a short lifetime as players quickly grow bored with them due to the unequal competitive playing field, but they are often able to make serious money during the initial buzz of excitement and engagement.

37. Ramin Shokrizade, "Mastering F2P: The Titanic Effect," *Gamasutra* (blog), October 16, 2016, https://www.gamasutra.com/blogs/RaminShokrizade/20131016/202489/ Mastering_F2P_The_Titanic_Effect.php (accessed February 6, 2018).

38. Ramin Shokrizade, "Monetizing Children," *Gamasutra* (blog), June 20, 2013, https:// www.gamasutra.com/blogs/RaminShokrizade/20130620/194429/Monetizing_Children.php (accessed February 8, 2018).

39. Ramin Shokrizade, "Secrets of F2P: Threat Generation," *Gamasutra* (blog), 10/05/15, https://www.gamasutra.com/blogs/RaminShokrizade/20151005/255285/Secrets_of_F2P _Threat_Generation.php (accessed March 15, 2018).

40. I have to admit to finding myself utterly flabbergasted that anyone in their right mind would pay anything for such a trivial, superficial effect that had no in-game advantage at all. The whole "skin" economy is a mystery to me.

41. Jeff Grubb, "Belgium Pushes to Ban Loot Boxes in Europe," VentureBeat, November 21, 2017, https://venturebeat.com/2017/11/21/belgiums-gaming-commission-pushes-to-ban -loot-boxes-in-europe/ (accessed March 16, 2018).

42. Ramin Shokrizade, "The Top F2P Monetization Tricks," *Gamasutra* (blog), June 26, 2013, https://www.gamasutra.com/blogs/RaminShokrizade/20130626/194933/The_Top _F2P_Monetization_Tricks.php (accessed February 6, 2018).

43. Charlotte Alter, "FDA Warns Antipsychotic Drug Can Cause Compulsive Sex and Gambling," *Time*, May 3, 2016, http://time.com/4317182/abilify-aristada-aripiprazole-sex -gambling/ (accessed February 6, 2018).

44. M. L. Nestel, "Patients Say Abilify Turned Them into Compulsive Gamblers and Sex Addicts," *Daily Beast*, November 28, 2016, https://www.thedailybeast.com/patients-say-abilify -turned-them-into-compulsive-gamblers-and-sex-addicts (accessed February 6, 2018).

45. For some fascinatingly revolting stories, see: MelCthefirst, "Casinos and Urine Soaked Carpets?" Straight Dope Message Board, December 15, 2002, https://boards.straightdope.com/ sdmb/showthread.php?t=150554 (accessed April 16, 2018).

46. For a good example of the toll slots can extract even upon very educated and self-aware people, read, Sandra A. Adell, *Confessions of a Slot Machine Queen: A Memoir* (Madison, WI: EugeniaBooks, 2010).

47. Game designers are often openly contemptuous of these sorts of high-spending players despite them being the mark for most of the current crop of popular free-to-play mobile games. For a fascinating insider look at how advanced some of these game companies can be with their targeting technology, see, Eli Hodapp, "'We Own You'—Confessions of an Anonymous Free to Play Producer," TouchArcade, September 16, 2015, http://toucharcade.com/2015/09/16/ we-own-you-confessions-of-a-free-to-play-producer/ (accessed March 15, 2018).

CHAPTER SIX: PROFESSIONAL LEAGUES AND THE RISE OF ESPORTS— ARE THEY STILL GAMES?

1. Johan Huizinga, *Homo Ludens: A Study of the Play-Element in Culture* (London: Routledge & Kegan Paul, 1949).

2. Justin Block, "We Shouldn't Be Surprised When NFL Players Retire Early Anymore," *Huffington Post*, April 8, 2016, https://www.huffingtonpost.com/entry/dbrickashaw-ferguson -nfl-early-retirement-no-surprise_us_5707c4d5e4b0c4e26a2273fa (accessed March 15, 2018).

3. Ryan Wilson, "Only 23, Another NFL Player Is Retiring Early because of Concussions," CBS Sports, April 7, 2016, http://www.cbssports.com/nfl/news/only-23 -another-nfl-player-is-retiring-early-because-of-concussions/ (accessed February 6, 2018).

4. Joe Osonitsch, "Why Does Everyone Hate Roger Goodell?" *Odyssey*, August 24, 2014, https://www.theodysseyonline.com/why-does-everyone-hate-roger-goodell (accessed March 15, 2018).

5. For some rather depressing details of backstabbing and general chaos, see the tales of a hall of famer, Warren Sapp: Warren Sapp and David Fisher, *Sapp Attack: My Story* (New York: Macmillan, 2012), pp. 78–92.

6. NFL player Willis McGahee, for example, was quite vocal about his dislike of both the city he was playing for (Buffalo) and the team's management but not his fellow players. For a sympathetic take on McGahee, who was later traded to Baltimore, see: Rick Maese and Bill Ordine, "Facing Down His Critics, " *Baltimore Sun*, March 25, 2007, http://www.baltimoresun .com/bal-mcgahee1217-story.html (accessed April 15, 2018).

7. Rupert Cornwell, "NFL: Forget Fans—Moving Rams to Los Angeles Is All about Money for Stan Kroenke," *Independent*, January 15, 2016, https://www.independent.co.uk/sport/us-sport/national-football-league/nfl-forget-fans-moving-rams-to-los-angeles-is-all-about-money-for-stan-kroenke-a6815131.html (accessed March 15, 2018).

8. Steve Almond, "Is It Immoral to Watch the Super Bowl?" *New York Times*, January 24, 2014, http://www.nytimes.com/2014/01/26/magazine/is-it-immoral-to-watch-the-super-bowl.html?_r=0 (accessed February 6, 2018).

9. The NBA is particularly rich in examples of both ends of the spectrum: Michael Jordan was famous for putting himself through insanely involved workouts even while he was widely recognized as the best player on the planet; Jon Koncak, alternatively, was given a ten million dollar contract in 1989, which was unprecedented at the time, particularly for a bench warmer. He was forever known thereafter as Jon Contract, and never lived up to his billing due to his general apathy and lack of desire to work on his game. He had made his money. For a more sympathetic portrait, from Jon's point of view, see: I. J. Rosenberg, "Ex-Hawk Koncak Forever Known as 'Jon Contract,'" *Atlanta Journal-Constitution*, April 18, 2015, https://www.myajc.com/sports/basketball/hawk-koncak-forever-known-jon-contract/CDhakPenuPxs2LFZNajhXI/ (accessed march 15, 2018).

10. Most of the third chapter is dedicated to a linguistic and historical tracing of the meaning of "play" in various languages.

11. If "purity of the game" actually exists . . . Typically the phrase is only used to justify a power play against players, or as a defense of the indefensible NCAA "amateur sport" racket whereby billions are made but student athletes pocket none of the proceeds. This is entirely in line with Johan Huizinga's claim that monetization destroys the fundamental quality of a game, and the NCAA has so cynically structured the college athletic landscape that it's hard to avoid seeing it as anything but an obvious cash grab.

12. Marcellus Wiley, ESPN analyst and former ten-year NFL player, often discusses how shocked fans would be if they knew how few NFL players actually enjoyed playing the game. ("How Do NFL Players Feel About Football?" *SportsNation*, ESPN, video, 1:15, March 2017, http://www.espn.com/video/clip?id=18901968 [accessed April 11, 2018].)

13. Peter Warman, "Esports Revenues Will Reach $696 Million This Year and Grow to $1.5 Billion by 2020 as Brand Investment Doubles," Newzoo, February 14, 2017, https://newzoo.com/insights/articles/esports-revenues-will-reach-696-million-in-2017/ (accessed February 6, 2018).

14. Daniel Rapaport, "What to Expect from the Booming Esports Industry in 2017," *Sports Illustrated*, February 9, 2017, https://www.si.com/tech-media/2017/02/09/esports-industry-expectations-billion-dollar (accessed February 6, 2018).

15. "Highest Overall Earnings," e-Sports Earnings, https://www.esportsearnings.com/players (accessed February 6, 2018).

16. I find the obvious, in-your-face gut appeal of UFC fighting a bracing contrast to the equally violent NFL, which is busy at all times downplaying the brutality of the game. You might look down on combat sports as nothing more than a primitive throwback, but at least the UFC

is honest about it—and more than that, revels in it. They are also rigorously equal regarding gender: if two women want to beat themselves to a bloody pulp in the "octagon," UFC is happy to promote and televise it.

17. Alice Lee, "7 Charts That Show the State of Youth Sports in the US and Why It Matters," Aspen Institute, February 24, 2015, https://www.aspeninstitute.org/blog-posts/7-charts-that-show-the-state-of-youth-sports-in-the-us-and-why-it-matters/ (accessed February 6, 2018).

CHAPTER SEVEN: THE DANGERS OF THE VIRTUAL

1. Oliver Emberton, "Life Is a Game. This Is Your Strategy Guide," *Oliver Emberton* (blog), http://oliveremberton.com/2014/life-is-a-game-this-is-your-strategy-guide/ (accessed February 6, 2018).

2. Loewenthal shamefully transcribed and published these games against Morphy but, crucially, changed one of Morphy's moves, resulting in what he claimed was a draw (turning one of his losses into a tie). This embarrassing episode is somewhat obscured by an unclear history, and it's possible that Morphy was aware of Loewenthal's intent and gave either overt or implied consent to the change. Still, Loewenthal was a grown man and should have taken his lumps with more grace, even if the person beating him was a child. For details of Morphy's life and death, see his classic biography: David Lawson, *Paul Morphy: The Pride and Sorrow of Chess* (Philadelphia: David McKay, 1976).

3. This is a common ability of chess prodigies, although Morphy seems to have been the first to display the gift. Many others have followed in his footsteps, with the current record being held by George Koltanowski who once played thirty-four blindfold games simultaneously. For details, see: Nick Ravo, "George Koltanowski, 96, Chess Master Known for Playing While Blindfolded," *New York Times*, February 13, 2000, https://www.nytimes.com/2000/02/13/nyregion/george-koltanowski-96-chess-master-known-for-playing-while-blindfolded.html (accessed March 15, 2018).

4. His fascinating obituary, written by a life-long friend, Charles de Maurian, in 1884, can be found here: "Charles de Maurian's Obituary of Paul Morphy," *Chess.com*, July 3, 2013, https://www.chess.com/blog/batgirl/charles-de-maurians-obituary-of-paul-morphy (accessed March 13, 2018).

5. This despite, or perhaps because of, his own Jewish heritage. Fisher's mother was Jewish, and by tradition and Jewish law Bobby was also Jewish, and therefore part of some sort of tiresome Jewish global conspiracy.

6. For a quick overview, you can start with the following short article; for more details, see almost any book about the history of chess grandmasters: Thorin Klosowski, "The Five Weirdest Chess Masters," *Westword*, April 29, 2011, http://www.westword.com/arts/the-five-weirdest-chess-masters-5785686 (accessed March 15, 2018).

7. Vladimir Vladimirovich Nabokov and Michael Scammell, *The Luzhin Defense* (New York: Vintage Books, 1990), p. 29.

8. Ibid., p. 43.

9. Ibid.

10. Andrew Salmon, "Couple: Internet Gaming Addiction Led to Baby's Death," CNN, April 2, 2010, http://www.cnn.com/2010/WORLD/asiapcf/04/01/korea.parents.starved .baby/index.html (accessed March 15, 2018).

11. Craig Mod, "How I Got My Attention Back," *Wired*, January 13, 2017, https://www .wired.com/2017/01/how-i-got-my-attention-back/ (accessed February 6, 2018).

12. Ibid.

13. Bianca Bosker, "The Binge Breaker: Tristan Harris Believes Silicon Valley Is Addicting Us to Our Phones. He's Determined to Make It Stop," *Atlantic*, November 2016, https://www .theatlantic.com/magazine/archive/2016/11/the-binge-breaker/501122/ (accessed February 6, 2018).

14. Cecilia D'Anastasio, "How Video Game Addiction Can Destroy Your Life," *Vice*, January 26, 2015, https://www.vice.com/en_us/article/vdpwga/video-game-addiction-is -destroying-american-lives-456 (accessed February 6, 2018).

15. Paul Thompson, "'Sorry' Mother Jailed for 25 Years for Allowing Her Daughter to STARVE to Death While She Played an Online Video Game," *Daily Mail*, June 7, 2011, http:// www.dailymail.co.uk/news/article-1394903/Rebecca-Colleen-Christie-jailed-25-years -allowing-daughter-Brandi-Wulf-STARVE-death-played-World-Warcraft.html (accessed February 6, 2018).

16. D'Anastasio, "How Video Game Addiction Can Destroy Your Life."

17. Ibid.

18. Matt Richtel, "In Online Games, a Path to Young Consumers," *New York Times*, April 20, 2011, http://www.nytimes.com/2011/04/21/business/21marketing.html (accessed February 6, 2018).

19. As seen from the previous chapter's discussion of "screen time" and game-playing hours increasing steadily almost from birth: six-month-olds are now messing around with iPads. See, for example, Alexandra Sifferlin, "6-Month-Old Babies Are Now Using Tablets and Smartphones," *Time*, April 25, 2015, http://time.com/3834978/babies-use-devices/ (March 15, 2018).

20. Jane E. Brody, "Smoking among Children Is Linked to Cartoon Camel in Advertise-ments," *New York Times*, December 11, 1991, http://www.nytimes.com/1991/12/11/us/ smoking-among-children-is-linked-to-cartoon-camel-in-advertisements.html?page wanted=all (accessed February 6, 2018).

21. John M. Broder, "F.T.C. Charges Joe Camel Ad Illegally Takes Aim at Minors," *New York Times*, May 29, 1997, http://www.nytimes.com/1997/05/29/us/ftc-charges-joe-camel-ad-illegally-takes-aim-at-minors.html (accessed February 6, 2018).

22. This institute lacks any awareness of the mind-blowing hubris involved in their mission statement: to predict varying future possibilities, select the most appropriate one, and guide

the worlds toward it. The first task is clearly impossible, the second rather creepy (do they really know better than anyone else what's "appropriate" or not?), and the third patently absurd. As a money-making venture for those involved it seems to be successful; for those on the outside it reeks of undiluted technophile wankery. What follows is part of its mission statement:

> IFTF is celebrating its 50th anniversary as the world's leading non-profit strategic futures organization. The core of our work is *identifying emerging discontinuities that will transform global society and the global marketplace*. We provide organizations with insights into business strategy, design process, innovation, and social dilemmas. Our research spans a broad territory of deeply transformative trends, from health and health care to technology, the workplace, and human identity. IFTF is based in Palo Alto, California (http://www.iftf.org/what-we-do/).

23. William Saletan, "The Computer Made Me Do It," *New York Times*, February 11, 2011, http://www.nytimes.com/2011/02/13/books/review/Saletan-t.html (accessed February 6, 2018).

24. Ibid.

25. Bruce Feiler, "She's Playing Games with Your Lives," *New York Times*, April 27, 2012, http://www.nytimes.com/2012/04/29/fashion/jane-mcgonigal-designer-of-superbetter-moves -games-deeper-into-daily-life.html (accessed February 6, 2018).

26. Andrew Moseman, "Jane McGonigal: The Gaming Fix for the Real World," *Discover*, January 25, 2011, http://blogs.discovermagazine.com/sciencenotfiction/2011/01/25/jane -mcgonigal-the-gaming-fix-for-the-real-world/ (accessed March 19, 2018).

27. As is true for self-help gurus the world over, evidence that the self-help actually helps (the obvious success of the guru in question) is taken as proof that the professed theory has wide applicability and must therefore be true for a true believer if they truly believe (and purchase the books or games or videos or whatever is being sold). As far as I can tell, most of the benefits of "gamification" have gone directly into the coffers of "gamification" gurus.

28. Feiler, "She's Playing Games."

29. Simon Parkin, "'SuperBetter' and 'The State of Play,'" *New York Times*, October 12, 2015, https://www.nytimes.com/2015/10/18/books/review/superbetter-and-the-state-of-play .html (accessed February 6, 2018).

30. Steven Johnson's *Everything Bad Is Good for You* (New York: Riverhead Books, 2005) does the same for television; he makes the absurd claim that modern television is so complex and rewarding that it actually increases your IQ so 'you should watch more.

31. Eliza Strickland, "Can Playing Tetris Ease the Symptoms of Post-Traumatic Stress?" *Discover*, January 7, 2009, http://blogs.discovermagazine.com/80beats/2009/01/07/can -playing-tetris-ease-the-symptoms-of-post-traumatic-stress/#.UUnw4VdIVQI (accessed March 18, 2018).

32. Saletan, "Computer Made Me Do It."

33. Foldit: Solve Puzzles for Science, https://fold.it/ (accessed February 6, 2018).

34. "Game Changer Manifesto," Dream Catalyst, October 10, 2015, http://dream-catalyst.org/game-changer-manifesto/ (accessed February 6, 2018).

35. Gloria DeGaetano, founder, Parent Coaching Institute, at ibid.

36. The 1999 book *Stop Teaching Our Kids to Kill* by Dave Grossman and Gloria DeGaetano (New York: Crown) is the crucial text for the Game Changer Movement; it argues precisely what you would expect given the title. Playing violent video games is nothing less than "teaching kids to kill."

37. "Game Changer Manifesto," Dream Catalyst.

38. Now that I think about it, this is an excellent way to extract money from gamers; the desire to communicate can sometimes feel overwhelming. Imagine using all your "radio time" for a given game, and you don't want to spend one dollar in-game to buy thirty minutes more. In the middle of the next mission you suddenly need to inform an ally about a tactical situation that recently arose. . . . A perfect time to squeeze one dollar from the player who is desperately trying to tell his friends not to enter a booby-trapped building.

39. Mark Duell, "Couple to Marry after Meeting Playing *Call of Duty* Online—Because She Kept Killing Him All the Time," *Daily Mail*, December 14, 2016, http://www.dailymail.co.uk/news/article-4032946/Couple-marry-meeting-kept-KILLING-playing-Xbox-game-Call-Duty-messaged-pleading-online-life-spared.html (accessed February 6, 2018).

40. D'Anastasio, "How Video Game Addiction Can Destroy Your Life."

41. "Game Changer Manifesto," Dream Catalyst.

42. For details, see Social Venture Network, http://svn.org/ (accessed February 6, 2018).

43. Games for Change Festival, 2018, http://gamesforchange.org/festival/ (accessed February 6, 2018).

44. Quandary Game, https://quandarygame.org/ (accessed February 6, 2018).

CHAPTER EIGHT: KEEP US SAFE BY GIVING THEM GAMES

1. Paul Bois, "The Kids Aren't' Alright: These 'Grand Theft Auto' Rampage Videos Are Disturbing" *Daily Wire*, October 3, 2017, https://www.dailywire.com/news/21883/kids-arent-alright-these-grand-theft-auto-rampage-paul-bois (accessed February 6, 2018).

2. Ibid.

3. "Grand Theft Auto 'Therapeutic' for Kids, Say Psychologists," *Telegraph*, August 27, 2013, http://www.telegraph.co.uk/technology/news/10268820/Grand-Theft-Auto-therapeutic-for-kids-say-psychologists.html (accessed February 6, 2018).

4. "Violent Crime Victimization," Child Trends, last updated December 2015, https://www.childtrends.org/indicators/violent-crime-victimization/ (accessed February 6, 2018).

5. Senate Committee on the Judiciary, *Comic Books and Juvenile Delinquency, Interim Report* (Comic Book Code of 1954) (Washington, DC: United States Government Printing Office, 1955), https://en.wikisource.org/wiki/Comic_book_code_of_1954 (accessed March 15, 2018).

6. "Speed Limit Increases Cause 33,000 Deaths in 20 Years," *Status Report* 51, no. 4 (April 12, 2016), http://www.iihs.org/iihs/news/desktopnews/speed-limit-increases-cause-33 -000-deaths-in-20-years (accessed February 6, 2018).

7. Patrick M. Markey, Charlotte N. Markey, and Juliana E. French, "Violent Video Games and Real-World Violence: Rhetoric Versus Data," *Psychology of Popular Media Culture* 4, no. 4 (2015): 277–95, https://www.apa.org/pubs/journals/features/ppm-ppm0000030.pdf (accessed February 6, 2018).

8. Within reason; part-time heroin use isn't suggested as a viable choice.

9. *Arcade Outsiders: Retro and Pinball Collectors Podcast*, http://arcadeoutsiders.com/ (accessed February 6, 2018).

10. *VideoGame Outsiders* Forum, 2017, http://videogameoutsiders.com/forum/index .php?PHPSESSID=0434b2f17814475a801e8dcb6042ea2b&topic=11828.0 (accessed February 6, 2018).

11. Ian Kellogg, "John's Arcade Kit," https://iankellogg.com/catalogsearch/result/ ?q=johns+arcade+kit (accessed April 10, 2018).

12. *Funspot: Largest Arcade in the World*, 2017, http://funspotnh.com/ (accessed February 6, 2018).

13. *The Kill Screens*, 2011, http://www.thekillscreens.com/ (accessed February 6, 2018).

14. *That Dragon, Cancer*, http://www.thatdragoncancer.com/#home (accessed February 6, 2018).

15. Vanishingly few athletes make the jump from high school directly to professional sports (famous examples include LeBron James), a process known as "prep to pro," which is now illegal under the new NBA bargaining agreement.

16. John McDuling, "A Guide to American College Football, the Multibillion-Dollar Business Where the Labor Is Free," Quartz, September 13, 2013, http://qz.com/257332/a -guide-to-american-college-football-the-multi-billion-dollar-business-where-the-labor-is-free/ (accessed February 6, 2018).

17. Paul Corcoran and Dennis M. Gephardt, *Eye on the Ball: Big-Time Sports Pose Growing Risks for Universities* (report; New York: Moody's Investor Service, October 10, 2013), https://www.insidehighered.com/sites/default/server_files/files/Sports%20Pose%20Growing %20Risk%20for%20Universities.pdf (accessed February 6, 2018).

18. Taylor Branch, "The Shame of College Sports," *Atlantic*, October 2011, http://www .theatlantic.com/magazine/archive/2011/10/the-shame-of-college-sports/308643/ (accessed February 6, 2018).

19. "Juvenal's Tenth 'Satire,'" http://www.crtpesaro.it/Materiali/Latino/Juvenal's%20 tenth%20Satire.php (accessed April 10, 2018).

20. John Locke, *Some Thoughts Concerning Education* (London: A. and J. Churchill, 1693), p. 63.

21. Ibid., p. 1.

22. Jake New, "What Off-Season?" Inside Higher Ed, May 8, 2015, https://www .insidehighered.com/news/2015/05/08/college-athletes-say-they-devote-too-much-time -sports-year-round (accessed February 6, 2018).

23. McDuling, "Guide to American College Football"."

24. Darren Eversen, "What the Rise of Southern Football Says about America," *Wall Street Journal*, December 5, 2008, https://www.wsj.com/articles/SB122843720586081461 (accessed February 6, 2018).

25. Soccer hooligans, rival sport team fights, gunfire outside stadiums, Giants fan killed by Dodgers fans, etc. For a rather extreme example see: Kristin J. Bender, Mark Gomez, and Joshua Melvin, "San Francisco: Dodgers Fan Fatally Stabbed in Fight with Giants Fans; Two Suspects Still at Large," *Mercury News*, September 25, 2013, https://www.mercurynews.com/ 2013/09/25/san-francisco-dodgers-fan-fatally-stabbed-in-fight-with-giants-fans-two-suspects -still-at-large/ (accessed April 10, 2018).

26. Alexander K. Gold, Austin J. Drukker, and Ted Gayer, "Why the Federal Government Should Stop Spending Billions on Private Sports Stadiums," Brookings, September 8, 2016, https://www.brookings.edu/research/why-the-federal-government-should-stop-spending -billions-on-private-sports-stadiums/ (accessed February 6, 2018).

27. Ibid.

28. Fred Coalter, *A Wider Social Role for Sport: Who's Keeping the Score?* (New York: Routledge, 2007), p. 1.

29. Ibid.

30. Ibid.

31. Amanda Ripley, "The Case against High-School Sports," *Atlantic*, October 2013, https://www.theatlantic.com/magazine/archive/2013/10/the-case-against-high-school -sports/309447/ (accessed February 6, 2018).

32. Ibid.

33. Ibid.

34. Ibid.

35. Elizabeth Kolbert, "Have Sports Teams Brought Down America's Schools?" *New Yorker*, September 5, 2013, https://www.newyorker.com/news/daily-comment/have-sports -teams-brought-down-americas-schools (accessed February 6, 2018).

36. "Education Spending Per Student by State," *Governing*, 2015, http://www.governing .com/gov-data/education-data/state-education-spending-per-pupil-data.html (accessed April 11, 2018).

37. Ray Downs, "Texas Town Opens Nation's Most Expensive High School Football Stadium," UPI, August 17, 2017, https://www.upi.com/Texas-town-opens-nations-most -expensive-high-school-football-stadium/7081503026585/ (accessed February 6, 2018).

38. Dennis Spellman, "Katy Football Stadium Spending Leaves School Board in a Bind," *Covering Katy News*, October 26, 2016, https://coveringkaty.com/education/katy-football-stadium-spending-leaves-school-board-bind/ (accessed February 6, 2018).

39. Charles Blain, "Much Needed Shakeup on Katy ISD Board," Empower Texans, May 9, 2014, https://empowertexans.com/quicktakes/much-needed-shakeup-on-katy-isd-board/ (accessed February 6, 2018).

40. Ibid.

CHAPTER NINE: FLOODING THE COLOSSEUM

1. James Brightman, "Game Industry Growing Four Times Faster than US Economy—ESA," GameIndustry.biz, November 11, 2014, http://www.gamesindustry.biz/articles/2014-11-11-game-industry-growing-four-times-faster-than-us-economy-esa/ (accessed February 6, 2018).

2. Ana Swanson, "Why Amazing Video Games Could Be Causing a Big Problem for America," *Washington Post*, September 23, 2016, https://www.washingtonpost.com/news/wonk/wp/2016/09/23/why-amazing-video-games-could-be-causing-a-big-problem-for-america/ (accessed February 6, 2018).

3. Ibid.

4. Ibid.

5. Mark Aguiar, Mark Bils, Kerwin Kofi Charles, and Erik Hurst, "Leisure Luxuries and the Labor Supply of Young Men" (paper; Madison, WI: University of Wisconsin-Madison, July 4, 2017), https://www.ssc.wisc.edu/~nwilliam/Econ702_files/abch.pdf (accessed February 6, 2018).

6. Ibid.

7. I'm not claiming nobody remembers what they did in a given game, they obviously do, but the excitement comes not from "having raced over the bridge at 100 mph while playing GTA 4" but from (virtually) experiencing this self-directed action. Remembering the incident is meaningful not because of the information but because of the emotion/activity associated with the incident. This is precisely the opposite of reading; reading itself is mostly invisible and almost impossible to quantify emotionally, but nearly everyone experiencing *Emma* (as the author intends, as written sequentially and in order) is more than capable of losing themselves in the story. Reading is both imaginative and passive; video games are, for the most part, imaginatively barren but crucially self-guided and interactive.

8. "Overall Leaderboards: Time Spent in GTA Online," GTA Online Stats, October 15, 2014, http://gtaonlinestats.com/leaderboards/timespentingtaonline (accessed April 1, 2018).

9. Keith Hopkins, "Murderous Games: Gladiatorial Contests in Ancient Rome," *History Today* 33, no. 6 (June 1983).

10. Nir Eyal, *Hooked: How to Build Habit-Forming Products* (New York: Portfolio, 2014), p. 1.

11. Holly B. Shakya and Nicholas A. Christakis, "Association of Facebook Use with Compromised Well-Being: A Longitudinal Study," *American Journal of Epidemiology* 185, no. 3 (February 1, 2017): 203–11, https://academic.oup.com/aje/article-abstract/185/3/203/2915143/Association-of-Facebook-Use-With-Compromised-Well?redirected From=fulltext (accessed February 6, 2018).

12. Olivia Solon, "Ex-Facebook President Sean Parker: Site Made to Exploit Human 'Vulnerability,'" *Guardian*, November 9, 2017, https://www.theguardian.com/technology/2017/nov/09/facebook-sean-parker-vulnerability-brain-psychology (accessed February 6, 2018).

13. I made it a personal rule after I first noticed this method being used to never click on any additional links and never to again visit a website that attempted this sort of sleazy, ham-fisted, click-increasing scheme. I wish more people would do the same. With sufficient numbers we could kill it and other profit-based behavior manipulations that are overtly annoying to the end user.

14. Paul Lewis, "'Our Minds Can Be Hijacked': The Tech Insiders Who Fear a Smartphone Dystopia," *Guardian*, October 6, 2017, https://www.theguardian.com/technology/2017/oct/05/smartphone-addiction-silicon-valley-dystopia (accessed February 6, 2018).

15. Ibid.

16. Ibid.

17. Ibid.

INDEX

Adams, Joe, 223

administrative (re)defining of common terms, 62–63

administrative solution to campus problems, 47, 49–50, 57

alcohol and choice, 63, 113

American Chess Championship, 168

Anderssen, Adolf (chess master), 168

animal play, 23–40

Antifragile: Things That Gain from Disorder (Taleb), 45, 50–51

arena combat, 148
    evolutionary development, 31
    Roman example, 32
    rules, 32

Atari, 87, 106

attention economy, 178–79, 234–35
    equilibrium of pain, 236
    generates poor outcomes, 235
    happiness not goal of, 236
    pull the plug, 239

beauty
    evolutionary role, 28
    in video games, 177

bees, scientific chops, 28, 38

Bion-M No. 1 (Russian spacecraft), 36

blindfold chess, 168

Bois, Paul, 204

Bosker, Bianca, 178

brain drain in academia, 49

Brichter, Loren, 238

bureaucracy's inevitable expansion, 49, 65

Burghardt, Gordon, 34–35, 37

"but actually" trope, 193

Call of Duty (video game), 181, 196–99, 201

Camel cigarette scandal, 185

Campbell, Bradley, 64

Candy Crush (video game), 103–41, 177, 183, 196, 197, 238
    addictive qualities, 123, 125
    backlash, 104–105
    cute by design, 132, 134
    difficulty level, 135
    gameplay, 120, 134
    in-game purchases, 126
    luck-based rather than skill-based, 122

manipulation methods, 105,
124, 235, 240

match three game, 106

money-focused, 133

outsourcing advertising to
players, 136

relative simplicity compared
to modern games, 108, 200

river bridge, 126

social network leveraging, 135

Carr, Nicolas, 94

Carville, James, 214

casinos, 18, 109–17

alternative "open" interior
design philosophy, 117, 123

chip use instead of fiat currency, 140

Friedman interior-design philosophy, 114–15, 123

Las Vegas growth stagnant due
to, 116

manipulative tricks, 115

ugliness by design, 114

unfair gaming odds, 113

Chatfield, Tom, 94

chess

insufficient to support a full
life, 174

link to insanity, 170–72

obsession in fiction, 172

child abduction scare, 45

chimpanzee play, 25–26

choice, necessary for play, 14

Clash of Clans (video game), 137,
177–78

Clery Act, 61

Coalter, Fred, 217

coddling, 57

1960s rejection of, 47

Haidt's theory of, 57

Taleb's theory, 52

*Coddling of the American Mind,
The* (Lukianoff and Haidt), 45,
46–50

college football, 162

effect on student-body composition, 212

leveraging nostalgia, 214

perverting education mission, 215

revenues and losses, 211

scholarship racket, 213

comic book

code, 203, 206–207

moral panic, 206

concept creep, 62

Conrad, Brent, 84

consumer manipulation, 113, 117,
123–24, 129, 132, 136–37, 142

Cornell University, occupation of
Willard Straight Hall, 47

Counter Strike (video game),
181–82, 199–200

Create a Comic (video game), 183

Cuphead (video game), 73–74

decision trees in video games, 96

DeGaetano, Gloria, 196

demonetization, 74–79

    driving bland content, 78

    policy, 77

Derrida, Jacques, opaque writing
    style, 27

Designing Casinos to Dominate the
    Competition (Friedman), 114

Diplomacy board game, 87

distressed monetization, 137

Dungeons & Dragons, 68–69

educational system failure, 221

Emory University, 54–56

EnVyUs (Overwatch team),
    150–60

esports economy, 148–49

Everything Bad Is Good for You
    (Johnson), 93–102

evolution, 16, 19–21, 23, 27–30,
    32–33, 38, 41, 44, 66

    play escaping function, 27

    theory of play, 25, 41

executive function, 42, 44

Eyal, Nir, 239

fairness

    evolution development,
      32–33

    in gameplay, 123, 126, 131

fantasy sports, 145

faux contrarianism, 99

FaZe clan (*Overwatch* team),
    150–60

fighting wren, 30

Fischer, Robert (chess master),
    170

fish (gamer), 103

Foldit (video game), 193–94

freedom, play requires, 14

free market effects on game design,
    200

Free-Range Kids: Giving Our
    Children the Freedom We Had
    Without Going Nuts with Worry
    (Skenazy), 45–46

Friedman, Bill, 114–16, 123–24

FrontierVille, "Dying Bambi"
    scenario in, 137

game(s)

    addiction, 20, 21n2, 141,
      174–76, 178, 181–86, 199,
      209, 230–31, 234–36,
      238–40

    algorithms to extend play
      time, 178

    character building, 210

    consciousness not required to
      play, 16

    controlling humans, 179

    court systems possible example
      of, 146

creation of a more convenient
reality, 21
definition, 12–13, 15–17,
26–27, 147
easy modern access to, 176, 233
economy in America, size of,
68, 88, 225
empty pleasure theory, 228
enabling social control, 232
inspiring unemployment, 71,
226–27
life played as a, 167–68
low informational content, 229
lure of pro leagues, 210
passive vs. active, 205, 209, 228
pro sports are not examples of,
147
short- and long-term effects, 229
targeting children, 184,
230–31, 233
time Americans spend playing,
70, 71, 84, 190, 225, 228–29
unethical free market forces,
185
Game Changer Movement,
195–96, 200
Games for Change Festival, 201
gamification
artificial structure placed on
reality, 192
definition of ugly term, 186
everyday life example, 191

Foldit success, 194
Groundcrew failure, 191
Jane the Concussion-Slayer
(video game), 188
lack of evidence of efficacy, 190
moral dependency of players,
192
relentlessly hierarchical, 192
requirements for success, 194
sports as an example, 188
SuperBetter self-help book/
game, 189
geckos
in orbit, 36
play example, 37
Gentile, Douglas, 182–84
Gladwell, Malcolm, 92, 94–95
Glyptemys insculpta (wood turtle),
35
Grand Theft Auto (video game),
106, 203–206
time spent playing, 230
Green, Ryan and Amy, 209
guilt reduction, 53

Haidt, Jonathan, 45–46, 48, 50,
52, 56, 66, 192
Harris, Tristan, 178–79, 236–37
Harrwitz, Daniel (chess master),
168
Helicopter Parent model, 45, 48,
50

Henderson, Roy, 219
high rollers, 110, 113
Hollywood, 72, 83
  cowardice of movie producers, 201
Homo Ludens (Huizinga), 143, 147
Hooked: How to Build Habit-Forming Products (Eyal), 233, 239
Huizinga, Johan, 143, 145

IAT (implicit bias test), 58–61
  IAT-based mediations have no effect on behavior, 59
in-app purchases, 124
insect play, 38

Jacobsen, John, 208
Jae-beom, Kim, 20
John's Arcade (YouTube channel), 208
Johnson, Steven, 93–102
Juvenal, 212

Katy (Texas) School District, 222–23
Kent State shootings, 47

LDShadowLady (Lizzy Shadow, YouTube user), 80–82
Lehman, Erik, 195–98
Locke, John, 212

loot boxes (gambling), 139–40
loricifera, 24
Lukianoff, Greg, 45, 46, 66
Luzhin Defense, The (Nabokov), 170–74

Major League Baseball, 149
Making Caring Common (project), 201
mammalian play, 38–39
Manning, Jason, 64
"Masque of the Red Death, The" (Poe), 90–91
McGonigal, Jane, 92, 186–95
Melville, Herman, 103
microaggression, 62, 64–65
Minecraft (video game), 80–83, 107, 109, 200
Mitchell, Robert, 24, 26, 27
mobile gaming, 72
Moby-Dick (Melville), 103
Mod, Craig, 177, 178
modern art, silliness of, 67
money game, 135, 140
moral dependency, 48, 52, 57, 192
moral outrage, 53–54
Morphy, Paul, 168–70
  death, 169
Moseman, Andrew, 187
multiplayer game
  enabling respect, 198
  features, 197

Nabokov, Vladimir, 170
NBA, 145–46, 211
    effect of money on players,
        147
NCAA, 163, 211–15
    scandals, 214
NFL, 15
    early history, 147
    not qualifying as a game, 145
    players sabotaging players, 144
    retirements, 143
Nimzowitsch, Aron (chess
    master), 170
nomenclature confusion (lin-
    guistic), 180
nonfiction book types
    explanatory, 92
    polemic, 92
    targeted, 92, 101
nontenured university faculty
    scandal, 49

offense, 48, 52–54, 56, 58, 62, 65
    sacred and holy, 52
opportunity cost, 85, 98–99, 218
Ottawa, University of, 61
Overwatch (video game), 68, 139
    broadcast features, 161
    pro tournaments relatable to
        players, 165
    spectator sport, 161
    team game, 162

tournament, 148, 150–60
ultimates, 155

Pachydactylus (gecko), 36
pain, possible function of, 29
Parent Coaching Institute, 196
Parker, Sean, 234
Pärt, Arvo, 67
Pearlman, Leah, 238
PewDiePie (YouTube user), 73
Pham, Emilee, 104
Pigface (turtle) 33, 34
    love of current, 35
    play with toys, 34
    self-injuring behavior, 34
planned obsolescence, 112
play
    animal, 23–40
    biological roots, 19, 42
    categories of, 25
    choice required, 14
    creates skills, 26
    definition, 13, 15
    deprivation of, 42
    English language limited in
        describing, 13
    evolutionary functional
        hypothesis, 20, 41, 44
    functional lack, 26
    freedom required, 14
    mediates horror of existence,
        28, 30

peer vs. adult play, 44
self-referential nature, 27
spontaneous nature, 15
rules not needed, 16
pleasure
difficulty of adults experiencing it, 18
functional effects, 38
limited by evolution, 29
play involves it, 18
Poe, Edgar Allen, 90–91
postmodernism (pretentiousness),
87
Premont Independent School
District, 218–22
Prensky, Marc, 93
Prius (video game), 20
Puzzle and Dragons (video game),
131

rats
long-term game planning,
39
peer vs. adult play, 44
play examples, 38
reading, power of, 229
wrestling pinning techniques,
39
*Reality Is Broken: Why Games
Make Us Better and How
They Can Change the World*
(McGonigal), 186

reality TV, looming death of,
83
relativity, extreme, 91
reward removal, 130–32
Roman games, 32, 148, 232
Rosenstein, Justin, 237
Rubin, Dave, 77

safety extremely high
in America, 46, 205, 207
on campuses, 53
Scott, George, 223
selection bias, 56
self-censorship on campus by
students, professors, 54
Settlers of Catan (board game),
68–69, 88
Shadow, Lizzy. *See*
LDShadowLady
shareware model, 124
shark (gamer), 103
Shokrizade, Ramin, 105, 113, 132,
136, 138
Singal, Jesse, 59
Singleton, Ernest, 218–19
Skenazy, Lenore, 45, 66
skill game, 140
slot machines, 18, 106, 113, 115,
123–24, 141, 236
attention economy parallel,
236
history, 117–19

players incorporated into mechanics, 19
profitability, 118
reduction to simpler form, 118–19
Social Venture Network, 201
solitaire, 17
Some Thoughts Concerning Education (Locke), 212
special reality of games and play, 14, 16
sports
    body/mind link, 213
    government spending on, 217
    harming education, 219
    hidden downsides, 221
    public funding of private stadiums, 215
Steinitz, Wilhelm (chess master), 170
Stolle, Troy, 97
Swanson, Ana, 71

Taitz, Jenny, 104
Taleb, Nassim Nicholas, 45, 50–52, 66
technological blindness, 102
TED talks, 187
Tetris (video game), 109, 117–23
    gameplay, 120
    mechanical play, 16
    random nature, 121
    simple graphics, 107

That Dragon, Cancer (video game), 209
threat generation, 138
Title IX, 50
Torre, Carlos (chess master), 170
Trionyx triunguis (turtle), 33
Trump "chalking scandal," 54–56
truth-seeking, 89

UC-Berkeley Equity and Inclusion Department, 65
UC-San Francisco bias definition, 58
UFC (Ultimate Fighting Championship), 163–64
    legitimization, 164
Ultima Online (video game), 97–98
unconscious bias, 58–60
unconscious mind, 65
    hubristic to muck with, 60
    unknown state of, 59
upgrading via pain, 129

victimhood, culture of, 64–65
violence, 203–207
    games inspiring it, 203
    Grand Theft Auto (video game), 204
    horror movies, 204
    simulated, effect on real world, 207

virtual reality, 105, 181, 233, 240
virtual world enabling escape, 132
virtue signaling, 53

Washington Center of Game
  Science, University of, 193
whale (gamer), 103, 111, 125,
  127, 141
Wilfrid Laurier University, 61
Williams, James, 237
Willow Warbler (*Phylloscopus
  trochilus*), 30
Wittgenstein, Ludwig Josef
  Johann, 17

Wittgenstein's ruler, 17
*Wonderland: How Play Made the
  Modern World* (Johnson), 93
Wynn, Steve, 116

YouTube, 72–78
    ad revenue total per million
      views, 74
    demonetization, 74–78
    libertarian argument to solve
      problem of, 78
    non-intelligent parsing of
      video content, 76
Yun-jeong, Kim, 20